GIVING

ALSO BY DR. DEBBIE RICH

Resurrected

Giving

Desperate Hunger Gets God's Attention

GIVING

YOUR KEY TO BREAKTHROUGH

DR. DEBBIE RICH

Without limiting the rights under copyright(s) reserved below, no part of this publication may be reproduced, stored in or introduced into a retrieval system, or transmitted, in any form, or by any means (electronic, mechanical, photocopying, recording, or otherwise) without the prior permission of the publisher and the copyright owner.

The content of this book is provided "AS IS." The publisher and the author make no guarantees or warranties as to the accuracy, adequacy or completeness of or results to be obtained from using the content of this book, including any information that can be accessed through hyperlinks or otherwise, and expressly disclaim any warranty expressed or implied, including but not limited to implied warranties of merchantability or fitness for a particular purpose. This limitation of liability shall apply to any claim or cause whatsoever whether such claim or cause arises in contract, tort, or otherwise. In short, you, the reader, are responsible for your choices and the results they bring.

The scanning, uploading, and distributing of this book via the internet or any other means without the permission of the publisher and copyright owner is illegal and punishable by law. Please purchase only authorized copies, and do not participate in or encourage piracy of copyrighted materials. Your support of the author's rights is appreciated.

Unless otherwise noted, all scriptures are from the KING JAMES VERSION, public domain.

Scripture quotations marked (NKJV) are taken from the NEW KING JAMES VERSION®. Copyright© 1982 by Thomas Nelson, Inc. Used by permission. All rights reserved.

Scripture quotations taken from the Amplified® Bible (AMPC), Copyright © 1954, 1958, 1962, 1964, 1965, 1987 by The Lockman Foundation. Used by permission. lockman.org

Copyright © 2024 by Debra K. Rich. All rights reserved.

Released July 2024
ISBN: 978-1-664457-744-8 (Paperback)
ISBN: 978-1-664457-745-5 (Hardcover)

Rise UP Publications
644 Shrewsbury Commons Ave
Ste 249
Shrewsbury PA 17361
United States of America
www.riseUPpublications.com
Phone: 866-846-5123

To Drs. Rodney and Adonica Howard-Browne: There are no words to express my respect, love, and gratitude for all you have been to me.

CONTENTS

Foreword	9
Acknowledgments	13
1. Revelation Knowledge of God's Provision	15
2. The Power of the Tithe	23
3. The Breaking of the Alabaster Box	39
4. The Lesser Giving to the Greater	77
5. Blessed to Be a Blessing	95
6. Stimulated Giving	111
7. You Are Not A Bird	125
8. If I Can't Build It, I Will Pay For It	137
9. Godly Contentment Or Lazy Faith?	151
10. God's Desire For You To Prosper	165
11. He's An Excessive, Too-Much God	175
12. God Provides Seed for the Sower	199
13. The Ravens Are Coming	211
14. Broken Once Again	223
15. The Two Streams Coming Together	233
16. Putting Out The Vessels	241
17. The Multiplication Of The Bread And Fish	255
18. It's All About The Offering	263
19. Recent Financial Miracles	293
20. Following in the Steps of My Pastors	299
21. Watching Over Your Seed	303
22. Additional Scripture Resources	317
Resurrected	323
About Debbie Rich	326

FOREWORD

BY DRS. RODNEY AND ADONICA HOWARD-BROWNE

God's Word does nothing for us until we grab a hold of it and DO it.

Debbie Rich had the call of God on her life from an early age, but through various circumstances, she was never able to fulfill that call and see the things she longed for in her heart. After years of heartache and a major personal tragedy, Debbie found herself at the bottom of the barrel. In fact, it was more like she was *under* the barrel and the barrel was on top of her!

When we met Debbie, she was a single mom of three boys with no money, no home, and driving a car that had already been written off by an insurance company after it went down the side of the mountain into a tree. She had a call on her life, but no one who believed in her—no one who expected her to make it—and they told her so. Indeed, several people tried to persuade her to quit the ministry and go back to where she came from—and these were her "friends"!

Debbie came to our meetings in Anchorage, Alaska, and God gave us a word for her—that it was not the end but only the beginning, and every promise that God had made her, from a child, would indeed come to pass!

Now, you can have a call and even a powerful anointing, but if you can't afford to get out of town, how are you going to take the Gospel into

FOREWORD

Jerusalem, Judea, Samaria, and the uttermost parts of the earth (Acts 1:8)? Debbie received an impartation of the anointing in our meetings that changed her life, but not only that, she grabbed a hold of the teaching on giving and being a blessing. Debbie knew about the blessings of giving in her head. But for the first time, it really dropped down into her heart and she purposed in her heart to boldly act on the Word and activate her faith through her giving. She began to give sacrificially, a habit that she continues to this day.

Because of Debbie's faith in God as her sole source and supply, and because of her faithfulness to give generously and cheerfully at every opportunity she gets, she has seen God perform miracle after miracle in her life. Debbie discovered that God has a good plan for her life—for hope and a future (Jeremiah 29:11) and she found the "key" that unlocked this great future.

You may know that God has a great plan for your life, but until you do something about it, you will never see your potential realized. You must decide that God's Word is going to work for *you,* and you have to *work* God's Word. Start doing what God's Word says to do—no arguments, no excuses!

Debbie walks in a realm of blessing in her life so far from her humble beginnings, and it is not by chance or because God has favorites. She stepped out to trust God and to honor Him in her giving without reservation, and she is living proof that He is not a respecter of persons, but He honors His Word and blesses with a harvest in proportion to the seed we have sown.

Through her radical giving, Debbie has experienced the blessing of the Lord in every area of her life—an increase in the anointing, material blessings, provision, and supernatural favor! Debbie's ministry has gone around the world, and on top of that, she has even seen God bless her by granting her the very secret petitions and desires of her heart.

If you will grab onto the truth of God's Word the way that Debbie has, you will be blessed beyond your imagination.

FOREWORD

It is a privilege and an honor for us to know Debbie and to watch God's grace in her life. We pray that you will read this book and receive its message. We dare you to take the challenge and act on the Word of God concerning giving.

Drs. Rodney and Adonica Howard-Browne

ACKNOWLEDGMENTS

When I first met Drs. Rodney and Adonica Howard-Browne, they had nothing to gain and everything to lose by encouraging this poor single mom. While most told me the call of God was over in my life, they said it had just begun.

You will read in this book how I caught the key to breakthrough. The key was given to me through these two people. I was called to go all over the world but didn't have enough finances to go down the street. However, I was set free by the anointing of the Holy Spirit that was upon Dr. Rodney. The anointing destroys the yoke of bondage.

Pastor Rodney, I will never forget how you stared down the faces of religious opposition in those meetings. You didn't care who didn't like it, who misjudged you and questioned your motives, or even who walked out. You knew that you had a job to do, and that was to teach the uncompromising Word of God and not water it down to please anyone. You knew that it would be worth it if just one would catch the key. I was that one, and I promise you that I will continue to run around the world with it and make duplicates of it.

Thank you for coming to Alaska in the dead of winter and laboring for all those weeks. Thank you for leaving your native land of South Africa to see America set ablaze with the fire of revival. Thank you for going where few dare and for persevering against all of Hell so that some of us could be set free.

I've watched you stand, and having done all to stand, stand. I've watched you in some of the greatest trials that anyone could face, setting an example for all of us.

I thank you for seeing in me and upon me what few people did. I thank you for your encouragement, vision, and leadership. I brag on you wherever I go. I believe you're called to lead the entire world into revival, and I, for one, will follow all the days of my life.

I'm so very honored and proud to be associated with you both and with Revival Ministries International. I know where I was touched and will always come back for more.

I also thank you for not only teaching me how to give by way of precept but also by way of example. I know of no greater giver in the entire world. I will continue to rub shoulders with you and let that tangible, transmittable anointing rub off on me. I want to give more and more until that day that we give our last offering and lay our trophies down at the feet of the Lord Jesus Christ and hear, *"Well done, thou faithful servant."*

ONE

REVELATION KNOWLEDGE OF GOD'S PROVISION

In November of 1992, I had a Holy Ghost encounter that forever changed my life. A friend invited me to attend a revival meeting in Anchorage, Alaska, conducted by Evangelist Rodney Howard-Browne of South Africa. There, I encountered the glory of God as never before. *"Joy unspeakable and full of glory"* was present in every one of his meetings. I had already been experiencing revival and joy in my life and ministry for several months. So, even though that manner of outpouring was intensified in his meetings, it was not foreign to me. However, I witnessed something that was very unusual. This man was teaching on giving, or stewardship, before receiving each offering. He took his time doing it, too! Since meetings were being held twice a day, we were getting quite an earful.

At first, I was irritated. I had never heard anyone teach on this subject before every single offering, nor had I witnessed anyone take so long to do so. Each teaching lasted from twenty to forty-five minutes. As Brother Rodney taught, several thoughts entered my head—thoughts that went like this: 'He's taking up too much time for this' or, 'This much teaching is simply unnecessary. I've never seen it done this way before, so it should not be done this way.'

After several minutes of negative thinking, other thoughts invaded my head. I started mentally rehearsing what a good "faith person" I was and the many stewardship classes that I had already taken in Bible school. After all, I graduated from a Bible school that emphasized faith and prosperity. I had a course called "Giving and Receiving" and had made an 'A' on the test!

I graduated with a perfect 4.0 grade point average. I could quote the Scripture verses that he was reading! So, of all the people in that auditorium, I did not need any more teaching on the subject of giving. I felt that I already knew as much or more about stewardship as Dr. Rodney Howard-Browne did. Besides, if this was how long his offering teaching was, how much time would he take on the "real" message?

After a while, though, I realized that not everyone in that church was as well taught as I was, nor were they the "faith person" that I was. So, giving Dr. Howard-Browne the benefit of the doubt and deciding that someone there might need the teaching, I began to really listen to the message.

Somewhere in the middle of all that pride, arrogance, blindness, and pure stupidity, the Holy Spirit spoke to me. Thank God for the Holy Ghost! I heard, "Debbie, you don't know this."

Shocked, I replied, "Yes, I do know this, Lord. Remember me, the one who had a course on it and got an 'A' on the test?"

He said, "You may have gotten an 'A' on the test, but you flunked the course. You have some head knowledge (or mental assent), but you do not have heart revelation. Look at your life. I sent this man here for your sake. I've called you to go all over the world, and you don't even have the finances to go down the street. How do you think you will accomplish this? Debbie, you have to begin to see Me as Jehovah Jireh, the Lord your Provider. Today, a table is being laid out for you. On this table is all you need in any area: healing, freedom, peace of mind, provision, joy, etc. You can pick and choose if you want, but you might as well have all of Me that you desire, including provision. This minister is giving you the key. Take it! He is teaching you out of the revelation that he has received. This is tangible, transmittable anointing. Repent, open up your heart, and I will set you free."

With that revelation, my eyes were suddenly opened. I realized what a Pharisee I had been and began to repent to the Lord for being so arrogant and blind. Here I was, judging Dr. Rodney when he had been trying to help me and everyone else in the room. I could not believe my presumption in thinking I was such an elite "faith person" when, in reality, I knew very little about faith or prosperity. The truth was, I was barely surviving. I was driving a totaled car and getting ready to move in with other people. I didn't have anything to bless anyone with, and I could not fulfill the call of God on my life. At that moment, I knew that what I had previously possessed was only mental assent, not heart revelation. It's difficult to believe how blind we can become if we're not careful. You know, when your heart grabs the truth, your life will become a living testimony of it.

After repenting, I listened to Dr. Rodney with a new eagerness. I knew that everything inside me had changed. At that moment, I heard him say two things: "As the seed of Abraham, you're commanded to be a blessing to the entire world," and "You can't bless anyone else when you don't even have enough for your own family." He also said that as a poor preacher in Africa, he called out to God and said, "Lord, if You will give me the key to breakthrough, I will make duplicates of that key, and I will pass them out to anyone who will take one by faith."

Suddenly, I knew that I would be a blessing to the whole world. I wanted to shout, "I took that key, and I know that I will be blessed to be a blessing." I was much more conservative in those days. I'm sure that if I had shouted that out loud, some patronizing preachers sitting around me would have patted me and said, "There, there now. Let's worry about living on our own and getting a better car before we declare that we will be a blessing to the whole world."

This, however, is a spiritual story, not a Cinderella story. My old, broken-down Chevy Cavalier did not turn into a brand-new Lexus. I still had to drive my old, totaled car. No one offered me a new home that day; I returned to the old trailer and was making plans to move in with a couple from my church. However, everything on the inside of me changed because I had received a heart revelation.

This change on the inside of me was so pronounced that it almost felt like physical poverty bands that had surrounded my heart and mind were being snapped. When things change on the inside, circumstances on the outside must begin to bow to that revelation knowledge on the inside. The enlargement begins on the inside of a person. It may take some time, but it will definitely happen. Today's church is embalmed with unbelief, and they continue to propagate the unbelief. But the Bible says in Isaiah 10:27, *"The yoke shall be destroyed because of the anointing."*

God rescued me from a life of poverty and lack that night. I have never been the same. My small thinking and poverty mentality were destroyed and replaced with faith in a big, big God. Hallelujah! Thank God for His mercy and grace. I never want to live outside of it.

What happened next is even more astounding. I once again distinctly heard the Lord speak to me. He said, "Debbie, I want you to teach about giving this same way everywhere you minister. This Word has to work in the villages as it works in the city. It must work for the red man and the black man like it works for a white man. It must work for a woman as it does for a man. It must work for the young and old like it works for the middle-aged, or it is not the Word of God." I began to argue with Him. Have you ever tried arguing with God? I can guarantee you that it is not a good idea.

I said, "Lord, I don't go to large churches like Dr. Rodney Howard-Browne does. I go to the villages of Alaska, where most missionaries don't even receive offerings, let alone teach before them. This will never fly there. They will think that I'm just a white woman coming to steal the last little bit that they have. They will run me out of the village."

I could see that not everyone was thrilled when Dr. Rodney taught stewardship in the large charismatic church that we were in. It would be worse in missionary territory. While I was arguing to no avail with God, Pastor Rodney stepped off the platform, walked up to where I was sitting and said,

"God told me to tell you that He is setting you free from poverty tonight. He also said to tell you that He is anointing you to teach this the same way that I am. He said to tell you that the Word of God must work in every nation, city, or village, or it's not the Word. It must work for the red man and the black man, or it's not the Word. It must work for a woman or child like it works for a man, or it's not the Word. It must work for the young and the old alike, or it's not the Word. The Word will work for anyone, anywhere! Also, if you do not teach it like this, He will hold you personally responsible for their poverty."

At that point, I swallowed hard, smiled, and said, "Yes, I just heard that somewhere." Deuteronomy 19:15 says, *"At the mouth of two witnesses, or at the mouth of three witnesses, shall the matter be established."*

What followed next was equally important. It was offering time. I realized that I had borrowed gas money to go to the meeting and had almost nothing. I checked my wallet and realized that I had only two quarters to put in the offering. People around me were putting in checks and bigger bills. (They made sure that I could see how much they were giving.) I knew that when I put two quarters in, those quarters would plunk like the lady with her last two mites in the Bible. It would be totally humiliating. I also thought about how fruitless it would be for Dr. Rodney's ministry. It could not contribute to doing any crusades. It would not even buy him a cup of coffee. He was already blessed. He was carrying a team with him. He would not even know that I gave it. While it would do him no good at all, it was my everything. I didn't even have milk for my children or gas in my tank. What would possibly be the purpose?

Thank God that those thoughts only stayed in my head for about two seconds. It took me much longer to type those words than they remained in my head. They were replaced by Holy Ghost thoughts. "Debbie, if you hold on to the little that you have, you will remain in this condition forever and never fulfill the assignment on your life. However, if you release it into My hands, in faith, you will never lack again."

Thank God that I surrendered my pride and plunked those two quarters into the bucket in faith and expectancy and never looked back. I gave one hundred percent. God doesn't look so much at the amount we give but at the percentage in comparison with what we have. I am sure that I gave more than some who were dropping in one thousand dollar checks in comparison with what they had in the bank. God honors that kind of sacrificial giving.

From that day forward, I have not backed off from teaching this message in any location that I have traveled, including the foreign field. I have now taught in most of the states of America, as well as fifty other nations. The Bible says in Romans 10:17, *"So then faith cometh by hearing, and hearing by the word of God."*

Since I hear myself teach on this subject almost every day and often twice a day, I have experienced faith coming fresh every day. God has given us many opportunities to act upon that faith as well. This area of His Word is very dear to my heart. Now, Pastor Rodney frequently asks me to teach on the subject of stewardship in his meetings. I thank God that he took the time and risked the offense of the people so that I could be forever changed. Now, I, too, can teach so that others can catch this message.

Will you be one of those who catch this message? Or will you be one who just reads this and then gains only mental assent? Will you be one who believes that this message may be fine for Pastor Rodney or for me, but it could never work for you? Worse yet, will you be one who refuses to believe, remaining exactly where you are? Will you remain with nothing more to share with a lost and dying world while you continue to criticize and judge those around you who have caught it? I hope not.

As for me, I did not wait to put into practice what I had learned but immediately began giving very sacrificially in Pastor Rodney's meetings. At first, seeing many around me give large amounts while I gave only a dollar or two embarrassed me. But I decided I would not be moved by my embarrassment. I cheerfully worshiped God in my giving and began mixing faith with it. I reminded God of His Word. "Lord, You are no respecter of persons. What You have done in Drs. Rodney and Adonica Howard-Browne's lives, You will do in mine. I believe I will be a blessing to the entire world. I believe that You will bless my socks off, so I may be a blessing." On some nights, I had more to give. Many times, however, I gave the last of what I had, but always very expectantly.

Even before I started receiving a salary from my own ministry, I persisted in giving sacrificially. I gave into other ministries, continuing to believe God would bless my own. I gave with joy and expectation, and it was only a matter of months before God began to bless me abundantly. In the last several years, God has taken me from being a single mother with a totaled car who lived in other people's homes to one who owns a car and a home of her own. God has allowed me to sow hundreds of thousands of dollars into His work all around the globe. Our ministry is putting people through Bible school, helping others start their ministries, contributing to new churches in foreign fields, and helping finance other ministries' soul-winning crusades.

It is too late to tell me that God's Word is not true! I have witnessed His faithfulness to me. It has been said that the man (or woman) with an experience is never at the mercy of the man with merely an argument. Thirty years ago, I knew I was in no condition to help anyone else; I didn't even have enough to help myself. Since catching a spirit of giving from Pastor Rodney, I have witnessed firsthand the provision of my wonderful God. I now have carried the same message to others around the world.

I am privileged to witness many others catching the same message. In the following pages, these same teachings will be presented to you. You, too, will have the opportunity to break out of your financial rut and begin to prosper until you also are a blessing to many. Remember, as Abraham's seed, you are commanded to be a blessing. The only way you can be a blessing is to be blessed.

I pray that God gives you ears to hear and eyes to see what you would otherwise be unable to comprehend. Grab this revelation with your heart, not just your head. Let revelation knowledge transform your life.

TWO

THE POWER OF THE TITHE

"For I am the Lord, I do not change [but remain faithful to My covenant with you]; that is why you, O sons of Jacob, have not come to an end.

"Yet from the days of your fathers you have turned away from My statutes and ordinances and have not kept them. Return to Me, and I will return to you," says the Lord of hosts. "But you say, 'How shall we return?'

"Will a man rob God? Yet you are robbing Me! But you say, 'In what way have we robbed You?' In tithes and offerings [you have withheld]. You are cursed with a curse, for you are robbing Me, this whole nation! Bring all the tithes (the tenth) into the storehouse, so that there may be food in My house, and test Me now in this," says the Lord of hosts, "if I will not open for you the windows of heaven and pour out for you [so great] a blessing until there is no more room to receive it. Then I will rebuke the devourer (insects, plague) for your sake and he will not destroy the fruits of the ground, nor will your vine in the field drop its grapes [before harvest]," says the Lord

> of hosts. "All nations shall call you happy and blessed, for you shall be a land of delight," says the Lord of hosts.
>
> MALACHI 3:6-12 (AMP)

The principle of the tithe is so important and yet so misunderstood. Some of you reading this are under the impression that you thoroughly understand this subject. I believe that a greater revelation of what it is about is coming to you as you read this book. Many know that they *should* tithe without ever understanding *why*. Some people have been browbeaten into becoming tithers. However, most who attend church do not tithe at all. These individuals are missing out on one of the greatest truths in the Word of God.

Statistics tell us that only about 5 percent of the Church tithes. These statistics refer to the entire Church around the world, including the Pentecostal, Charismatic, and full-Gospel denominations. This is a shocking indictment of the state of the Church. However, think about what the church has been able to do with only 5 percent of the Church tithing. The Church of the Lord Jesus Christ has triumphed through the ages, with only a few obeying this basic commandment of God.

Many churches and Bible schools have been built, missionaries launched to the four corners of the earth, and people from many countries have heard the Gospel. When global catastrophes have occurred, the Church has stepped forward with financial aid. The Church has fed millions, rebuilt homes previously destroyed by fire and floods, and helped multitudes of families in financial distress. This has been accomplished because *a few* chose to obey the Word of God in regard to tithing. If all of this has been accomplished by only 5 percent, how much more could we do with 100 percent of the Church tithing? I choose to believe that more of the Church will make the decision to do what is right. Until then, I will be part of the 5 percent. Will you? Tithing is a privilege. Even if the Bible did not promise us anything in return, I would continue to tithe. I choose to honor God; therefore, I worship Him with the first fruits of all that He has given me.

Some believe that tithing is strictly a principle of the Law. A man came up to me after a service, wanting to argue this point. He said that because I taught from Malachi, chapter 3, that morning, I was putting people back under the Law. He let me know that he did not plan on abiding by a "Law principle." I assured the gentleman that tithing was a biblical principle that ran from Genesis to Revelation.

We see this in Genesis 14:18-20 when Abraham tithed to Melchizedek hundreds of years before the Law was established. In a unique way, even Adam tithed in the Garden of Eden. God told Adam that he could eat of any of the trees in the garden, but one. God let Adam know that one tree was off-limits and belonged only to God. He was letting Adam know that he was only a steward, not an owner. Since creation, God made it clear that He wants the first of our love, worship, time, family, and finances. He is a jealous God who will compete with no other gods.

I continued to explain the principles of tithing to this man. I told him that even though my text was from the Old Testament, tithing was a principle for all times. However, if he wanted me to preach only from the New Testament, he needed to come back that night for the evening service. He agreed to come back to the next service. That evening, I shared from the Gospel of John about a woman of the New Testament who forgot all about Old Testament giving and gave what was equivalent to a year's wages (John 12:1-8).

Mary's brother, Lazarus, was raised from the dead through Jesus' ministry. Even her own life had been transformed. She knew that giving an Old Testament tithe of 10 percent was not sufficient to express her thanksgiving and worship. She was not questioning whether she was still required to give 10 percent. For her, 10 percent was not the end of giving; it was just the beginning.

The Bible tells us that this woman decided to give a year's wages. She made the decision to go way beyond Old Testament tithing. She was living in a new day when the New Covenant was being ushered in. She was not debating whether she was required to tithe off of the gross or net, as many do today. The heart of a giver does not try to meet the basic requirement but goes above and beyond the basic requirement. In this New Covenant, established upon better principles, the Old Testament 10 percent is simply where we begin.

After I shared this with the gentleman, he was no longer upset about giving an Old Testament tithe of 10 percent. He did not like the fact that I taught from the New Testament about a woman who gave a year's wages. He was not ready to talk about giving his all, as was seen in the New Testament widow woman's giving of her last two mites (Mark 12:42).

Today, in the New Testament Church, we really should not even have to bring up the issue of the Old Testament tithe. The Old Testament tithe was a requirement for a people who, in actual standing, were only God's servants. Today, those of us who are born again are God's children, with a new and better covenant established upon better promises. God promises to withhold no good gift from us (Psalm 84:11). We are born again (1 Peter 1:23) and filled with His Spirit (Ephesians 5:18). We have been redeemed from Hell (Revelation 5:9). Our names have been written down in the Lamb's Book of Life (Revelation 21:27). We have been seated in heavenly places with Christ Jesus (Ephesians 2:6) and the Devil is under our feet (Ephesians 1:20-22). We have joy unspeakable and full of glory (1 Peter 1:8). We have peace that passes all understanding (Philippians 4:7). God has given unto us all spiritual blessings (Ephesians 1:3) that pertain unto life and godliness (2 Peter 1:3). We will spend eternity (Romans 6:8) on streets of gold with gates of pearls (Revelation 21:21). Seeing that God has already given us His best, Jesus Christ, His only Son, why should we have a problem giving Him a mere 10 percent?

God could have required us to give back all 100 percent, or 90, or 75. God could have said that He was God, and we would just have to do this with no promise of a harvest. After all, 100 percent of everything we have belongs to God. The Bible says that the earth is the Lord's and the fullness thereof (Psalm 24:1). He owns the cattle on a thousand hills (Psalm 50:10).

God owns the air that we breathe, the feet that take us to work, and the hands with which we work. It is by Him that our hearts continue to beat and air is drawn into our lungs. We would find out rather quickly how truly dependent we were upon Him if God ever withdrew His grace from our lives. However, our good God does not operate that way. Our God is a God of blessing.

God's entire plan is for our good and not for evil. He is not a bully. He is a Provider, a Healer, a Father, a Savior; He is the Lover of our souls. When God asks us to do something, it is always with our best interest in mind, and it will always bring us the very best benefits. So why, then, should we begrudge God a mere 10 percent of what already belongs to Him? Why, then, would we argue with a good God about anything? There is a wealth of promises in God's Word. Malachi, chapter 3, is full of such promises.

Verse 6 is where we will begin our study for this chapter. In that verse, God reminds us that He never changes. This is another reminder that tithing will never end. When God declares something, He does not change His mind later, deciding that it was a bad idea. If God desired for us to honor Him in such a way back then, He still desires it today.

In verse 7, God reminded Israel that they were backslidden and had been for a while. He proceeded to tell them how to rectify that problem. There, the question is raised, "How should they return to Him?" I would have expected Him to say something like, "With sackcloth and ashes," or, "Return with great fasting and prayer." Typically, in one way or another, we would have expected to see a dramatic display of repentance. And, believe it or not, that is exactly what we do see, just not in the usual way.

We see throughout the Old Testament that when people backslide, they quit tithing. When they quit tithing, they backslide. Which one comes first? It is evident that they occur simultaneously. In this passage, God let Israel know that if they truly desired to repent, they would begin to tithe again. One of the first evidences of backsliding is when a person stops tithing. By the same token, one of the first evidences of repentance is that the person resumes tithing once more. Remember the old adage, when you have a person's pocketbook, you have their heart? Giving is a very practical way of displaying our hunger and honor for God. Hunger for Him is not just displayed in what we say, for we already know that words come cheap. Hunger for God is displayed in what we do and what we do not do.

It is no coincidence that the Bible reveals how closely the heart and the pocketbook are intertwined. Jesus tells us that if we cannot be trusted with simple mammon, we cannot be trusted with the true riches (Luke 16:11). What are the true riches? They include the glory, the anointing, God's joy, signs and wonders, and the healing power of God. Jesus said in Matthew 6:21 that where your treasure is, your heart will be also. It is no wonder, then, that in the 3rd chapter of Malachi, God told Israel that the way to return to Him was through tithing. We come to realize that once we can relinquish what is most precious to us and become a giver, God has our hearts.

In verse 8, God told His people that they had been robbing Him. What strong language! Today, many would even find such language offensive. They consider their money as their own when, in reality, it belongs to God. They would become indignant at God's audacity to suggest such a thing. They might shrug it off, saying, "This is my money and certainly not the serious offense you're making it out to be."

However, we are all stewards of God's money. His plan is for us to be blessed if we will simply become the best stewards that we can be with what He has entrusted to us. He calls the people who don't tithe, thieves and robbers.

When I think of someone committing robbery, I envision armed men in ski masks forcefully entering a shop, demanding that everyone, "Stick 'em up!" Then, they would command the clerk behind the counter to hand over the money. This is precisely the terminology that God chose to use for people who did not tithe.

Verse 9 tells us that Israel was cursed with a curse. It declares that the disobedient brought a curse on the entire nation. I am sure that, at that time, there were remnants of people still tithing. God has always had a remnant of the obedient. Not every single person was backslidden. Yet, the disobedience of the majority was bringing a curse upon the whole nation. Therefore, God lumped the entire nation together in common disobedience, stating, *"You are robbing me, even this whole nation."* The Bible tells us in Galatians 5:9, *"A little leaven leaveneth the whole lump."*

Some would mistakenly say that verse 9 is only referring to Old Testament Law. However, the Bible tells us in the New Testament that we are the Body of Christ, jointly fitted together. What one does directly affects the other. So we must all work together.

That is why it is so important that we all work together in unity. On any given Sunday morning, what the worship leader does affects the congregation, and vice versa. We cannot sit back and let the ministers worship and do everything for us. That would negatively affect the corporate anointing in the entire church. When it is time to stand, we must stand. When we are praising God, it is best that we all clap and sing. The more we get corporately involved in the service, the better.

How well the congregation responds with *Amen* affects the preaching. How well that minister preaches affects the congregation. How well the children behave affects the teacher. How well the Sunday school teacher teaches affects the children. None of us are an island to ourselves. I must be obedient to God, not just for my sake but also for yours. My lack of obedience can affect you.

Verse 10 states that all the tithes must be brought into the storehouse. *The Amplified Bible* says that a tithe is the whole tenth of your income. The term tithe comes from the Hebrew word meaning *tenth*. It is not a twelfth, not a fifteenth, not a twentieth or less, but a total of a tenth. Many people just drop something into the offering plate once a week, lackadaisically unconcerned about the amount. It is as though they are simply tipping God. However, God is a holy and awesome God. Not only is God not interested, but He is actually insulted by our "tips." Remember, God calls anything less than the 10 percent tithe "robbery."

God tells us to bring the tenth into the storehouse. Where, today, is our storehouse? Our storehouse is the place where we receive our spiritual food, i.e., the local church to which we are committed. Some people actually give a tenth of their income, but that tenth is divided between the person, ministry, or institutions of their choice. Or they may divide their tithe between several ministries, once again believing that it is their prerogative to do so. They could not be more wrong.

I remember once holding a revival in a place that I will leave unnamed. Before the Sunday morning service, I asked the pastor if he would like for me to teach before the tithes and offerings were received. Now, not only was he a friend of Pastor Rodney's who clearly knew how we taught, but he also knew he could trust me, and my teaching could only benefit his church. So, I did not expect him to waver. However, he thought for a few moments, hesitating before agreeing that I could teach. Halfway into the offering teaching, he burst out laughing. I knew that this pastor yielded to the Holy Spirit easily and frequently got quite drunk in the Holy Ghost. Still, I perceived that something I said had specifically prompted his outburst. But I continued on, and we had a good service.

Afterward, the pastor and I engaged in conversation. As we were talking, he asked if I had noticed his laughter. When I told him, "Yes," the pastor related that his church had recently sent several evangelists out into the ministry. Shortly before the morning service, he had been informed that some of his congregation had begun tithing to these evangelists and relatives who were in the ministry elsewhere. The pastor had wanted to address this specific issue in the service. However, he knew that if he let me teach before the offering, he would miss that opportunity.

The pastor's outburst of laughter was in acknowledgment of the Holy Spirit, who, very aware of the problem, had me address it with no prior knowledge of the issue. It was actually much better that I addressed it because the people knew that I had no knowledge of the situation. Therefore, they knew that the instruction came from the heart of God. The pastor was overwhelmingly delighted that God brought this out into the open, exposing and correcting the church's error. Thank God for the Holy Ghost!

Verse 10 also mentions *why* we should bring the tithe back into the storehouse. God is so good! Not only does He tell us what to do, but He also tells us why. God always has our best interest at heart. He says that when we bring the tithe into the storehouse, there will be food in His house. Now, I don't know about you, but I like good food. I don't want just any kind of food. I want to have the best food I can have. The Bible speaks of both the meat and the milk of the Word. I want rich, hearty food that is both palatable and nutritious.

Many congregation members feel that responsibility for the spiritual food we eat rests entirely with the pastor. They pray and ask God to get a hold of their pastor so that he will preach better. Perhaps they even hope that the pastor will fast and pray in order to become sensitive enough to give them just the right food. They certainly don't want stale manna. What these people do not realize, though, is that they share in the responsibility for good food being in the house. In this passage, God does not say that the pastor must fast and pray so that the congregation will be fed good food. It says that *if we tithe*, there will be food in the house. This gives us one more reason to become excited about tithing.

The Bible also tells us that through tithing, we can prove God. Notice that the Bible didn't say to *try* God. Many individuals will hear a good message on tithes and offerings and decide to try it. They will tithe on Sunday and expect their broken refrigerator to be fixed by Monday morning. If it is not, they will get discouraged and quit tithing, saying, "I should have known that this wouldn't work for me. It only seems to work for some." Then they give up on the Word of God.

I want you to know that anyone can try God for a few hours, days, weeks, or even years. It does not take any tenacity or faith to *try* something. It is when the going gets rough, and your faith is being put to the test, that others will see whether you are going to prove Him. The Bible says that even the Devil believes and trembles. It says that after you have done all to stand, you must stand. You must continue on believing to prove God.

You must continue to tithe even when it looks like you are going under. You must press through financial setbacks, failing economies and predictions, well-advising friends, and all of Hell that will try to get you distracted from proving Him. Proving God takes faith, patience, determination, commitment, and tenacity. You must know that you know, that God is true, and every man is a liar. It will be worth it to prove Him! Will you be one to prove Him or one who only tries Him?

Perhaps you have heard of a man by the name of J.C. Penney. Many do not realize that he was a Christian who gave God all the glory for his success. The story is told that he was a firm believer in the Word of God and, therefore, in tithing. When the Great Depression of the 1930s hit America, his business and everyone's businesses around him were dramatically affected. About this time, a friend of his opened a store across the street. When the Depression began to seriously affect business, his friend came to him. He told Mr. Penney that because of the Depression, he had decided to quit tithing. He then asked Mr. Penney if he was going to follow suit. Without hesitation, J.C. Penney answered that because they were in the Depression, he was going to double his tithe. Eventually, Mr. Penney's friend lost his store. What happened with J.C. Penney and the prosperity of his great chain of stores made history. There is great power in obedience and faith in God's Word.

Robert G. LeTourneau was a prolific inventor of earthmoving machinery and the founder of LeTourneau Technologies, Inc. His factories supplied machinery, which represented nearly 70 percent of the earthmoving equipment and engineering vehicles used by the Allied forces during World War II, and more than half of the 1,500-mile Alcan Highway in Canada was built with LeTourneau equipment. Over the course of his life, he secured nearly 300 patents relating to earthmoving equipment, manufacturing processes, and machine tools.

His pastor told him that God needs Christian businessmen to support His work. He realized that everything God had done for him was for the glory of God and decided to implement the ideas in his head. He said, "God is going to be my business partner." He and his wife ended up giving God 90 percent and only lived on 10 percent. This is something we should all aim for.

God is such a good God. He is infinite, omniscient, omnipresent, and omnipotent. As finite humans, we give ourselves far too much credit. God set up the principle of tithing for our benefit, not His. Tithing was initiated to give us an opportunity to prove Him and to be blessed. If we don't tithe, God will not go broke. He will not have to hock some of the pearly gates or fire half of the angels. God will not be forced to liquidate the golden streets just because people disobey Him. He will still be God, and He will still be on the throne tomorrow, just as He is today.

God went on to say that He would open up the windows of Heaven for us. In Bible days, windows were open spaces with curtains hanging over them, not glass panes, as we know today. If someone wanted to look out the window, he or she would have to draw back the curtain so that what was available could be seen. Sometimes, someone else would open the window for them as they went to look out. In our text, God is saying that when we tithe, He will personally pull back the curtain so that we can look through at what is available to us.

Just think! As you tithe, God pulls back the curtain, and you begin to see what He has for you. It will remain hidden until you take this step of obedience. That's why fresh revelation knowledge comes when we obey God by tithing. It becomes an exciting adventure. Beyond the curtain, we can finally see all that God has made for us and keeps available for those who love Him.

The *Matthew Henry Commentary* made an interesting note about God opening up the windows of Heaven:

> Very sudden plenty is expressed by opening the windows of plenty. We find the windows of plenty. We find the windows of Heaven opened to pour down a deluge of wrath in Noah's flood in Genesis 7:11. But here they are opened to pour down blessings, to such a degree that there should not be room enough to receive them. So plentifully shall their ground bring forth that they should be tempted to pull down their barns and build greater, for want of rooms as in Luke 12:18.

I find it interesting that God uses the very same expression about pouring us out a blessing as He does when He speaks of pouring out the deluge, or Heaven's floodgates, during Noah's flood. Yet, God says that He will pour out such a blessing that we won't have enough room to receive it. He means what He says.

Verse 11 says that God will rebuke the devourer for our sake. This is an awesome promise. The Bible tells us in Colossians 2:15, *"And having spoiled principalities and powers, he made a shew of them openly, triumphing over them in it."*

Jesus already defeated the Devil and made a show of him openly. In Bible days, when an army defeated another army, they dragged the defeated foe through the streets, their foot on the defeated ones' necks. They wanted everyone to see who the victor was and who the defeated foe was. That is what the Bible is referring to when it says that God made a show of them openly. If Jesus has the keys of death, Hell, and the grave, and the Devil is a defeated foe, then I don't have to try to defeat the enemy. I only have to occupy the land that God has already given me.

In addition, the Bible tells me that God will rebuke the enemy. He does a much better job than I could ever hope to do. However, there is a qualification for God rebuking the Devil. First, I must be in obedience to God; I must be a tither.

Verse 12 tells us that all the nations shall call us happy and blessed. A tither is a blessed and happy person. When I am holding revival and begin teaching on giving, I can almost tell who is tithing and giving and who is not. The people's faces give them away every time. The only people who have problems with giving are the ones who don't give. The same is true of revival. The only people who have problems with it are not in it. The only people who hate joy are those who don't have any.

Several years ago, I was meditating upon the conditions and subsequent promises of Malachi 3. As I meditated, I became puzzled at the reluctance of God's people to become true tithers. I started wondering why born-again, Spirit-filled people, who had been given eternal life, would even hesitate to give at least the amount that Old Testament people gave. So, I began to pray, asking the Lord about it. He responded and showed me the reason. I heard the words, "How many of those people do you think are really saved, Debbie?" I was so surprised by God's response. I said, "Lord, surely You are not accusing people of not being saved or born again based upon their lack of giving?" I received the same question back from Him again. I quoted verses from the Bible to the Lord about how to become born again. I pointed out that according to Romans 10:9-10, a person must only believe in their heart and confess with their mouth the Lord Jesus Christ, and he or she would be saved. Finally, after several moments, I received more revelation from the Holy Spirit. The Lord reminded me that many individuals say things with their mouths that they do not believe; therefore, the things that they say never take root.

Suddenly, I could see a picture of people coming through the gate of Heaven to stand before God. If God were to ask them why He should let them into Heaven, I could hear and see people saying things like, "Oh, that's easy. Your Word says in Romans 10, verses 9 and 10, that all I must do is confess with my mouth and believe with my heart. I know the day I did that. I walked up an aisle in front of people and did just that."

Then God would reply, "Oh, you believe in My Word, do you? Did you also believe Malachi 3, where I said that if you tithed, I would open up the windows of Heaven for you and pour out a floodgate blessing that there would not be room enough to receive?" They would answer, "No, Lord, I didn't believe that part, but I do believe Romans 10, verses 9 and 10."

In this vision, God asked, "Did you also believe My Word in Philippians 4, verse 19, that speaks of My meeting your needs according to My riches in glory? What about Luke 6, verse 38, that says that as you give, men will give back to you good measure, pressed down, shaken together, and running over?"

"No, Lord. I must admit that I struggled in believing those parts, but I really did believe Romans 10, verses 9 and 10. That's all that really counts, isn't it?"

I could see God inquiring further, "Did you believe what I said in the 28th chapter of Deuteronomy about how I would bless you coming in and going out? Did you believe the part of 2 Corinthians, chapters 9 and 10, which spoke of giving? Did you believe Me in Third John, that as you gave, My desire was that you would prosper and be in health even as your soul prospered?

"How about what I put in Galatians about sowing and reaping, or the parts of My Word that talk about becoming good stewards? Did you believe Me when I said that where your treasure was, your heart would be also, and about seeking first the Kingdom of God and My righteousness? What about giving you power to get wealth like it says in Deuteronomy 8? What about all of those giving and tithing Verses found in both the Old and New Testaments? Did you believe any of them?"

I could see many people sadly responding, "No, Lord. I couldn't really believe any of those passages, but I insist that I believe the ones about salvation."

Then God replied, "You are trying to tell Me that you believe what My Word says about eternal salvation, even though it is something of another world that you cannot taste, see, hear, feel, or smell. You can believe it by faith, but you cannot believe the rest of the passages of My Word that talk about an easy, tangible thing like money. Did I not say that if you cannot be trusted with natural mammon, you couldn't be trusted with the true riches? You do not believe Me for salvation. You have only been fooling yourself. You may have said something with your mouth, but your heart never really believed. You don't know Me at all."

Some of you may think that this is a little harsh, but it is what God revealed to me by His Spirit. No wonder so much is said in His Word about giving. No wonder many serious things took place in His Word as a result of people's hearts not being right when it came to giving. Remember Cain, Ananias and Sapphira, and Judas. I am not making a legalistic, religious judgment here. I would not presume to do so. However, I think it serves as a good reminder for all of us to check our hearts in certain areas. Giving is a true revealer of the heart.

I realize that some have only known legalistic, religious Christians, never hearing good teaching on this subject. However, after a while, as God begins to reveal His Word to us by His Spirit, we must make adjustments and grow up. There is no condemnation to those reading this book who may not have been tithers and givers. Instead, this is an opportunity for repentance and adjustments, victory and freedom.

As quickly as you get this under the Blood of the Lamb, God has forgotten that you were not a tither. You get to start out fresh from this day on. Hallelujah! You, too, get a chance to prove Him. He will not let you down. Who knows? One day, you might be writing your own book about what a good and faithful God He has become to you. This will be the Holy Ghost adventure of a lifetime!

The next several verses of this passage are equally important. Many individuals legalistically obey God but are not willing or cheerful about it. As soon as they give, these people begin to complain and murmur against God. They knowingly or unknowingly make accusations against Him. They begin by saying that the wicked are more blessed than the righteous and it doesn't pay to serve God.

It may look as if the wicked are getting away with a lot right now, but they aren't. There are a lot of things going on behind the scenes that we don't know about. These people may have money, but we do not know what fear they fight on the inside about losing it. Sometimes, there is tremendous guilt associated with how they made their money or how much they neglected their families. We must always keep our mouths lined up with God's Word and stay on His side. We must speak of God's promises, His faithfulness, His mercy, and His grace unto His own children. As the old saying goes, "Payday may not always be on Friday, but payday is coming." One day, everything will be made right. Do not be envious or jealous of the unrighteous. Just stay faithful, obedient, and true.

Verse 16 reminds us that God is listening as we speak to one another about Him. He makes a book of remembrance to include us when we speak highly and faithfully of Him. God promises to spare us in the day of calamity. This is just one more good reason to stay on His side. I will speak of the goodness of God all the days of my life. Of course, the only way we can do that is if God's promises have been tried and proven in our lives.

Won't you join me in proving that God is faithful to His Word? If you are not a tither now, won't you become one? If you are already a tither, make it a goal to give above the tithe. Many men and women have achieved giving not just 10 percent but giving 90 percent and living on only 10 percent. That has become my goal as well. I trust that after thorough examination, you will be as blessed as I have been by this tremendous Word of God.

THREE

THE BREAKING OF THE ALABASTER BOX

This teaching on the subject of giving is my favorite. I am most known for this teaching. I hear quite often, "Evangelist Debbie, I don't know of anyone who can teach this as you do." Other ministers have told me that they took good notes and tried to teach it the same way and could not. They ask why that is. I believe that the answer is quite simple. I become Mary in the story because I have been her many times, as God has asked me to break open many alabaster boxes in holy worship to Him. This is a revelation to me. It is a way of life for me. It is not a nice teaching. That is why the glory of God comes into the room in a very real way when I teach it. God is well-pleased.

Scholars tell us that out of the three and one-half years of Jesus' ministry on this earth, only twenty-seven days are recorded. It's no wonder that John tells us in John 21:25, *"And there are also many other things which Jesus did, the which, if they should be written every one, I suppose that even the world itself could not contain the books that should be written."* So, the Holy Spirit had to make a decision about what to include in the holy Bible and what to leave out. He included three separate alabaster box breakings among the four Gospels—not one, but three. They are broken by three different women in three different locations and with different people present. Most people think it is the same alabaster box breaking but it most definitely is not. This tells me that the breaking of an alabaster box is near to the heart of God, and He thinks it is of utmost importance. Anything that God thinks is important is important to me. This is not a side-subject to the Gospel. It is front and center and a big part of the Gospel. Jesus tells us in Matthew 26:13b that *"Wheresoever this gospel shall be preached in the whole world, there shall also this, that this woman hath done, be told for a memorial of her."* By teaching this in this book, I am preaching the Gospel.

There are different details that serve to bring out different important points in each of the alabaster box breakings. However, my favorite to teach from is John 12:1-8. Let's look at this powerful passage of Scripture.

> Then Jesus six days before the passover came to Bethany, where Lazarus was, which had been dead, whom he raised from the dead.
>
> JOHN 12:1

This occurred just six days before Jesus would be crucified. Whatever the Father wanted to be accomplished in Jesus' life must be accomplished in this last week. It follows that every event of this last week was especially important, and the Holy Spirit, the Author of our Bible, was making sure that only the most important events would be recorded. Details are important, or they would not have been included. We are also told that Jesus went to Bethany and to the home of his dear friends, Lazarus, Mary, and Martha, a man and his two sisters. The entire family was close to Jesus, and He stopped there often on His way to Jerusalem. They were close friends who cared deeply about one another. We are also given the detail that Lazarus was the one who had been dead, but Jesus raised him from the dead. The Holy Spirit wanted to make sure that we are reminded of what took place in the raising of Lazarus from the dead because it is a central point to this story.

Can you imagine what it was like for Martha and Mary to watch their brother deteriorating by the hour as he sank closer and closer to death? I am sure that they sent word to Jesus that Lazarus was sick and expected to die. They had watched Jesus heal countless people, stop funerals and raise the dead, and perform many miracles. I am sure that they would have expected Jesus to come and heal their brother, especially if He knew that it was His good friend Lazarus. However, it did not happen. Jesus checked in with His Father to see if He should go heal Lazarus. The Father said no, and Jesus could only do what He saw the Father do and say what He heard the Father say. The day came when Jesus was told that Lazarus was dead. Jesus checked in with the Father again and now was given the okay to go heal Lazarus. When Jesus arrived, Lazarus was dead and stinking in the tomb because he had been dead for four days. It seemed to the sisters that Jesus was four days too late. However, it is important to realize that He is never late. He is always on time.

The sisters were deep in grief and mourning when they saw Jesus walk up to the tomb. I am sure many thoughts ran through their heads. They were human. Possibly they thought, 'Why did You bother to come now when it is too late? Why did You let us down by allowing our brother to die when You healed others? Did You come now just to cry with us?' Jesus walked directly to the tomb and commanded, *"Lazarus, come forth."* It is a good thing that Jesus called his name, or everyone who was dead would have come out of their tombs. Mary and Martha watched with amazement as Lazarus walked out of the tomb, alive, raised from the dead, and healed of whatever sickness had taken his life. However, he came out of the tomb, still bound in grave clothes. Jesus gave another command, *"Loose him and let him go."* Now he was free and unfettered, as well as alive and healed. The sisters were so overcome with joy and gratitude that they began to think of ways to thank Jesus. They thought of a way. They would invite him to supper. It would be a very special one for one purpose: to thank Him for raising their brother from the dead.

> There they made him a supper; and Martha served: but Lazarus was one of them that sat at the table with him.
>
> JOHN 12:2

For the Bible to give us these details, they have to be paramount to this story. We would not need to know about the supper or Lazarus being raised from the dead unless it was central to the revelation of this passage.

Here, we have a powerful story of worship through giving. Jesus had touched and changed Mary's life in a wonderful way. She would never be the same. She loved Jesus and desired to let Him know how much. She, along with her brother and sister, had invited the Lord to their home just to let Him know how much they loved Him. This time, they weren't asking Him for healing or to raise someone from the dead. They wanted only to express their gratitude and to love Him.

They must have been southerners for it to be called supper instead of dinner. The first thing that I want you to realize is that this family was not wealthy. Wealthy Jewish families had the servants prepare the supper. In this case, the ladies were doing it themselves, which proves that they did not have much money.

I am sure that Martha was nervous and distressed about making sure the supper was perfect.

> Now it came to pass, as they went, that he entered into a certain village: and a certain woman named Martha received him into her house.
> And she had a sister called Mary, which also sat at Jesus' feet, and heard his word.
> But Martha was cumbered about much serving, and came to him, and said, Lord, dost thou not care that my sister hath left me to serve alone? bid her therefore that she help me.
> And Jesus answered and said unto her, Martha, Martha, thou art careful and troubled about many things:
> But one thing is needful: and Mary hath chosen that good part, which shall not be taken away from her.
>
> LUKE 10:38-42

Martha was concerned with many acts of service. She was probably busy dusting, vacuuming, and preparing the perfect meal. I am sure that she was going through her recipe book to look for the most gourmet meal that she could prepare. The dessert had to be something over the top. Jesus was coming, and that meant that it was not the night for Kentucky Fried Chicken and paper plates. It was the night to bring out the best china. Martha believed that the house had to be spotless. This was no ordinary evening. They felt that they could not make a supper that would adequately say "thank you" the way they wanted. However, they would try their very best.

We do not have the details about the conversation at the table or details of what happened later. However, I can imagine some of what must have taken place. Mary, Martha, Jesus, and Lazarus were all present at the table. We don't know the table seating placement, but there must have been a lot of staring at the table. When Jesus and Lazarus exchanged stories and conversation, as well as laughs, the sisters had to be thinking, 'Look at our brother laughing and eating and telling stories. We were just at the tomb where he was dead and stinking. How can this be? It is only because of the one sitting across from him, Jesus. He has done this thing for us. He has wrought this miracle.' They would look at their brother and then look at the One who gave them the miracle. I imagine that there were tears of joy at the table as well.

I once had the privilege of eating at a table where a man who had been raised from the dead at a Reinhard Bonnke meeting was present. As I heard the story of him being dead for three days and even being embalmed, I enjoyed watching him eat, chew, and swallow. It was an incredible experience that I will never forget. Actually, people should find my chewing and swallowing fascinating. On March 26, 2006, I had a saddle pulmonary embolism hit my lungs and fill up every lobe of my lungs. It cut off all oxygen to my body in a moment. I was flown by helicopter to Tampa General Hospital and told that I would not survive the night. I actually left my body three times that night and could see the paramedics working on me. I was healed by the power of God, and you can read about that in my book, *Resurrected: Overcoming Death, Destruction, and Defeat*. The fact that

I left my body should cause people to enjoy watching me eat or do anything.

I can imagine how Mary and Martha were feeling. They must have felt that the supper was inadequate to thank the man who had raised their brother from the dead.

As Martha began to clear the dinner and do the dishes, Mary was thinking of how she wanted to take the worship to another level, above a nice supper. Compared to the depth of her gratitude, Mary might have felt that even her best attempts to express her feelings would sound shallow. I am sure her sister became somewhat annoyed at the glazed look of love and worship on Mary's face as she contemplated how she could thank and worship Jesus. Martha probably said something like, "Mary, please get that look off your face and come out here and help me with the dishes." Mary could have replied, "I'm sorry, I'll be there in a moment, but I have to take worship to another level first."

Maybe she looked at Jesus and said, "Master, I know that everyone tells You that they love You, but I must try again. I love You, I really do. I thank You for what You did for our family and for Lazarus. Do You know how much we love, honor, and exalt You?" Maybe she realized afterward that words sometimes come cheap. Just days after this, people would be calling out to Him, *"Hosanna, King of the Jews,"* and then would a few days later yell, *"Crucify Him."* Sometimes, words do not mean very much. No wonder the songwriter Charles Wesley expressed it this way, "O for a thousand tongues to sing my great Redeemer's praise." Thank God that today, we have the gift of tongues to help us pray and worship. Mary must have thought, 'There must be a better way to express this.' She longed to let Jesus know that nothing could compare with the love she had for Him.

Maybe she decided to give Him a holy kiss on each cheek. Perhaps she would try singing a worship song to Him, much like one that we might sing today: "In moments like these, I lift up my hands to Jesus. In moments like these, I sing out a love song to Jesus." I can picture the tears flowing down her face as Mary poured herself into the song. Still, it wasn't enough. She realized that anyone could sing to Him, whether heartfelt or not. No, she would need another expression of worship—one that would leave no doubt as to how she felt and how thankful she was that Jesus had forever changed her life. It would need to be expressed in a more sacrificial way. She pondered as to what else she could do. Perhaps she did a meaningful Israeli dance for Him or sang for Him. She still felt that all of these deeds fell short of what she was trying to describe from her heart.

For many years, there was a popular praise chorus that almost every Pentecostal and charismatic church sang. It was called *When I Think of His Goodness*. The song had several verses to it that went something like this:

> When I think of His goodness and what He's done for me
> When I think of His goodness and how He set me free
> I want to praise, praise, praise, praise, praise, praise, praise
>   all night, all night.

The next verse was...

> I want to jump, jump, jump.

And then...

> I want to clap, clap, clap.

Many churches continued to add verses such as...

> I want to run, run, run,
> I want to dance, dance, dance,
> I want to twist, twist, twist,

As the visiting evangelist, I wanted to sing, "I want to rest, rest, rest." I was exhausted from multiple action verses. Sometimes, I felt as though churches were trying to outdo each other in add-on verses. It was their way of saying, "Some people only love You enough to clap and sing. We love You more. We love You enough to jump, run, dance, twist, shout, and more." I can appreciate what they were trying to express. However, how sacrificial is it really to jump or dance for a few minutes unless you are physically handicapped in some way? As I thought on this, I began to wonder why no one ever sings, "When I think of His goodness and what He's done for me, when I think of His goodness and how He's set me free, I want to give, give, give, give, give, give, give all night, all night." As soon as I asked this within my heart, I heard the Holy Spirit say, "That's because it is so much easier for people to jump or shout or clap than it is to give." Yet, the Bible does not say that God so loved the world that he shouted, clapped, or danced. He gave His only. He did not have an extra couple of sons. He gave His only and His best before we ever responded to Him.

Giving represents our entire lives, eight hours away from home on a daily basis, of blood, sweat, and tears. Giving is one of the highest forms of sacrificial worship that exists. Your mortgage, utilities, children, vehicles, vacation, retirement, wardrobe, and playtime are all asking for those finances. But when you put God first in holy worship, He is well pleased.

I am sure that Mary ran out of ways to express her gratitude and worship. She was probably frustrated that she was not able to adequately let Him know that He was her everything. Then, suddenly, she remembered her precious alabaster box that was kept in a secret location. She thought, "That's it! I know what I must do."

> Then took Mary a pound of ointment of spikenard, very costly, and anointed the feet of Jesus, and wiped his feet with her hair: and the house was filled with the odour of the ointment.
>
> JOHN 12:3

We don't know from where Mary purchased the alabaster box. Was it her inheritance? Did she work a year for it? Was she saving it for a rainy day? Was it for her future? It may have had great sentimental value. Was she planning on passing it down to someone else? We do not know. We only know that it was very costly. The Amplified Bible says that it was very expensive. Again, the Holy Spirit is giving us details that He wanted to be included in the holy Bible. The fact that it was costly must be very important. This was not superficial worship; this worship was premeditated and costly. This worship was the kind where the rubber meets the road.

Many times, I hear people say, "It's not how much we give that is important; it's only the thought that counts." That is a ridiculous statement, and you cannot find anything like that in the Bible. You can only find it in the book of "I Say So." I would like to see that person tell that to their banker when only making a partial mortgage payment: "I don't think I should have to pay you that expensive amount. I had a nice thought about you today." Try telling the same thing to the grocery store manager: "I know my groceries amount to $200, but I feel like only giving you about $15. It's the thought that counts, and I had a great thought about this grocery store today." They will ask if your momma knows you are here. We only get this ridiculous when it comes to the things of God. It is time the Body of Christ wakes up and understands what worship is all about.

I want you to think about a husband and wife on their anniversary. She decides to lavish him with the best gift that she can afford. She goes out of her way to either buy or make a card that expresses her love. She prepares an over-the-top dinner of all of his favorite foods. She even buys clothing that she knows he would love and puts it on. After the dinner, gift, and card, she tells him how much she loves him. She now wonders what he will give her, and he says while walking away, "I had a nice thought about you today." I don't think she would feel very loved in return. Our God has lavished us with everything, and when we come back with nothing but an excuse that it is the thought that counts, He will not feel very loved.

Where there is much love, great sacrifice always follows. Our entire hearts are in this kind of worship. It is so costly that unless you were moved by the Holy Spirit, you could not do it. We see that with the widow woman who gave her last two mites, which was one hundred percent. We see it again with King David, who said that he would not give the Lord anything that did not cost him. My Bible says that God so loved the world that He gave. When we love like He loves, we become like Him. We are not going through religious motions. This is the kind of worship that requires everything. It is the essence of true worship.

It only took seconds to break open her alabaster box, and yet, we are still smelling it in the church over two thousand years later. I studied about alabaster and found out why it is so expensive. It is mined from deep within the earth, usually in Egypt, in Bible days. It is delicate and has to be handled very precisely. It must be twisted and turned, and then twisted and turned again until it is on the surface of the earth. God is after our hearts, and in this Western society, our finances are wrapped around our hearts. When we are worshipping or sitting under the Word of God being preached, God is turning and twisting our hearts until He has them in His hands for good. We see here that He had Mary's heart.

Mary poured this expensive perfume and oil mix that was worth a year's wages upon the One she loved so much. How much would a year's wages be today? I think $50,000 would be a conservative amount in 2024. Yet, it is hard for us to imagine any perfume costing that much to just pour it all out in a moment.

I want you to imagine that you were there that night when Mary lavished Jesus. Would you have a problem with someone pouring a year's wages of $50,000 on Jesus? Most people suddenly grow angelic wings when asked this question. They reply, "Of course not. It's for Jesus." None of us would have a problem with someone lavishing Jesus with such extravagance because He is the Son of God. If He were physically here, we would love to worship Him in such a way. The problem, though, is that physically, He is no longer here. Currently, He is seated at the right hand of the Father.

What if the same person poured $50,000 worth of perfume on your pastors? Would you have a problem? Most people would. They would consider that a waste. "That's too much for any preacher." Let's take it a step further. What if a person off the streets whom you do not know walked into a church service where you were attending, and someone poured $50,000 of perfume on that stranger? Would you now have a problem? Most would. Yet the Bible says in Matthew 25:40, *"And the King shall answer and say unto them, Verily I say unto you, Inasmuch as ye have done it unto one of the least of these my brethren, ye have done it unto me."* The way we give to God is through His people and His ministries. He counts that the same as if we are giving directly to Him.

No one has a pole long enough to reach into Heaven for you to give directly to God. It must be done through His servants. Yet, many in the Church fail to realize this and criticize people who are lavish givers and criticize the ministers who receive the gifts. They call it a waste. People do not realize that the Bible says that God's servants who teach and preach the Gospel are worthy of double honor. That is speaking of finances. People also do not realize that their own prosperity is tied to the honor they give to those who are called to lead them.

After Mary poured this expensive perfume on Jesus, she knelt down in front of Him and began to wipe His feet with her hair. That perfume ran down her hair, her hands, arms, and clothing. She began to shine and smell just like Jesus. The same anointing and fragrance that she was pouring on Him could not help but get on her, too. Within minutes, she was covered with the same fragrance. When you worship Jesus with your giving, that precious oil runs all over you. The worship that you pour out comes back around you and lavishes you, as well. It causes you to look, think, smell, and do just like Jesus. The anointing douses you in His presence, His glory, and His love.

The Bible tells us that the entire house was filled with the fragrance. Do you realize that offerings have a fragrance? The anointing has a fragrance. It goes before you and permeates and changes everything. We see many times in the Scriptures that offerings have a smell. When the animals were sacrificed under the Old Covenant, the smell came up before the Father as sweet incense. It resulted in the fire coming down and consuming the sacrifice. It was a very holy time, a sacred worship. Philippians 4:18 says, *"But I have all, and abound: I am full, having received of Epaphroditus the things which were sent from you, an odour of a sweet smell, a sacrifice acceptable, wellpleasing to God."* Some offerings smell sweet to the Lord, and some actually stink. I want to make sure that every offering I give to Him is a sweet smell unto His nostrils.

Just days later, Jesus went to the whipping post for my healing and your healing. The whipping post was a gruesome torture that most did not survive. It is described as being just as tortuous, or possibly more so, than the crucifixion. Many criminals did not survive the whipping post to go to the cross. Yet, He was willing to endure it for the joy that was set before Him. Every stripe was for our healing. The Bible says in 1 Peter 2:24, *"Who his own self bare our sins in his own body on the tree, that we, being dead to sins, should live unto righteousness: by whose stripes ye were healed."*

The process of the torture of the whipping post was so ugly. The Romans were sadistic professionals. They felt they were the best at punishing the victim. One writer wrote that the mere anticipation of the whipping caused the victim's body to grow rigid, the muscles to knot in his stomach, and the color to drain from the face. It caused his lips to draw tight against his teeth as he waited for the first sadistic blow to come across his body. This was considered to be one of the most feared and deadly weapons of the Roman world. The mere threat of a scourge could cause a crowd to become silent and the most hardened criminal to recoil at just the prospect of being scourged.

He was bound to a two-foot scourging post. They draped the victim's body over the top of that post so that his back was completely exposed. His arms were wrapped around the post with a chain. His hands were tied to a metal ring, and his wrists were securely shackled to keep the body from moving. He couldn't wiggle or dodge the whip's lashes. Once the victim was secured, they began to put him through unimaginable torture.

The whip consisted of a short wooden handle with several eighteen- to twenty-four-inch straps of leather on the handle. At the end of the leather were pieces of metal, glass, wire, and jagged fragments of bone. Most often, two torturers were selected to whip the person at the same time from different sides. As these dual whips struck the victim, these leather straps with their sharp, jagged objects would cut deeply into the flesh, shredding his muscles and sinews.

The artwork we see of Jesus with a few scratch marks on His back is so terribly wrong. No one would have a picture or painting on their wall of the way He actually looked. He was completely shredded.

Every time the whip pounded across the victim, these straps of leather would curl around his torso, imbedding into his abdomen and upper chest. As each stroke lacerated the sufferer, he would try to thrash around. However, he was unable to move because his wrists were held bound so tightly by the metal ring above his head. He was helpless to escape the whip and would scream for mercy, that the anguish would come to an end. Every time the torturer struck a victim, the straps of leather attached to the metal handle would cause multiple lashes as the sharp objects sank into the flesh and then raked across the victim's body. The torturer would jerk back, pulling hard, in order to tear whole pieces of human flesh from the victim's body. The victim's back, buttocks, stomach, upper chest, back of legs, and face would soon become completely disfigured. Historical records describe a victim's back as being so mutilated after a Roman scourging that his spine would be exposed.

Records show the bowels of a victim would spill out. A church historian wrote that the veins were laid bare, and the very muscles, sinews, and bowels were open to exposure.

If the scourging wasn't stopped, the slashing of the whip would eventually fillet the flesh completely off the victim's body. With so many blood vessels sliced open, the victim would begin to experience a profuse loss of blood and bodily fluids. The heart would begin to beat harder and harder as it struggled to get blood to parts of the body.

He would bleed profusely. It was like pumping blood through an open hydrant. There was nothing to stop the loss of blood from pouring through the victim's open wounds.

That loss of blood caused the victim's blood pressure to drop drastically. He would experience tremendous thirst because of the massive loss of bodily fluids. The victim often fainted from the pain. Eventually, he would enter into a state of shock. Frequently, the victim's heartbeat would become so erratic that he would die of cardiac arrest. The entire body chemistry went out of whack because the person bled profusely.

The amount of torture that He endured should convict us to not have any tolerance for sickness or fear of it. Jesus paid too much of a price for our healing for us to become lackadaisical about accepting sickness and disease.

The stench of blood, sweat, ripped flesh, and dirt must have been overwhelming, even for sadistic torturers. They must have thought, 'There has to be a better way to make a living.' This horrendous smell would almost overpower them at times. As the scourging continued and the stench was great, all at once, a sweet smell broke through. It was a wonderful fragrance of perfume and oil that came to the surface and flooded the ugly atmosphere. It changed everything. It must have confused the two men who were involved in the scourging. "What is this beautiful fragrance that I smell in the middle of ugly stench?" They were smelling the fragrance of the "Lily of the Valley."

Jesus was going through something so unimaginable and was thinking, 'No one takes My life from me. I lay it down. I trust My Father. This is a cup that I have to drink for mankind. I am drinking it for the sins of the entire world. It's a bitter cup, but I am willing.' Then, He caught a whiff of that beautiful fragrance. He was blessed and sustained as the smell brought Him comfort in the middle of His toughest hour. He smelled it and remembered that one lady loved Him and poured her worship on Him. One woman recognized what He came to the earth to do. She came back to thank Him for what He had done for her and her family. She went to great expense as she humbled herself to lavish Him in front of the religious crowd. He remembered her worship, her offering, and her love. In one of His worst moments, one woman's sacrificial love was sustaining Him.

Pastor Rodney Howard-Browne preached on this on New Year's Eve in 2022. He said that it was interesting that this took place right after Mary broke the alabaster box of precious perfume and poured it on His head. It's all about sacrifice and consecration. Notice that the consecration came right after the offering. Pastor Rodney has found over the years that the offering results in a tangible thing in the natural realm, but the spiritual thing results in the consecration of the person. You say, "Yes, but Jesus wasn't giving an offering," but He was. He was giving Himself. He was about to pour out just like the woman poured the perfume, she took what was precious to her and poured it on Jesus. The fragrance filled the house. God is always interacting with man. When Abraham was willing to sacrifice Isaac, He called it worship. Mt. Moriah and Mt. Calvary were close to each other, and as Abraham was about to plunge the knife into his son, God spoke to him, and Abraham saw in the spirit Jesus Christ hanging on a cross for mankind, and he called the place Jehovah-Jireh (The Lord Himself will provide). Because Abraham was willing to sacrifice his son, God was willing to sacrifice His. Mary is symbolically pouring out, and just days later, Jesus would be pouring out His entire life's blood.

At Gethsemane, as His attackers came to arrest Him, they witnessed that fragrant smell because He was already anointed with the fragrance of the perfume. They had never smelled anybody like this before. There is a fragrance to the anointing of God. When the anointing comes into the room, it changes everything.

Previously, another alabaster box pouring took place at the house of Simon the Leper. Leprosy represents sin. When the perfume filled the house, they were not able to smell leprosy anymore. They smelled the sweet Rose of Sharon.

It is interesting that the three alabaster box breakings were all done before Jesus was scourged and crucified. They were offered as worship but also to anoint His body for burial. Later, we see other women going to the tomb to anoint His body for burial. It was the right thing to do, according to religion. However, they would not get the opportunity. They missed their moment because they were waiting for the proper religious timing. When they arrived at the tomb of Jesus, surprise! *"He is not here. He is risen."* Only three women were able to prepare His body for burial. They did not wait for the proper day or the religious obligation. They worshipped Him while He was alive. Mary did not wait until the bills were paid, the retirement was in place, the kids were educated, or any other thing that people wait for. She traded her future for His present presence. She said, "I don't know about tomorrow, but I have Him here with me today, and today, He will know how much I love Him, how thankful I am for His love and mercy, and how grateful I am for what He has done for our family. I will worship Him today and not wait for some religious holiday."

It only took Mary one moment to break open the alabaster box, but we are still smelling it in the church over two thousand years later. It is a memorial unto her love and worship. In fact, Matthew 26:13 says, *"Verily I say unto you, Wheresoever this gospel shall be preached in the whole world, there shall also this, that this woman hath done, be told for a memorial of her."* So I am preaching the Gospel by writing what this woman did.

Many people only give when they are manipulated or told to do so on a certain day or because needs have been listed and they feel obligated. When I was growing up, we had something called "Missionary Sunday." I believe it was once a month. We would save coins in a jar and bring the jars to church on that last Sunday of the month and pour out our change for the missionary. I believe it usually amounted to about $30. We did that because it was the proper Sunday to do so. It was expected and relieved us of guilt of not properly giving to missions. We never gave to the missionary in between "Missionary Sundays."

Many people only give when there is a building fund going on. There is usually a paper thermometer on the wall with paper mercury showing where we should be each month in regard to finances for the building fund. It usually showed that we were greatly behind the goal. In July, the paper thermometer showed we were only where we were supposed to be in January. People would feel guilty and try to give some to bring the paper mercury up on the paper thermometer. We were giving because of a certain need, not because of love for the Lord in holy worship. The Church must be taught that we are to be givers every day in worship to the Lord, not just when a need is presented. That is why most pastors have to constantly present a need. If they don't, the people quit giving. So, after the church is built, they must build a garage, and then buy buses to put in the garage, or the giving ceases. That is completely wrong. When people understand that giving is worship, there will be a constant flow to do everything that every ministry is called to do.

Many times, when the Bible points out different offerings, we see two opposite offerings displayed. One reveals a person with a right heart that is surrendered to God, and the other reveals a selfish and wicked heart. We see it over and over again: Cain and Abel, Esau and Jacob, the widow with the last two mites and the Pharisees, the rich young ruler and Zacchaeus, and more. We see it displayed in this story once again with the heart of Mary and the heart of Judas.

> Then saith one of his disciples, Judas Iscariot, Simon's son, which should betray him,
> Why was not this ointment sold for three hundred pence, and given to the poor?
> This he said, not that he cared for the poor; but because he was a thief, and had the bag, and bare what was put therein.
> Then said Jesus, Let her alone: against the day of my burying hath she kept this.
> For the poor always ye have with you; but me ye have not always.
>
> JOHN 12:4-8

You would have thought that those witnessing this worship would have been thrilled at this display of love and followed suit themselves. It is hard to imagine that anyone would have a problem with the spirit of giving, but in this biblical story, someone did. It was Judas, the man who was about to betray Jesus. The Bible could have only said that somebody had a problem with Mary's display of worship with the alabaster box breaking without revealing who it was. Instead, the Holy Spirit, the Author of our Bible, makes sure that we understand that it was none other than Judas. He does not stop with that detail. The Holy Spirit goes on to tell us that it was Judas who was about to betray Jesus. Why is this such an important detail? It is important because we must understand that everyone has either a heart like Mary's or one like Judas'. They both have spiritual descendants. Everyone in a church today is of one family or the other. I must ask each person who reads this book, which one are you more like?

Judas tried to sound spiritual. No one ever identifies themselves as a thief and a betrayer. Even people who are about to split a church or leave a church will always do it with a so-called spiritual explanation. They use "Christianese." Most of us who have been around church circles for any length of time have noticed that many people pray or prophesy in King James English. The reason for that is they think it sounds more spiritual and will be received as being more spiritual. I think they believe that God speaks in King James English. I have noticed that they may not say much of anything, but if they add a "th" to the words, people marvel, "ahh" and "ooh." For instance, they may say, "God sayeth unto you that He loveth thee-eth." People start shouting and say, "Did you hear that? God loves us!" I would hope that they already knew that God loved them. The Bible has already told us that. Knowing how people are, if Judas were living now, he would have used King James English. He would have said, "Jesuseth, thou knowest that I loveth to giveth moreth than anyoneth that I knoweth. I loveth offeringseth. Howevereth, as the practical and wisesteth maneth on your boardeth, I musteth protesteth to thiseth wasteth, and telleth youeth thateth this could've-eth been soldeth and giveneth to the pooreth. Buteth, insteadeth, it was wastedeth upon making youeth smelleth goodeth, and noweth it is goneth. Don't you agree-eth?"

Notice that Judas did not say, "Jesus-eth, thou knowest-eth that I am a thief-eth and an embezzler-eth, and I am mad-eth at this woman's worship-eth of You-eth because-eth I cannot steal-eth more-eth." People never say, "Pastor-eth, I am about to split-eth your church-eth wide open-eth. I am selfish-eth and hate-eth to tithe-eth." They usually say, "Pastor-eth, I have your back-eth." What they really mean is that they are behind you with a knife, ready to stab you in the back. People may fool themselves, but they cannot fool God. He knows every motive. One day, every motive will be exposed.

Judas was Jesus' treasurer. He had been stealing out of the purse (embezzling), and no one realized it but Jesus. That is another stewardship teaching that shows Jesus was not poor. You do not hire someone to be your treasurer if you never have any treasure. Can you imagine Jesus asking Judas on a regular basis, "How much money do we have in the bag?"

"Nothing, boss, like yesterday and the day before."

It is ridiculous to think that Jesus would have an accountant when there was never anything to account for. Another proof that Jesus was not poor, is the fact that Judas could embezzle, and nobody ever noticed. You have to have some extensive funds for anyone to be able to embezzle.

The fact that Judas was stealing probably led to him selling Jesus for about $23.71. He probably thought that no one could take Jesus away. He had seen Him escape crowds before. He undoubtedly thought that he could replace what he had been stealing, and Jesus would be fine and none the wiser about what he had been doing. He thought that he could repent later and everything would be fine. However, Mary put a wrench in his plans. If the perfume had been sold and the proceeds put into the bag, Judas could have helped himself to the funds. Now, he not only didn't have access to the finances from the perfume but was agitated and convicted about Mary's lavish worship. It was in great contrast to his own black heart, and instead of repenting, his heart grew even more hardened.

I believe this is where the root of offense entered Judas. That is something we must constantly guard against. Offense is very costly. Let's look a little deeper into the betrayal of Jesus by Judas. It has everything to do with his attitude during the alabaster box breaking. Judas regularly called Jesus *didaskalos*. That word in Greek is the word for master or teacher. Judas did not call Jesus "Lord." There was some area of surrender that he was never willing to surrender. When did the Devil put into Judas Iscariot's heart the thought to betray Jesus? The Bible says he was a thief anyway. He held what was in the bag and was dishonest with the money.

It happened when he took issue with Jesus about the money. Judas became obsessive about being offended at Jesus for allowing such a waste on Himself.

The Bible says how the Devil put into the heart of Judas Iscariot that seed of betrayal (John 13:2). The Devil still puts this into the hearts of the people.

I heard a great Bible teacher by the name of Rick Renner teach on the whipping post and the crucifixion quite some time ago. He has studied this subject and has a lot of revelation. The word devil is *diabolos* in the Greek. It means to strike, to strike, and to strike. It's the word *dia*, which means to penetrate, and *blos*, which means to throw. So, every time you see the word "devil," it's a job description. It means to strike the mind until he penetrates, in a weak and vulnerable moment. When he gets through, he has injected a seed of betrayal. In the Greek, it means hurled into. It seems like the Devil had been looking for an opportunity for betrayal. When Judas got offended, he opened the door to the Devil. The offense often opens the door. When Judas got offended over money, the door was opened. Satan hurled betrayal into the heart of Judas. Then Judas sat around the table at the Last Supper. He pretended to be in covenant with Jesus when he had already broken the covenant in his heart. In a weakened moment, the enemy struck! The Devil put a seed of betrayal in his mind.

The enemy comes to penetrate. Jesus talked about offense when sharing the story of the sower in Mark 4, where He talked about things the Devil uses to steal the Word. Notice that offense is at the top of the list.

Satan finally penetrated Judas's mind. He had been trying to bombast that mind for a long time, striking again and again. It may be that Judas had a weakness in his character that the Devil knew about. Until that time, he may have been able to resist that, but now the enemy had penetrated the mind of Judas Iscariot.

A seed of betrayal had been sown into the mind of Judas Iscariot. He's one of the twelve disciples and the treasurer. He and Jesus talked every day about the money. They would have had a very close relationship. Very often, when the Devil wants to hurt you, he uses those closest to you.

When deception is sown into you, you begin to look for confirmation to support your deception. Many times, people find that support from other offended people. People become so deceived that they believe they are doing the right thing. Judas was as deceived as deceived could be.

The enemy is looking for a way to get inside you. Very often, he uses finances. It is a known fact that more church splits occur over financial issues than anything else.

If you are offended, you and your ministry will go no further until you repent from your offense. God will use these things to reveal something in your character that needs to be changed. Repentance will solve the problem every time.

What if Judas Iscariot had repented instead of taking the road of suicide? Peter practically did the same thing as Judas, but he repented instead of killing himself.

God's plan is for restoration. So, if you have been a Judas, you need to go back to the person whom you've offended or betrayed and make things right. Repentance opens the door for the blessing of God to begin to operate in your life again. The Bible says that where there is strife, there is confusion and every evil work (James 3:16). God wants us to be vessels of honor.

God had a desire for Judas to be a vessel of honor, but he went out and killed himself. If we do not repent, we end up eliminating ourselves and taking ourselves out. We need to be like the prodigal son and say, "What I'm doing is wrong." Don't blame it on anyone else. Instead, get on your knees, repent, and cry out to God.

In the ministry of Jesus, all the demons of Hell were trying to stop Him. What a key position Judas had, and yet, the Devil took him out. Quick repentance and the admittance that he was wrong could have fixed everything. However, pride stopped it, and pride goes before destruction

(Proverbs 16:18). Don't run from Jesus when you sin, but instead, run to Him.

Jesus was struggling under such intense spiritual warfare before He ever went to the cross. He sweat great drops of blood. That is a medical condition that physicians can explain. It only exists in people who are under the highest stress and pressure. Jesus was going through a war. This is why angels came and strengthened Him. He could not depend on His own disciples. In the middle of Jesus' ordeal, while He was a bloody mess, Judas Iscariot came with a multitude of men. The Greek word for multitude meant three to six hundred soldiers. How many soldiers did they think it would take to arrest Jesus? When they said that they were looking for Jesus of Nazareth, Jesus said, *"I am He!"* The same word is used here that was used when God revealed Himself to Moses in Exodus 3 and said, *"I AM THAT I AM."*

> ...And Judas also, which betrayed him, stood with them.
> As soon then as he had said unto them, I am he, they went backward, and fell to the ground.
>
> JOHN 18:5, 6

The Bible says that there was such a blast of divine power that the soldiers were smacked to the ground and hurled all over the place. This display of power demonstrated that they had no power to arrest Jesus. The only way it could happen was for Jesus to lay His life down. Jesus heals and says, *"Don't you understand that I could call twelve legions of angels?"* One legion is six thousand to seventy-two thousand. In the Old Testament, one angel killed one hundred eighty-five thousand men. These men didn't have the power to take Jesus. He laid His life down. They tied a rope around Him like a lamb to the slaughter. They led Him to Caiaphas. In that moment, it looked like He was being led by the end of a rope, but in reality, He was being led by the Holy Ghost. In other places where alabaster boxes were broken, we see that the disciples called the women's worship waste.

> But when his disciples saw it, they had indignation, saying, To what purpose is this waste?
>
> MATTHEW 26:8

> And there were some that had indignation within themselves, and said, Why was this waste of the ointment made?
>
> MARK 14:4

It is so interesting that one person's worship is another person's waste.

When I looked up synonyms of waste, I was given these words: garbage, debris, trash, rubbish, junk, dust, sewage, and litter. Waste means giving too much for something that is not worth it. It means to use or expend carelessly, extravagantly, or for no purpose. It means that the object or person has no or little value to you. On the other hand, sacrifice means giving up something extremely costly for something of greater value. People only give to something they value. Some only see value in what fulfills their natural desires, such as a house, car, boat, vacation, retirement, clothing, hobbies, children, etc. If they don't see our Lord as valuable, they will not give to Him. Again, we give to what we value.

When I was pastoring, I taught for a few weeks on the subject of the honor of God. I came to realize that the words *honor* and *glory* are very similar in meaning. Where you find God being honored, you will find His glory. The word *glory* in the Old Testament is the Hebrew word *kabod*. It means weight, splendor, or copiousness. It also means abundance, heaviness, and honor. His glory is associated with His goodness. His manifested presence has a lot to do with how much we honor Him. There is an honor principle in the Bible:

> ...but now the Lord saith, Be it far from me; for them that honour me I will honour, and they that despise me shall be lightly esteemed.

1 SAMUEL 2:30

The definition of honor is heavy, weighty. Notice that these are some of the same meanings as the word translated glory. It means to value, precious, costly, expensive, to prize, or to revere. If you honor something, you mean that you value it, and it is precious and valuable to you. If you treat the things of God as precious and valuable and important to you, God will treat your things as precious, valuable, and important to Him. However, if you despise His things, you shall be lightly esteemed. Just through ignorance, we can fail to appreciate Him and His things. If you use the expression "so what," you can be biblically despising. "So it's church time again, offering time, so what?"

The word honor is related to heaviness. Honor and glory have to do with the ancient system of bartering. They bought and sold in the marketplace with precious metals. Everything had to be weighed on scales. When they asked, "How much does this cost?" they were told that it was so many shekels. The payment was with heavy metals. The person had to put gold or silver on one side and balance it out with what they were purchasing. If it was really valuable, they had to put a lot of gold on the scale to balance the scale out. We need to pray, "Lord, I want Your values and priorities to be mine. Help me to see things and value them the way You do."

We read in 1 Thessalonians 2:13 NKJV, *"For this reason we also thank God without ceasing, because when you received the word of God which you heard from us, you welcomed it not as the word of men, but as it is in truth, the word of God, which also effectively works in you who believe."* Paul is thanking God because you received God's Word not as the word of men but as the Word of God, which effectually works in you who believe.

If we want to see a greater move of the Spirit, we must learn to reverence Him. We must learn to honor the anointing and honor the Holy Ghost, or there will be limitations, and He won't manifest Himself to us. Jesus said in Matthew 7:6, *"Do not give what is holy to the dogs; nor cast your pearls before swine."* What does He mean? Pigs do not appreciate pearls. You can give your pet pig a ten-thousand-dollar string of pearls or a gravel rock, and he doesn't know the difference. It has to do with knowing what's valuable and what is not valuable. It has to do with knowing what is holy and what is not holy.

When the Lord finds people who appreciate what He's given them, and they use it for His Kingdom, He keeps giving them more. The Lord doesn't want His holy things despised. His things and His words are precious and valuable and should be treated as such. He says that those who don't value and appreciate, He will despise them. Some definitions of the word despise are to make light of, to disesteem, to regard as insignificant, and to make nothing of. It's not just that you're disgusted with something. You don't appreciate it or honor it. The lack of honor is despising it, and there is no in-between. You honor, or you despise.

> "Again, the kingdom of heaven is like treasure hidden in a field, which a man found and hid; and for joy over it he goes and sells all that he has and buys that field.
> "Again, the kingdom of heaven is like a merchant seeking beautiful pearls, who, when he had found one pearl of great price, went and sold all that he had and bought it."
>
> MATTHEW 13:44-46 (NKJV)

Faith is also inseparable from honor. God's looking for a people who, when He gives His Word through human vessels, say, "That's the Word of God; that's what changes your life." They will esteem and honor it. He opens their heart to understand and have faith.

He gives them revelation to receive it and get saved. Others say, "Awe, that's just a preacher. All we need is another preacher." They don't appreciate the Word of life and are not given a heart to understand or the faith to receive. The Lord says, *"Take heed what you hear, for with the same measure you mete, you will receive"* (Mark 4:24).

When you hear the Word of the Lord, the degree of honor, faith, and respect that you show will determine the measure of life, blessing, and the revelation that you get out of it.

Why do some get so much out of what they hear, and others who have access to the same thing do not? Many are in the same place as they were years ago. They haven't made progress or developed. What's the difference? The difference is in how they esteem it.

Did they value and honor it? If you treat the things of God as ho-hum, He won't come to you. The people who value, honor, and treasure the things of God will draw God to them. I can say that I treasure, esteem, and honor the call of God and the anointing of God upon my life. I honor His presence, His faithfulness, grace, favor, and long-suffering that He has bestowed upon me.

Mary understood thankfulness and honor. She valued Jesus. She valued His presence. That resulted in sacrificial worship. Judas and the other disciples did not honor or value Him as they should. No wonder they couldn't stand with Him, just days later, when He needed them most. You only give to what you honor and value. They took His presence for granted. They became too familiar with the anointing on His life and did not appreciate Who they had in their midst.

> Why was not this ointment sold for three hundred pence, and given to the poor?
>
> JOHN 12:5

Our job is not to take care of everyone on this earth who may not even be living for Jesus or operating in His principles. We could empty out everything we have for the homeless, and they would probably be homeless again tomorrow. They may spend it on alcohol, drugs, illicit relationships, or other things. Meanwhile, we would have nothing the next day, and nothing would have been accomplished. Jesus said in Matthew 26:11, *"For ye have the poor always with you; but me ye have not always."* There is definitely a time to give to the poor, but it must be Spirit-led as it needs to be in all giving. Our job is to ask, "Are we found at His feet, satisfying His heart?" That's what He wants.

> Then said Jesus, Let her alone: against the day of my burying hath she kept this.
>
> JOHN 12:7

Judas obviously thought that Jesus would commend him for his suggestion to rebuke Mary, sell the perfume, and put it in the bag. However, Judas was wrong. Jesus said that she was to be left alone, and He went even further:

> Verily I say unto you, Wheresoever this gospel shall be preached in the whole world, there shall also this, that this woman hath done, be told for a memorial of her.
>
> MATTHEW 26:13

Jesus not only refused to rebuke her, He commended her and made sure these alabaster box breakings were recorded in His holy Word for the Church to learn and understand what worship and giving are all about. He even went further than that. He said that wherever the Gospel is preached, this will be told of this woman. I am preaching the Gospel to you right now. All three of these women are still being remembered. Judas is also being remembered, but for a very different reason. Jesus will never be on the side of the tightwad, selfish person. He will be found on the side of the giver.

On many occasions, I have seen people begin to lavish upon Jesus, much as Mary did. As they do it, the whole house becomes filled with the sweetness of that worship, and people come to Jesus. You will be blessed by some of these testimonies. A recent occurrence that took place in Russellville, Arkansas, is fresh in my heart.

Bethel Assembly of God is, and has been for several years, a church on fire. The congregation is actively contending for revival and the supernatural.

The pastors, Earl and Janine Helton, have become accustomed to seeing God move in a big way. However, before we came in to hold a revival, they had not been exposed to a lot of teaching on giving. Therefore, they had not heard of people taking time every night before the offering to teach extensively. After the first night of revival, they told me, "Debbie, we know this is why you are here. We've never heard anything like this before, but please feel free to teach us in this area. This is the missing component in our church. We know we have to get this before we will have the means to take revival out to the people as we have been called to do. We are so enjoying this."

So, I taught and taught again on giving. And each night as I did, I could feel faith building in the air. I watched as, from beginning to end, the congregation drank in the message. I usually teach for up to an hour on stewardship before the offering and then preach another message along the subject of revival after the offering. But during the offering, God so moved in this area of worship that in a couple of the meetings, giving was the only message I shared.

On Friday evening, during my sermon, a man who was obviously moved (the visiting pastor of another church) ran to the altar with his offering. As I continued preaching, I watched much more of the congregation run up to the altar with their gifts as well. They refused to wait until I was through preaching. God was so moving on them that they couldn't wait another minute to worship Him with their giving. I noticed that along with monetary offerings, other costly gifts, such as jewelry, were being placed on the altar as well.

Then Pastor Earl, a professional golfer who taught lessons on the side, got up and left. When he returned, he was weeping. He walked up and placed a set of Big Bertha golf clubs on the altar that had taken him years to accumulate. Knowing how much those clubs meant to him, his congregation was deeply moved and so continued to give.

A young man on the worship team brought a beautiful, newly purchased guitar to the altar. Another young man laid down a pair of expensive sandals that he had just purchased that week. Meanwhile, a lady in the congregation sat thinking about a friend whose car had been repossessed, wishing she had a car to give her. Suddenly, another lady ran up to her, handing over her car keys and saying, "God just told me to give you my car." The first lady was so excited! She was able to give that car to her friend in need.

Then, the son of the woman, who had just handed over her car keys, told his mother that God had instructed him to buy her a car since she had given hers away. As the people all over the congregation began to weep, I gave an altar call for the best offering of all—souls in total surrender to God. The altars filled, and we had a wonderful time. The pastors told us that the finances given that Friday evening were more than had ever been received in an offering.

The following day, I had to depart for my next revival in Troy, Missouri. On Sunday, Pastors Earl and Janine left a phone message, stating that they urgently needed to talk to us about how giving was continuing in their church. We were able to get back to them on Monday and heard an outstanding report.

When the pastor started the next service, he felt that he should first give an altar call. Five people responded to that call for salvation—individuals for whom the church had been praying for several years! Included was the husband of the lady who gave her car away on Friday night. That lady shared how she dreaded going home to tell her unsaved husband that she had given her car away. However, much to everyone's surprise and delight, it is precisely what brought him to church and to the Lord. He said that a God who could be that real to his wife was a God worth knowing personally.

Another man who came to God that morning said that he had been in one of my services earlier that week. He loved the teaching and had not been able to get away from it. He said that what I had taught about God giving His best gift, Jesus, is what affected him most. So, he had returned to give his heart to Jesus. Hallelujah! We are finally in a day when the Church is learning how to sacrificially give until the glory comes in and people are drawn to Christ.

On Sunday morning, the pastor, following God's guidance, proceeded to teach the people about giving. Once again, a spirit of giving broke out in their congregation. Pastor Earl saw the glory of the visible presence of God manifested so strongly that he could hardly see the congregation. One of the men who had just gotten saved left the service. When he returned a few minutes later, he was carrying a guitar that he gave to the young man who had given his at the altar on Friday night. Once again, people gave away jewelry, not just on the altar, but also to one another.

Pastor Janine placed a silver bracelet on the altar. When she went back to her seat, someone tapped her on the shoulder and handed her a gold bracelet worth much more than the one she had just given. The person who gave it to her had not even seen her give hers away. Someone laid a shofar (ram's horn) on the altar, and another young man on the worship team gave him his saxophone. Then someone came up to the pastor and gave him one thousand dollars toward the building fund for their new youth building.

Pastor Earl had planned to have a groundbreaking ceremony for the new youth building after the Sunday morning service. However, God so moved in the service that time did not permit it, so they postponed the groundbreaking until that evening. Pastor Earl was the last one out of the building that morning, and he locked the doors behind him as he left. He was also the first person back inside the building that evening before the groundbreaking ceremony. When he returned, Pastor Earl found a note on his pulpit that he knew had not been there earlier. The note instructed him to go down to the golf store and pick out any set of golf clubs that he wanted. It went on to say that the clubs were already paid for. The pastor said that he'd never before seen such hunger in his congregation. Some who had just been saved that Sunday morning were already in the line to be filled with the Holy Spirit that Sunday night.

I must share with you once more about a time I broke open an alabaster box. In January of 1999, I was attending Dr. Rodney Howard-Browne's Winter Campmeeting in Tampa, Florida. God was speaking to me every morning and evening about sowing more than ever in preparation for a big harvest year coming up. I continued to give daily in those meetings, beyond anything I rationally could afford to give. I gave personally, as well as from the ministry account. I gave on credit cards. I pulled money out of every place I could think of. My finances were already almost depleted before the Campmeeting had even begun because we had several weeks off the road due to the Christmas season. However, I had made up my mind a long time ago that I would sow even more in a time of famine.

I received a phone call on the last day of the meeting. It was from the pastor of the Church where I was supposed to go next. He told me that he was concerned about the upcoming meeting. He said that because of several circumstances, he was afraid I would not receive enough in the offerings. He knew that I paid my own expenses and had been giving at the Campmeeting and felt he should warn me that I may not receive my plane fare in the offerings. I assured him that he was not to worry and to allow me to trust God.

I went into the last Campmeeting evening after that call. I was touched in a great way when Pastor Rodney taught that night on giving. I told the Lord that I desperately wanted to break open an alabaster box but had nothing left. Then I looked down and noticed the beautiful black pearl necklace that I was wearing. It was expensive and not paid for yet. I would yet be paying for it for another couple of years. It was the only expensive piece of jewelry that I had ever purchased for myself, and it held great sentimental quality because of where I purchased it. I suddenly realized that it was an alabaster box.

I took it off, without any hesitation, and gave it. I let my tears run down Jesus and wiped His feet with my hair. I left that Campmeeting knowing that I had worshipped Him with everything I had.

The next day, before leaving for my revival, I received a call from Pastor Rodney. He said, "Debbie, I am sowing radically for my Good News New York crusade. I need a miracle. I felt led today to give you five thousand dollars. Could you come pick it up?" I told him that I would be right over.

I went on to the revival, about which the pastor had been concerned that I might not receive enough to pay for our plane tickets. The revival extended and lasted for two weeks. Many answered the altar calls from the first Sunday morning on. It was glorious. The church congregation is about one hundred fifty people. At the end of the two weeks, I received an offering of twenty thousand dollars. It was one of the most miraculous offerings that I ever received. In addition, I received a second offering on the last Friday night for Pastor Rodney's Good News New York crusade. It was five thousand dollars.

The following day, after the revival, the pastor approached me about a dinner invitation. He said that there was a couple in his church who had been so touched and changed during the revival. They owned a jewelry store and wanted me to go to the store and pray over it and bless it. They also were wondering if I would go to dinner with them later. I answered that I would. I went to their store. The owners were not there at that time. I blessed the store and asked God to bless the owners abundantly so they would have even more to sow. After praying, I noticed the most beautiful ring I had ever seen in one of their display cabinets. I walked over and looked at the price, and laughed to myself. I thought, 'Don't even think about it, Debbie.' I walked away.

At dinner that evening, they began to thank me for coming. They gave me their testimonies of how their lives and others' lives had been impacted. They told me that they had a gift for me as a token of their appreciation. As I opened the beautifully wrapped box, my eyes could not believe what I saw. It was the very ring I had been looking at. I asked them how they knew I had been looking at that ring, and they just smiled.

As I was putting the ring on my finger, I heard the Holy Spirit say these words on the inside, "Debbie, I watched you break open your alabaster box at the Campmeeting. You never asked Me for anything except souls. You did not say you were sowing a piece of jewelry for another piece. Your heart is set on Me and My Kingdom, but I want you to know that I see all of it. I also want you to know that because I have your heart, I can let you have some things. I know that you continue to break open alabaster boxes. With this ring, I'm telling you that I know your heart."

Please do not misunderstand what all of this is about. It is not about getting bracelets, guitars, or golf clubs. It is not about just giving at offering time or getting blessed. It is about seeking God's Kingdom and righteousness first and then having all these other things added unto you. It is about living to be a blessing and living to give, not giving to live. It is not about what we have to do to be blessed. It is about what we get to do in this covenant. I get to be a blessing. And as I live to be a blessing, I get to see other lives touched and changed. I am able to worship God in such a way that it not only touched His heart but the hearts of others around me. In the process, that same anointing can't help but run down me as well.

If I did not have one promise in the Word of God about being blessed in return, I would still want to worship Him in this way. Even if God did not say I would reap a harvest, or that as I gave, He would cause men to give back unto me, good measure, pressed down, shaken together, and running over, I would still give like this. Even if He didn't say that He would meet all my needs according to His riches in glory, I would still want to worship in this wonderful way. I thank God that these promises are included, but that is not why I've chosen to give as I do.

My name has been written down in the Lamb's Book of Life. I have been redeemed forever. I have inherited eternal life and get to be with Jesus forever. I have been plucked out of the kingdom of darkness and translated into the Kingdom of light. I have received joy unspeakable and full of glory, and peace that passes all understanding. No, I don't have to be told my duty in giving; it is an awesome privilege. Giving is no longer something that I dread. It has become one of my favorite forms of worship.

The day could come when your very life could depend upon your giving. It did for me. I mentioned earlier that I had a pulmonary embolism attack my body in 2006. My pastors, Drs. Rodney and Adonica Howard-Browne, were holding meetings at Oral Roberts University in Tulsa, Oklahoma, when they received the news that I had been flown by helicopter to Tampa General Hospital. They were told that I was not expected to live. Pastor

Rodney was approaching the pulpit when he was given the note. He went to pray and heard the Holy Ghost say, "Debbie is going to be fine. You don't have to pray." When his wife, Pastor Adonica, went to pray, she heard, "Debbie is going to be fine. I can't do without her. She's a giver."

A few days later, both of them came to the hospital to see me in the intensive care unit. They came straight to the hospital after landing in Tampa in the early hours of the morning. When they told me what the Lord had spoken to Pastor Adonica, I was shocked. It sent my theological mind into a tailspin. I knew that we cannot buy our healing. Jesus already paid that horrible price at the whipping post. For a moment, I did not understand. Then Pastor Rodney began to talk to me about Cornelius in the Bible.

> And said, Cornelius, thy prayer is heard, and thine alms are had in remembrance in the sight of God.
>
> ACTS 10:31

It was Cornelius' praying and giving that got God's attention. We aren't buying our healing or anything else with our giving. Jesus purchased for us every good gift and every spiritual blessing. However, our giving puts us in God's remembrance and builds a memorial unto God. It gets God's attention. He loves our worship and inhabits it. Our giving speaks on our behalf.

I believe that it puts us in a better position to receive for many reasons. A giver has an intimate relationship with God. He or she becomes very sensitive to the Holy Spirit. We hear from Him and can obey quickly. A giver is one who operates in the faith realm. You must be able to quickly obey and give amounts that cause your head to go on tilt. When a person gets used to yielding in one realm, it allows them to understand how to yield in other realms. Faith works the same in all areas. You need faith to receive the healing that Jesus already paid for. A giver is also a receiver. The hand that is outstretched in giving is the same one that is outstretched to receive from God all that we need.

Pastors Rodney and Adonica took my hand while they were telling me this. Immediately, buzzers went off, and my blood pressure returned to normal. When I arrived at the hospital, I had absolutely no blood pressure. Later, it went up to fifty over thirty, but that is obviously too low. When they touched my hand and told me what God had said about me, a miracle occurred. I was flying around the world again in three weeks. I had been told that I would never preach again, would never fly in a jet again, and would be connected to oxygen for the rest of my life. What a miracle to be preaching the Gospel with no oxygen. I am so glad that I am a giver and that God says that He can't do without me. I will continue to be a giver for all the days of my life. I will see that increase and increase from glory to glory and faith to faith. I will lavish my Lord, who has done so much for me, with everything that I have. Some may think that I take too long to teach on giving. I am teaching people how to pour out onto our Lord and Savior. If you don't like that, you are more of the family of Judas than of Mary. Maybe He has not been as precious, faithful, loving, merciful, and gracious to you as I know He has been to me. Maybe you think that I make way too big of a deal of giving in worship to my Lord. If that is the case, all I can say is to use the words of a well-known Christian song by CeCe Winans called "Alabaster Box." Some of the words are as follows:

> I've come to pour my praise on Him
> Like oil from Mary's alabaster box
> So don't be angry if I wash His feet with my tears
> And I dry them with my hair, hmm
> 'Cause you weren't there the night He found me
> You did not feel what I felt
> When He wrapped His love all around me and
> You don't know the cost, not of this oil
> In my alabaster box

Growing up, we realized that worshipping through singing was holy. We looked forward to the preaching of the Word and to the altar service and always enjoyed prayer time. However, offering was never an anticipated part of the worship service; it seemed like more of an interruption. Somewhere in the middle of all that holy glory, we had to deal with the natural "carnal area" of giving. It seemed something we had to figure out how to do in order to keep the lights on and the preacher paid. There were bills to be paid and practical matters to attend to, but how we hated having to interrupt a wonderful service to do it. Somehow, holy worship, the true meaning of giving, had been lost.

God did not invent this giving thing to make sure that Heaven and His Kingdom didn't go broke. Are you kidding? He owns the cattle on a thousand hills. The earth is His and the fullness thereof. He paves His streets with gold and makes His gates out of pearls. He calls Himself El Shaddai, the God of more than enough. Another name is Jehovah Jireh, the Lord your Provider. God has never known lack. If no one gives, He will not go broke. God will not have to hock one pearly gate or take up any of His golden streets to make another payment on Heaven. Our giving is not how He survives. What He gives us is the opportunity to worship Him through giving and, in turn, an opportunity to be blessed.

Instead of an interruption, the offering needs to be elevated to its true status, one of holy worship. I believe that offering time is as holy as it gets in a service because offering time is when we become very serious and consecrated. We become very focused on who God is and what He's done for us. With our offerings, we lavish our worship upon Him. If it is a holy worship, it should become a very important part of the service. We should look forward to it and rejoice and be glad in it.

The Body of Christ must be taught that this is not a part of the service to treat lightly. Rather than being an interruption to the glory of God in a meeting, the offering is actually one of the focal points of worship.

Personally, I believe that as we begin to learn what true giving is all about, all such attitudes are subject to change. I trust that you, too, will become a Mary-type giver, a true worshipper whose heart is in the giving. You will begin to live to outgive God at any cost. Before we begin this race with God, we already know that He will win. It is exciting, nevertheless, to try and outgive Him. God delights in such worship. In the Old Covenant, God dwelled within the praises of His people. In this New (and better) Covenant, God dwells within the people of praise. I am one of those people. Won't you join me in becoming a worshipper as never before?

FOUR

THE LESSER GIVING TO THE GREATER

When the queen of Sheba heard of [the constant connection of] the fame of Solomon with the name of the Lord, she came to prove him with hard questions (problems and riddles).

She came to Jerusalem with a very great train, with camels bearing spices, very much gold, and precious stones. When she had come to Solomon, she communed with him about all that was in her mind.

Solomon answered all her questions; there was nothing hidden from the king which he failed to explain to her.

When the queen of Sheba had seen all Solomon's wisdom and skill, the house he had built,

The food of his table, the seating of his officials, the standing at attention of his servants, their apparel, his cupbearers, his ascent by which he went up to the house of the Lord [or the burnt offerings he sacrificed], she was breathless and overcome.

She said to the king, It was a true report I heard in my own land of your acts and sayings and wisdom.

I did not believe it until I came and my eyes had seen.

> Behold, the half was not told me. You have added wisdom and goodness exceeding the fame I heard.
>
> Happy are your men! Happy are these your servants who stand continually before you, hearing your wisdom!
>
> Blessed be the Lord your God, Who delighted in you and set you on the throne of Israel! Because the Lord loved Israel forever, He made you king to execute justice and righteousness.
>
> And she gave the king 120 talents of gold and of spices a very great store and precious stones. Never again came such abundance of spices as these the queen of Sheba gave King Solomon.
>
> The navy also of Hiram brought from Ophir gold and a great plenty of almug (algum) wood and precious stones.
>
> Of the almug wood the king made pillars for the house of the Lord and for the king's house, and lyres also and harps for the singers. No such almug wood came again or has been seen to this day.
>
> King Solomon gave to the queen of Sheba all she wanted, whatever she asked, besides his gifts to her from his royal bounty. So she returned to her own country, she and her servants.
>
> 1 KINGS 10:1-13 (AMPC)

This is a lesson of the lesser giving to the greater. There is much to be learned from this story. It is one of my favorite texts on the subject of giving.

The first verse tells us that the queen of Sheba had heard of Solomon's name in connection with the name of the Lord. Every time she heard about the greatness of Solomon's wisdom, she heard about his big God and how He was blessing Solomon. The queen of Sheba heard that it was because of Solomon's God that he had this wisdom. She also heard that because of their awesome God and Solomon's reign, gold became so plentiful that the silver was stacked up in the streets. Israel was blessed, blessed, and blessed under Solomon's reign. The queen of Sheba heard that Solomon's God was Jehovah Jireh, the Lord his Provider.

We can find several lessons in this first verse. We find that our name should be spoken in connection with our God's name, and our name should bring glory to His name. When people hear our name, they should automatically associate it with the God Whom we serve. If our name comes up in conversation, it should make people think of everything associated with our God. They should say something like, "I don't really know that person, but he sure is full of joy. He says it is because of his God and the joy that his God gives." They might say that you are an overcomer, one who is full of peace, or someone who walks in honesty and integrity. Whatever it is, when your name is brought up, it ought to consistently convey to others your good association with the name of the Lord.

The queen of Sheba heard that Solomon's God had been so very good to him. She came to see if the reports were exaggerated. The queen had no idea what she was about to find out. Let me ask you, how long has it been since someone came to check out your God? Did they hear you were so blessed that they could not believe it? Did they come as skeptics, unable to believe that anyone's God could be *that* big and *that* good? It's good food for thought, isn't it?

Solomon and the children of Israel were good examples of God's goodness and blessing to His people. It was wise of the queen of Sheba to check out the reports of blessing firsthand and not to accept someone else's word for it. She knew she would have to take some time and really examine things to know if what she had heard was true.

The queen of Sheba arrived prepared to give. The custom of the day required a queen to bring gifts to a king and vice-versa. The Bible lists for us in detail the gifts she brought: gold, spices, and more. Before presenting her gifts, the queen decided to begin her investigation in depth. Verse 4 tells us that she finally got to the heart of the matter, inquiring of Solomon all that was on her mind. The queen of Sheba listened first to the king's great wisdom, and for his part, Solomon did not hide anything from her.

The most important thing we can give to someone else is what God has given us on the inside. It is more important than any outward sign of blessing. To "show God off," we need to operate in wisdom. You cannot prosper materially or physically without operating in God's wisdom. The spirit, soul (the will, intellect, and emotion), and the body are all interconnected. What affects one affects the other. To be successful on the outside, one has to be wise on the inside. The person who is flaky, undisciplined, and unwise does not succeed in life. In many charismatic churches, we sing, "I've got something on the inside, working on the outside. Oh, what a change in my life." When God's wisdom is at work on the inside, it will bring about changes that will be seen and heard on the outside.

In 1 Kings 3:9, the Bible states that King Solomon asked God for an understanding heart to judge His people so that he could discern between good and bad. In the Hebrew language, *understanding* means hearing. Solomon was asking God for a listening heart. A listening heart results in godly wisdom. When a person learns to hear the voice of God and then is a doer of that Word, he will operate in godly wisdom. It brings about blessing and abundance in every area of life.

Apparently, the queen of Sheba was very impressed with Solomon's wisdom, but her examination did not end there. The queen looked at the house he had built. Some think only spiritual qualities are important. They think that people only look to the changes in their character in order to gauge how big God is. Actually, what the world really wants to know is whether our God is big enough to bless us outwardly in this natural realm. When the queen of Sheba saw how beautiful, ornate, and expensive King Solomon's house was, she was astounded. Her conclusion must have been, "Yes, when I hear Solomon's wisdom and see the house that he's built, I can only conclude that his God is good to him. His God is, indeed, a very big God."

The queen needed more convincing, however. So, she continued her exploration by scrutinizing the food they were eating. She, again, saw that God was so very good to Solomon and Israel. They were eating very well—

extremely well. Their God did not expect them to barely get by because He is El Shaddai, the God of more than enough.

Then, the queen of Sheba checked out the seating of King Solomon's officials and the decorum of his servants. She was impressed with how many servants he had. King Solomon had countless servants because he fed hundreds at his table every day. They all stood at attention, attending the king and his court with honor and dignity. They were submitted to his authority and kept proper rank at all times.

This is another lesson worth learning for the Body of Christ. The world is watching us to see if we truly have servants' hearts. The Church needs to learn the lessons of submission and authority. When visitors see that we do not honor them whom Christ has put in authority over us, it leaves a bad taste in their mouths. We should not be climbing over one another, vying for positions. We should be submitting ourselves to one another with brotherly love, as the Bible teaches. The queen of Sheba could see that Solomon's servants were performing their jobs with proper decorum.

Next, she observed their clothing. King Solomon was known not only for his great wisdom but also for his resplendent and royal apparel. His servants were dressed in the best clothing of the day. Indeed, their clothes were a sight to behold! Again, you might be surprised to realize that the care with which you dress can reflect to others how good and gracious your God is to you. Some people are watching to see if our God can only supply us with used, rummaged clothing or if He can and will dress us to show forth His goodness. I realize that we seem to be living in an era of more casual dress in church. I have even been in one or two churches where the pastors wore Bermuda shorts and sandals to service. At first, I was a little surprised but decided that this was their prerogative. I am all for people being comfortable in worship. It does amaze me, though, how many people will dress their best to go to the office and then throw on any old thing to go and worship God. If someone's best is blue jeans, so be it. I do believe that when they come to church, those jeans should be clean and should be the best pair that they own.

For me, dressing my best is not a religious tradition. It is the acting out of my personal conviction that, in every area of life, I should give God my best. I represent the King of kings and the Lord of lords. Every day and night that I stand up and teach the Word of the Lord, I am doing so as a minister of the Most High God. I'm not going to throw on any old thing to try to dress down. I want it known that my God supplies me with beautiful, flattering clothing. This is not a matter of me trying to show off. It is a matter of me showing off the goodness of my God.

Evidently, when the queen of Sheba checked out the clothing worn in Solomon's kingdom, she saw some beautiful clothes. Note how the Bible specifically mentions her observation of the clothes the children of Israel wore. She looked at natural things to determine if what she had heard about Israel's God was true. The queen went on to look at Solomon's cupbearers. Most Bible commentaries say that this was referring to the expensive metal from which the wine cups were made. It probably also referred to the fine juices that were being served in them. And she continued to be impressed with what she saw.

Then, the queen of Sheba decided to watch how King Solomon walked when he went up to offer sacrifices. This passage is probably referring to the humility and reverential manner in which the king approached the sacrifice for his God. However, after reading several Bible commentaries on this verse, I came to certain conclusions. This passage was not just referring to the actual method that the king used while ascending to the sacrifice. It was most probably referring to a special arched viaduct that King Solomon had built. That viaduct was very impressive and gave the king a private entrance to the west end of the temple from his palace. The viaduct had a massive arch; some of the huge stones have been found today. Never before had the queen witnessed such a display of God's greatness as she saw that day.

The queen of Sheba also observed the sacrifices. The original translations of this passage say that this is referring to the great holocaust involved in the sacrifice. King Solomon did it up right! He offered up many animals when he sacrificed; it was no small service.

When it came to checking out King Solomon's blessings, it is apparent that the queen of Sheba was detailed, leaving no stone unturned. Verse 5 says that once she had seen it all, she was breathless and overcome. The King James Version says, "There was no more spirit in her." It appears that after checking everything out, the queen fainted. She was so overcome by the goodness of God and His blessing upon the king and his country that she could no longer stand and lost her breath.

When was the last time anyone fainted after observing how big your God is to you? I would like to think that, to some degree, people are overcome when they see where God has brought them from. I have had family members stand in awe when they came to my home and saw my car. They remembered when I was driving a "totaled car" and was living with other people. Now, others live with me, and I have given vehicles away. Hallelujah!

Verses 6 and 7 quote to us what the queen of Sheba declared. She declared that everything that had been told her was true. She did not believe it until she came and saw it with her own eyes. Most people give exaggerated reports about things. People like to brag and exalt themselves and what they believe. Because of that, the world is not going to take our word for it when we say that our God is good. They are going to be like the people from Missouri who are famous for saying, "Show me." The queen declared that the only problem with the reports she had heard was that the half had not been told. That reminds me of an old song that we used to sing, "It is joy unspeakable and full of glory, and the half has never yet been told." With a God as big as ours, it is impossible to describe even half of His love, His goodness, His grace, and His mercy to us. At best, we can only make attempts. Everyone will have to experience God's goodness for himself or herself. However, we should make them so intrigued, so curious by what they see and hear that they, like the queen of Sheba, must come to check Him out.

The queen went on to state that King Solomon's men and servants were happy. She liked happiness and joy. The world is looking for happiness and joy. They are tired of depression and people looking miserable. That is why they look for happiness in an alcohol bottle, drug injection, or in an illicit relationship. That is why they look forward to weekend parties. They want to be happy.

Sometimes, people are afraid of the joy we experience in our meetings, thinking that it will "turn people off." I have found that the only ones turned off by it are the religious crowd. The more joy we have in our meetings, the more we see people running forward to become born again.

In verse 9, the queen of Sheba eventually made a declaration about Solomon's God. She proclaimed, *"Blessed be the Lord your God, Who delighted in you and set you on the throne of Israel! Because the Lord loved Israel forever, He made you king to execute justice and righteousness."*

The word *blessed* in Hebrew means prospered. The queen of Sheba acknowledged that Solomon's God was a God of blessing and that He had, indeed, blessed all of Israel. God loves us today and desires to prosper us because of that great love. You notice that the queen did not say that because God loved Israel, He cursed Solomon. Yet, that is what some today would teach. They make God out to be a thief who steals, kills, and destroys. Yet, time and time again, the Word of God makes it clear that Satan is the killer, stealer, and destroyer. God brings life and blesses, prospers, heals, and restores. Do not confuse their job descriptions.

"And she gave...." Verse 10 is a key verse. After the queen became convinced of how big God was and how much He had blessed Israel, she couldn't wait to give. This is where the principle of the lesser giving to the greater comes in. The queen was a very wealthy woman herself, and yet she heard that King Solomon was even more blessed. After checking it out, the queen of Sheba found that not only was the king more blessed than she was, but he was also twice as blessed as she had been told.

At that point, the queen could have "copped an attitude." She could have thought, 'He is more blessed than I am. Why should I give to him? I have my own needs to worry about. I only help people who are not as blessed as I am. That makes more sense. I'm going to take my gifts and go home.' This is carnal thinking, and that's when jealousy surfaces. We find ourselves thinking, 'Why should I give to them? They are more blessed than I am. They probably don't even have to work a real job, and they probably make more money, have a nicer home, and drive a better car than I do.'

No one's flesh likes to give to someone we consider more blessed than ourselves. We give to people that we consider lower than ourselves in one way or another. Pride motivates such giving. It makes our flesh feel good. Everyone likes to give to a person we feel might not survive without our pious gift. We have done our good deed for the day, and our flesh is exalted.

There *is* a time to give to the poor. The Bible speaks of that kind of giving, too. However, there is also a time to give to someone who is more blessed than you are. There is nothing in that kind of giving to exalt the flesh.

The queen of Sheba recognized that God was blessing Israel, and He was on their side. She was smart enough to want to get involved with that kind of blessing and, in turn, their God. She knew better than to be on the opposite side. At that moment, the queen had more revelation than a lot of Christians in the church have today. The queen of Sheba came to Israel prepared to give and, after checking everything out, did so. Bear in mind that, at this point, the queen could have changed her mind. She could have decided that Israel did not need her money. Actually, it was quite obvious that King Solomon did not need the queen's money. That was simply not the point.

The queen needed to invest in King Solomon, Israel, and their big God. She needed to hook up with anointing, blessing, provision, and success. The queen of Sheba needed to become involved with God's glory. Giving was the avenue. The Bible tells us that she gave one hundred twenty talents of gold, spices, and precious stones. Rare wood was also given, with which the king made instruments of music and pillars for the house of God.

It is interesting that gold and spices are the same gifts that would be given to another King, the King of kings, hundreds of years later. These are the same gifts that were brought to Jesus. He does not need our gifts, either. It is our heart that God wants, and many times, the surrender of the heart is displayed in sacrificial giving.

When the queen finished her giving, King Solomon did a very interesting thing. He turned around and began giving back to her. He gave the queen of Sheba whatever she wanted and whatever she asked for. Now, I cannot imagine how long it would have taken to unload all of the goods the queen gave and transfer them. I am sure that the parade of giving of gold, wood, spices, and stones took a very long time, perhaps even hours, to finish. Then, when the queen's servants finally finished unloading her boats, King Solomon's servants started loading them back up again, doing the same for her. Note that several things were going on.

First of all, King Solomon expected and then accepted the queen of Sheba's gifts. King Solomon knew that he was going to bless the queen, and she would be greatly increased by that giving. The king did not object with false humility. He did not say, "I couldn't possibly accept all these gifts from you when I am more blessed than you." The king just sat there and let the queen continue to give. When she had finished, King Solomon turned around and asked her what she wanted. He did not merely ask the queen of Sheba what she needed but what she wanted. This biblical principle is seen time and time again in the Word of God.

Remember the Shunammite woman in the Book of 2 Kings, chapter 4? She and her husband loved God and His glory and loved His prophet, Elisha. The couple loved him so much that they decided to add a "prophet's chamber" onto their home. They did not do this because they wanted something out of it or wanted anything in return. They built the chamber only because they loved the glory. The Bible tells us that they did it painstakingly. It cost them finances, time, labor, blood, sweat, and tears. But it was more than worth it to them. It would house the glory of God that was upon His servant, Elisha.

When they finished, the prophet, through his servant, asked the couple what they desired. At first, they answered that they wanted and expected nothing. This had been a labor of love. The prophet continued to press the couple until they admitted that, for a long time, they had wanted a son. The prophet told them that a year from then, they would conceive, and she would bear a child. This couple made room for the glory, and the glory, in turn, came back on them and asked, "What do you want?" The same glory with which they gave blessed them in return. That is a God principle.

We see this same principle in the Book of John, chapter 12, as we read about Mary and her alabaster box. The same sweet anointing that Mary gave got all over her hands, hair, and feet. She smelled like Jesus before she was through. It affected not only Him but her hair as well. By the same token, if you hang out with givers, that spirit of giving will get all over you. Oh, how God desires that the Body of Christ comes into this revelation!

For several years, I have had the privilege of being close to my pastors, the Howard-Brownes. I have never known such unselfish givers in my entire life. I have also never known people of greater vision and faith. Thank God! I believe that their giving spirit came all over me.

I will never forget an incident that happened in our church several years ago. Pastor Rodney was preparing for his Good News New York crusade, which was only months away. He had become acquainted with Rev. Bill Wilson of New York. Pastor Bill had the largest Sunday school in America, a church with over twenty thousand children. It was Pastor Rodney's desire that our church become better equipped to win the lost. So, he invited Pastor Bill to come to Tampa and share the art of soul-winning with our church. Pastor Wilson told Pastor Rodney that he was very busy, and if he were to be able to come at all, it would probably be without much notice of his arrival. Pastor Rodney agreed.

Sure enough, on very short notice, Pastor Rodney received a call from Pastor Bill. With not enough time to advertise or inform most of our church of the special speaker, our crowd was not what it could have been under more ideal circumstances.

As Pastor Bill gave a portion of his very moving testimony, there was hardly a dry eye in the house. Pastor Wilson shared how, at the age of nine, his mother left him on a street corner. Three days later, a Christian man came by and picked him up, sending him to a Christian youth camp where he came to know Jesus Christ as Savior. For years since, Pastor Bill had been picking children up in the Bronx of New York, introducing them to that same Savior. He is a very real person with a passion for souls, one who does not tolerate church politics.

When Pastor Bill finished sharing, Pastor Rodney received an offering for him. Our pastor advised us that our church had already purchased two buses for Pastor Bill's Sunday school outreach, which cost fourteen thousand dollars each. He went on to say that he invited Pastor Bill to come speak for two reasons—to bless us and also that we might be a blessing. Pastor Rodney said that before Pastor Wilson arrived, he had already determined that we would buy two more buses for his ministry. Therefore, Pastor Rodney already had a $28,000 check made out to Pastor Bill's ministry. He advised us that whether the $28,000 came in the offering or not, he was still going to give Pastor Bill that check.

Most of the congregation knew that our pastor could not afford to give such a generous offering at that time. The congregation knew that Pastor Rodney had great expenses and bills that he did not yet know how he would pay. Millions of dollars were still needed for his New York crusade. Yet, when Pastor Rodney could afford to give the least, he made the greatest determination to give into someone else's vision.

We were so touched by his generous heart that the same spirit of giving came upon most of us. I can only speak for myself when I say that I dug down and gave in a big way. Apparently, though, others in the congregation did the same. When the offering was counted, an usher excitedly relayed the total to Pastor Rodney. Our pastor, in turn, told us that from a crowd of approximately four hundred people, $20,000 had been received. We were elated, knowing that our seed was going into good ground.

At the time, I was sitting in the front row, only inches away from Pastor Rodney. What happened next is forever etched on my mind and heart. I saw our pastor's entire expression change, and I knew that God was talking to him. I witnessed tears filling his eyes as he began to speak again. He said, "There has been a change of plans. We are still giving Pastor Bill the $28,000 for his ministry. However, we are also giving him the $20,000 that came in tonight." Pastor Rodney walked over to Pastor Bill and handed him both checks. He informed Pastor Bill that the former one was for his ministry, but the latter one was for him personally.

Pastor Bill wept profusely. He said that he could not take the check given to him personally. But our pastor insisted, rehearsing the fact that Pastor Bill had been living in the back of a warehouse for years and didn't even own a car. Pastor Rodney said that it was time Rev. Wilson was blessed and that The River at Tampa Bay wanted to be a part of that blessing.

Then Pastor Bill asked to speak. He shared with the crowd that this was the first time he had been blessed in such a tremendous way. He was visibly moved. He related that he had once been asked to go on television and help raise money for a major ministry. He was promised that some of the money raised would come back to his kids in New York. While he helped raise millions of dollars, not one cent came back to his kids.

Pastor Bill said he was used to the "same 'ole, same 'ole" when it came to church politics and phoniness. He said that when he first heard of Pastor Rodney and the joy that bubbled forth in his meetings, he thought to himself, 'Great! This is all we need, another charismatic fad to hit the Church. I am not into this laughter stuff. I am into winning souls that will count for all of eternity.'

However, later, when he met Pastor Rodney, he discovered how genuine his ministry was. Pastor Bill said he observed our pastor's heart and his compassion for the lost, discovering that Pastor Rodney was, indeed, very real. He had never seen such a giving heart. I couldn't help thinking to myself, 'Yeah, you just met my pastor.' By then, there was not a dry eye left in the house.

I was once again so honored to be associated with such a man of God. I took notice that the more our pastor saw God's anointing on Pastor Bill, the more he wanted to get involved. And he did exactly that. Disregarding his own personal needs and those of his ministry, he hooked up with God's blessing upon Pastor Bill's ministry. He gave into another man's vision before his own. And I must tell you, God did not leave Pastor Rodney hanging. As our pastor considered another man's ministry first, God met his need for the New York crusade.

I have witnessed my pastor doing something very similar on many occasions. There have been times when he was hundreds of thousands of dollars behind with his own budget and yet sowed that much, and more, into another man's ministry. For instance, he did that several times with Evangelist Reinhard Bonnke. He so believed in the soul-winning ministry of Brother Bonnke that he was compelled to give into his ministry before he took care of his own ministry needs.

Most people would find it very difficult to give in that manner. However, Pastor Rodney learned this principle a long time ago. It is important to give in faith to greater anointing and harvest. Anyone can take care of his own needs first. It takes a real man or woman of God to believe in meeting someone else's needs first. Pastor Rodney understands the principles of God and His Word enough to know that, rather than looking at his own circumstances, he needs to get involved with someone of greater scope and vision. God has always met Pastor Rodney there with a miracle, just in time. God is bigger than our circumstances, but it is necessary to get involved in what God is doing in order to experience how big He is.

I, too, have taken to heart this principle of the lesser giving to the greater. When my pastor was preparing for Good News New York, I, in turn, decided that I would sacrifice my own needs to give to his crusade. So, every week that we held revival, I either gave up some of my own offerings or received a second offering for his crusade. Typically, when people know that a special additional offering is going to be taken, they give less in the first offering. So, even when we received a second offering, it cost us to do so. Sometimes, we gave the whole week's offering to the Good News New York crusade. In fact, for one week, we held two services a day and gave our entire $25,000 offering to the New York crusade.

There were many times during those weeks that I did not know how I would pay my own staff and ministry bills. But Pastor Rodney's ministry and crusade were a greater influence and scope than mine. His faith was greater, and his need was greater. I was the lesser giving to the greater. Not only that, but I took a week off to attend the New York crusade, paying my own expenses while we were there. In addition, I gave in the offerings while I was there. I did not have funds in my bank account at the time, so I put my giving on the credit cards.

I could have said that I had my own needs and problems to be concerned about and that Pastor Howard-Browne would have to trust God for himself. I did not sacrificially give as I did just because I love the Howard-Brownes or because they had been good to me. Because of the scope of their ministry, I would have given anyway. I believed in what they were doing and accomplishing. I found it interesting that during that outreach, we saw almost 50,000 souls come to Jesus Christ. I gave or raised funds right at $50,000 toward that crusade. That means that I have an investment of one dollar per soul. Again, God supernaturally met *both* Pastor Rodney's and my ministry's needs.

A year later, Pastor Rodney held another gigantic crusade in Shreveport, Louisiana, that again lasted six weeks. And, once again, I sacrificially gave at a time when I was being financially stretched. This time, I took two weeks off from my own crusade schedule to join Pastor Rodney there to offer my encouragement and help for the crusade. In fact, in the natural, it looked impossible. That was one of the reasons that I knew it was imperative to give. During that Shreveport crusade, we saw over 59,000 souls come to Christ. When I saw those people come to the Lord in New York and Shreveport, I rejoiced in the privilege of giving to a ministry greater than my own. Most will only give to someone else after their own needs are met. Even the world will do that. I want to do better.

Now, I will be very honest with you. I continued, for an extended time, to pay credit card bills from my giving toward the last crusade. I do not regret it at all. With each payment, I remember the looks on the faces of the souls that I witnessed coming to Christ. Oh, what a privilege it is to be used in such a way.

It is important for us to be prudent and wise. I'm not telling you to go out and run up extreme credit card bills in your giving. Some people could read this, take it out of context, not listen to the Holy Spirit, and fall into a huge mess. Do not do this out of desperation. Do not run up bills trying to pressure God into "bailing you out." It is imperative that you hear from the Holy Spirit and listen to His voice in these matters.

There was another time that Pastor Rodney led the way in giving in a time of crisis. Pastors Rodney and Adonica were leaving to go on an African crusade. He asked me to conduct the mid-week church service in Tampa. He confided to me that they needed a great financial miracle that week and asked me to believe God with them for that miracle. He also told me that I should receive an offering for myself after I received the church's offering. I did not feel to tell him that I, too, was in need of a great financial miracle that week. I received the church's offering and then my own. In the middle of the service, Pastor Rodney broke into our service by way of streaming on the internet. He gave a report of how well the meetings were going. We heard about many coming to Christ in the meetings, as well as being filled with the Spirit and refreshed. At some point, he told of how he was led to give an African pastor $100,000 for a church building. He was teary-eyed with joy as he conveyed the report. I knew more than anyone in our church how much he could not afford to do that. I was so moved. I found out that I had a miracle offering that night in the church. God spoke to me to follow my pastor's lead in giving. I gave my entire offering back to the church. I could not afford to do that, just as Pastor Rodney could not afford to do what he did. However, neither one of us could afford to disobey God. Can you guess what happened next? Pastor Rodney received a miracle, and so did I. This is how we live. It is an exciting adventure.

Remember, the enemy will continue to press all of us in this area of giving. He will say that even though God supernaturally met our needs last year, this year will be a different story. He will remind us of our own pressing needs or say that we are giving too much. He might even say that we are the only ones giving like that. I can tell you I refuse to backslide in this or any other area. When these thoughts come to me, I get even more determined to give. No matter the growing needs of my own ministry, I want to give more every year. I will forget about my lesser needs and continue to give to the greater.

My hope is that you have received revelation knowledge from this chapter. If you have never considered the subject of giving in this manner before, remember that revival is all about change. We are changing in the ways we think about and do things. We are all growing and going from glory to glory. I no longer want to give only if I have extra funds available or if the persons I am giving to have less than me. I will always consider it a privilege to give into a greater work of faith than that in which I am involved. I trust that you will, too.

FIVE

BLESSED TO BE A BLESSING

And it shall come to pass, if thou shalt hearken diligently
 unto the voice of the Lord thy God, to observe and to do
 all his commandments which I command thee this day,
 that the Lord thy God will set thee on high above all
 nations of the earth:
And all these blessings shall come on thee, and overtake
 thee, if thou shalt hearken unto the voice of the Lord
 thy God.
Blessed shalt thou be in the city, and blessed shalt thou be in
 the field.
Blessed shall be the fruit of thy body, and the fruit of thy
 ground, and the fruit of thy cattle, the increase of thy
 kine, and the flocks of thy sheep.
Blessed shall be thy basket and thy store.
Blessed shalt thou be when thou comest in, and blessed shalt
 thou be when thou goest out.
The Lord shall cause thine enemies that rise up against thee
 to be smitten before thy face: they shall come out against
 thee one way, and flee before thee seven ways.
The Lord shall command the blessing upon thee in thy store-

> houses, and in all that thou settest thine hand unto; and he shall bless thee in the land which the Lord thy God giveth thee.
> The Lord shall establish thee an holy people unto himself, as he hath sworn unto thee, if thou shalt keep the commandments of the Lord thy God, and walk in his ways.
> And all people of the earth shall see that thou art called by the name of the Lord; and they shall be afraid of thee.
> And the Lord shall make thee plenteous in goods, in the fruit of thy body, and in the fruit of thy cattle, and in the fruit of thy ground, in the land which the Lord sware unto thy fathers to give thee.
> The Lord shall open unto thee his good treasure, the heaven to give the rain unto thy land in his season, and to bless all the work of thine hand: and thou shalt lend unto many nations, and thou shalt not borrow.
> And the Lord shall make thee the head, and not the tail; and thou shalt be above only, and thou shalt not be beneath; if that thou hearken unto the commandments of the Lord thy God, which I command thee this day, to observe and to do them:
> And thou shalt not go aside from any of the words which I command thee this day, to the right hand, or to the left, to go after other gods to serve them.
>
> DEUTERONOMY 28:1-14

Deuteronomy 28 is one of the most exciting texts of blessing in the Bible. It displays the character of God in a wonderful way and demonstrates God's unequivocal willingness and desire to prosper His people. Yet those who would propose a poverty mentality would argue that the promises in this chapter could only be applied to Israel. While there are Bible verses that apply to Israel exclusively, this is not one of those passages. In order to understand a verse, we must interpret it with other verses.

The entire chapter of Galatians 3 explains how we, the blood-bought Church who are born again, are the seed of Abraham. Galatians 3:9 says, *"So then they which be of faith are blessed with faithful Abraham."* Other verses confirm that we, today, are the children of Abraham:

> Know ye therefore that they which are of faith, the same are the children of Abraham.
>
> GALATIANS 3:7

> And if ye be Christ's, then are ye Abraham's seed, and heirs according to the promise.
>
> GALATIANS 3:29

> For he is not a Jew, which is one outwardly; neither is that circumcision, which is outward in the flesh:
> But he is a Jew, which is one inwardly; and circumcision is that of the heart, in the spirit, and not in the letter; whose praise is not of men, but of God.
>
> ROMANS 2:28, 29

> Therefore it is of faith, that it might be by grace; to the end the promise might be sure to all the seed; not to that only which is of the law, but to that also which is of the faith of Abraham; who is the father of us all.
>
> ROMANS 4:16

So, we see that we receive God's promises of blessing to Israel, plus some.

> But now hath he obtained a more excellent ministry, by how much also he is the mediator of a better covenant, which was established upon better promises.
>
> HEBREWS 8:6

Abraham was indeed a very blessed man. God commanded him to be a blessing. God told Abraham that through him, the nations of the world would be blessed. However, Abraham could not become a blessing unless he himself was blessed. At one point, Abraham became so wealthy that the land could not contain both him and his nephew, Lot. They had to separate because of the abundance of their flocks and herds. Now, that's some kind of blessing. When was the last time that you had to separate yourself from someone else because you were too blessed?

I will always remember the first time I heard Pastor Rodney Howard-Browne teach on the subject of giving. He was referring to the blessing of Abraham. Pastor Rodney pointed out that we, the Church today, are Abraham's spiritual seed. And as the seed of Abraham, we are commanded to be a blessing. He went on, reminding us that we could not bless anyone else if we did not even have enough for ourselves. That is why it is so important to be blessed. It was not for us but for others.

In January of 1994, I attended Dr. Rodney Howard-Browne's Winter Campmeeting at Carpenter's Home Church in Lakeland, Florida. At the end of the Campmeeting, something special took place that I had never witnessed before. Pastor Strader had faithfully served the Body of Christ for many years. His car was in the shop with mechanical problems. That car had too many miles on it and was no longer a feasible vehicle. It was time for him to be blessed. Dr. Howard-Browne learned of the situation and wanted to be a blessing to the man who had so blessed him. So Dr. Rodney honored Pastor Carl in a very special way.

Carpenter's Home Church seated ten thousand people and was full that night. At a certain point in the service, the big auditorium doors opened, and a new car was driven in. I couldn't decide which man I enjoyed watching more, Dr. Rodney or Pastor Carl. I saw tears running down Dr. Rodney's face as he took joy in presenting Pastor Carl with the gift of a new car. Pastor Carl looked like he was in shock, as were many of us in the audience.

What a moment! Most of the congregation were enjoying seeing the man of God being blessed and another man of God living to be such a blessing. As for me, I never thought I would see such an hour. How thrilling to witness such a generous blessing! I remember determining that I would bless others in the Body the same way.

Some say that it is selfish to believe in God for blessings. Such belief could not be farther from the truth of God's Word. The enemy propagates these lies in an effort to keep the Church in poverty. The Devil doesn't want to see anyone who loves God get blessed because he wants to keep Christians from becoming a blessing to others.

The Devil is happy for his rock singers, the Mafia, and Hollywood to rake in millions of dollars. He promotes wickedness. But he is determined that the Church will have no funds with which to build Bible schools and churches. It thrills the Devil when we are unable to launch missionaries, send our youth to Bible camps, or take the Gospel around the world. When we do not have enough funds to spread the Gospel or to help anyone else, we are prevented from doing serious Kingdom business. The teaching and belief that Christians are to be poor, rather than blessed, is one of Satan's greatest tools to stop the Church of the Lord Jesus Christ.

I am not talking about expecting to be blessed if we do not make Christ the Lord of our lives. I am talking about focusing on serving God and pleasing Him. As we obey God, we should expect that what He has already promised will come, and blessings will follow.

I thank God that spiritually, I am a daughter of Abraham. Born again by faith, I am not just a servant of God; I am His very own child. I can expect that God will do at least as much for me as He promised to do for Israel, who were only His servants. The only requirement was to obey Him. In fact, the Bible tells me that I have a better covenant established on better principles.

I believe this example will make the greater covenant come alive for you. Let's say that I walked over to one of my sons and gave him a ten-dollar bill. Let's say that I told him it represented an old covenant with him. Suppose, then, that I walked over to a second son, handing him a five-dollar bill. Let's say that I told him it represented a new and better covenant with him. I promised the second son that what I gave him was better, though it obviously was not. Now, I know what my sons would say and what anyone else's son would think. The second son would say that if what he was given represented a new and better covenant, he would rather go back to the old one.

God did not say that the New Covenant was better for no reason. In the New Covenant, God did not take promises away. If God had done that, we might as well be back under the Old Covenant. Under the New Covenant, we have everything that people under the Old Covenant had and more. Today, we have not only the physical and material blessings that Israel enjoyed, but we have eternal salvation as well. It is not a tradeoff. We do not give up the physical and material promises of the covenant just because we have the blood of Jesus. We have Israel's promises plus new promises. That is why it is a better covenant, established upon better promises, just as God said.

Let's take a closer look at some of the material blessings that have been promised to us. In Deuteronomy 28:1 (AMP), we have the keyword on which the rest of this text is based. That word is *if*. The Bible says, *"If you will listen diligently to the voice of the Lord your God."* This is key in terms of blessings, prosperity, healing, wisdom, anointing, giftings, ministry, and anything else that pertains to God.

God has a different plan for each of our lives. To step into that plan, we must be able to hear from God and become obedient to what we have heard. God may speak to one person about creative ideas and inventions. He may give someone else direction regarding the stock market. (God gives better "inside" advice than anyone else can give you.) With another person,

God supernaturally connects them with others to bring money to him or her. But it rests on this: each person must hear from God and be obedient to His voice. No matter how much you give or how many verses about prosperity you memorize, you will never prosper without hearing and then obeying the voice of God.

If you are a born-again believer, you are part of the Body of Christ. What you do affects me, and what I do affects you. As the Body of Christ, it is important that we all remain sensitive to the voice of God and stand ready to instantly obey. We each have a role to play; no man is an island to himself. Your obedience is an important part of your provision and an important part of others receiving their miracles as well. Remember, steps of obedience will ultimately lead you into the provision of God in every area of life.

> For I know the thoughts and plans that I have for you, says the Lord, thoughts and plans for welfare and peace and not for evil, to give you hope in your final outcome.
>
> JEREMIAH 29:11 (AMPC)

To walk out the plan, we have to be people who hear and obey God's voice. Otherwise, we will find ourselves walking in the flesh and reaping the harvest of the flesh. Even then, God is such a merciful Father that He will restore us and help us start all over again.

Verse 2 of Deuteronomy 28 says that all of these blessings shall come upon us and overtake us. I get very excited about verse 2. Anything that overtakes me must be moving faster than I am. As I meditate on this verse, I like to picture several athletes racing in the Olympics. One runner may be in the lead, but eventually, he notices someone overtaking him. Out of the corner of his eye, he can see a runner rapidly approaching. No matter how much the first runner tries to stay ahead, he cannot. The reason he cannot is because the athlete overtaking him is running faster than he is.

What a picture we have here in the Word of God. No matter how fast I am running this race for Jesus, His blessings are chasing me down at an accelerated pace. Hallelujah! I cannot stay out of the way of those blessings no matter how fast I run. They are hunting me down and will eventually find me and run me over. I will get smacked from behind and will have to turn around to see what hit me. When I do, I will see that I have been overtaken by another wave of blessing. I do not have to be constantly looking for those blessings or calling them in. All I have to do is listen to God when He speaks and willingly obey His voice. God's blessings will find me.

Lately, as I have been running around the world at a fairly quick pace, I have not been looking for God's blessings. Yet, because God's Word promises them, I expect those blessings. I do not have the time or energy to go out looking for them. I am too busy loving and obeying God and doing His work, which He has called me to do. But no matter how fast I run, I can never go fast enough or far enough to escape God's blessings. Whether I am in a third-world country, the Canadian or Alaskan Arctic, or the jungles of South America, wherever I go, those blessings seem to find me. I'm not out searching for them; those blessings are hunting me down. Knowing that takes a lot of pressure off, so I can concentrate on going where God directs me and saying what He tells me to say.

Teaching at the River Bible Institute in Tampa, Florida, is one of my favorite things. The students there are so hungry. I know that I will help multiply Dr. Rodney Howard-Browne's ministry, as well as multiply the giftings that God has given me. Then, that same anointing will be transferred all over the earth. It is somewhat sacrificial to take time out of our busy schedule to come home to Tampa and teach for several weeks. While the honor does outweigh the sacrifice, I do not financially bring in what we would have had we stayed out on the road. However, when I am home, I do not even think about that. I just enjoy obeying God and teaching. I am not looking for a blessing; rather, I am looking to be a blessing.

On just such an occasion, I was teaching for four weeks. At the same time, I was continuing to give offerings in the church services pastored by Dr. Rodney Howard-Browne. One Sunday, Pastors Rodney and Adonica asked me to be their guest for dinner after church. When I arrived at the restaurant, Pastor Adonica was there, but Pastor Rodney was not. She informed me that he had stopped at a store to do some shopping but would join us later. Once we were seated, Pastor Adonica went ahead and ordered dinner for her husband. While I did think it rather strange that Pastor Rodney would invite me to dinner and then stop to shop first, I quickly put it out of my mind. After some time, he walked behind me, lifted a box up over my head, and dropped it down on the table in front of me. Inside that box was the brand-new laptop computer on which I have written this book. What a surprise! I was not asking for any blessing, but the blessing just found me.

During that same period, after teaching class one night, I was called to the back of the auditorium. A couple was waiting for me with a garment bag in their hands. I did not know them, but they told me they were students in my class and had been very blessed by my teaching. They said that they had something for me that they hoped would fit, but I was free to keep it, sell it, give it away, or do whatever I wanted to with it. I expected the item to be a dress, but I was quite surprised when they unzipped the bag. Out fell a stunningly beautiful full-length mink coat. I discovered that it fit perfectly. I have short arms and frequently need to have sleeves shortened. It is very unusual for clothing to fit. When I tried this coat on, I discovered that even the sleeves fit perfectly. It was as though the coat had been made just for me. Once again, I knew that the blessings of God had chased me down and overtaken me. There I was, out minding God's business. I wasn't asking for a mink coat or even sowing for one. I was sowing for more souls into God's Kingdom. The computer and the coat were just extra blessings that overtook me. God was minding my business while my eyes were on the goal line.

Verse 3 tells us that we will be blessed in the city and in the country. Some people think that the only way they can be blessed is if they live in a prosperous city with a lot of industry. No, that is a lie from the enemy. God is not dependent upon your job, government, or location. He is Jehovah Jireh, regardless of where you live or what is happening around you. It is better to be in the middle of a warzone in the will of God than to be out on a peaceful farm outside the will of God. It is all about being where God wants you to be, when He wants you there, doing what He wants you to do. Then, you will be full of joy, protected, healed, and prospered.

God told me a long time ago that if He could only prosper someone in the middle of a metropolitan city in the United States, His Word would be a lie. However, God's Word is not a lie—God's Word is true. God's promises are yes and amen! God can prosper you in a village where there is no industry. God can prosper you living out on a farm alone, raising your children. God can prosper you in another nation, even if it is a third-world country. God can do it if you are a missionary serving in a poor nation. I have seen it happen time and time again. Do not ever look to your circumstances, but only to Him. He is a big God.

Verse 4 promises that the fruit of our body will be blessed. I am so glad that God promised to bless not only me but also my children. All of this is included in the blessings of the Law.

God promises in this verse to bless the fruit (or, in the Greek, reward) of our ground. Our farms and gardens are included. Any land that you own or rent would be included. I stand upon this promise when I am preaching the Gospel in a foreign land. At that moment, I am using that ground, and I ask God to bless that ground because I am standing upon it.

God promises in this same verse to bless our animals. He specifically refers to cattle, sheep, and oxen (kine). The inference, though, is that God will bless the animals that belong to and mean something to us. Your pets would fall into this category. Even your goldfish should be blessed!

God promised, in verse 5, to bless our basket and our store. God has promised to bless our storehouses. When you are a giver, it is all right to have savings accounts. God will bless your dividends and mutual funds. He wants you to prepare for your future. God will bless your storage places and make sure that you have enough.

Verse 6 promises that we will be blessed coming in and blessed going out. God is promising to bless all of our endeavors. God will bless your trips, vacations, mission trips, and shopping trips. You do not have to fear engine failure, airplane crashes, or car wrecks. When you are serving God, He is with you and will bless all that you do.

God even promises to deal with our enemies. We are to love them and let God take care of them. God handles things in ways we couldn't even dream of. He has promised to give us favors and to cause our enemies to be at peace with us. If they pursue in stubbornness, God will make them retreat from us and not bother us.

God has even promised to bless all that we set our hand to do (verse 8). Some people think that God can bless their job only if it is a prestigious one, with a great salary. However, God will bless you scrubbing toilets for minimum wage if you will dare to believe Him. You may start out there, but as you work hard, continue to be a giver, and trust God, you will not stay there. Dare to believe that God will be true to His Word.

When we become prosperous, God desires that we continue to work in His Kingdom. We dare not become lazy and complacent. We're not trying to get blessed enough to retire but to re-fire! When we stop putting our hand on anything, God quits blessing. We need more undertakers. I'm not referring to funeral parlor managers but to people who will undertake jobs, ministries, and projects.

The Bible declares that if God's people will obey His commandments, God will make them a holy people unto Himself. Once again, we find the word "if." God is establishing the terms of the relationship. He was, is, has always been, and will always be a jealous God who will not share His people with anything or anyone else. We are to adore God and His righteousness. We can place nothing before Him. We get to partake of God's glorious holiness. Clearly, being Jewish did not automatically make that people holy. Rather, they had to make a decision to follow the Lord's precepts and commandments. It would become evident that in so doing, they were a holy people belonging to God. The ultimate blessing comes in being declared a holy people unto the Lord. It is the blessing upon which all the other blessings in the Word rest. In Matthew, we find it stated this way:

> But seek ye first the kingdom of God, and his righteousness;
> and all these things shall be added unto you.
>
> MATTHEW 6:33

When we prize God's righteousness, His holiness, and His Kingdom above all else, the other blessings will come. When you and I are blessed, those blessings will point to our God. People will know that we serve a good God, and they will want to serve Him too.

That is another reason we should want to be blessed, so that our blessing will help lead others to Christ. God has put something in the heart of man that automatically causes him to want to be blessed. The world is not turned off by our blessings. The world is turned off by lack and poverty. Until we are blessed, we cannot really point others to a good God who takes care of His people.

You and I have a responsibility to continue to be blessed to be a blessing. We are Abraham's seed. God will anoint us to get wealth so that He may establish His covenant in the earth. He will give us creative ideas, witty inventions, great wisdom and insight, favor with man, promotions, and inheritances. He will cause the world to bring provision to us without even knowing why. God will enable you to find money lying on the ground. As you continue to seek His Kingdom and His righteousness, God will command His blessing upon you. He will add all of these things to you so that you can be a vessel by which He can dispense His goodness into the earth.

In restaurants, I've bought dinners for people I didn't know, and God used the opportunity to bring those people to Him. It's awesome to have God provide, but it's even more awesome to be someone else's provision, both spiritually and materially.

One day, my pastor went to the store to pick up some groceries for his wife. He dressed casually and wore sunglasses in hopes that no one would recognize him. As he was walking down one of the aisles, a lady came up to him and asked, "Aren't you Dr. Rodney Howard-Browne?" At first, he was disappointed that he had been recognized. But, as he noticed the lady putting groceries in her cart, he suddenly felt led to give her a hundred dollars. Overjoyed, she told him this story. Her pastor had asked her to host missionaries who were coming to church. She didn't want to let him know that she had no money or groceries, so she told him that she would be happy to. God told her to go fill her cart at the grocery store, and He promised He would pay for it. She was out grocery shopping in faith. That night, Pastor Rodney became her source of blessing as he obeyed God. What a way to live! You can live that same way, too.

I can recount another time my pastor was used to be a blessing. He went with his wife, Pastor Adonica, to a clothing store and while there, he noticed a man trying on several suits. The man made the comment that he better not buy any. Pastor Rodney asked him why he should not buy one. The man replied, "Because I am a pastor." Pastor Rodney felt led to buy the suits for him, as well as two shirts and two ties to go with them. The man was a total stranger to him. The gentleman proceeded to ask Pastor Rodney his name. When he told him that he was Dr. Rodney Howard-Browne, the man broke down weeping. Pastor Rodney felt in his heart that the man had probably been one who had heard negative things about him and had criticized him.

It is just like God to ask us to bless someone like that. Doing so helps keep our hearts right so that we do not become reactive to criticism and persecution. It is also one of the ways God works to soften the hearts of our persecutors.

Pastor Rodney has been used this way quite often. On one such occasion, he was in Virginia Beach, eating lunch. He suddenly felt that he must go to a computer store. He thought that he would go to Circuit City and could not find one. He ended up going to another computer store. He began holding a conversation with the clerk behind the counter. He suddenly knew, by the Spirit of God, that he must give the man two hundred dollars. He did, and the man disappeared. It took him ten minutes to find him. Upon finding him, he noticed that the man was crying. Pastor Rodney began to inquire as to why he was weeping. He found out that the man had recently gone through a divorce and had fallen on hard times. He was exactly two hundred dollars short on his rent, and the landlord had told him that it must be paid that very night, or he would be thrown out. What a big God and what a way to live—being led by the Holy Spirit and willing to be a conduit for someone else to be blessed.

In case anyone would still dispute the fact that God wants to materially bless us, verse 11 takes care of that once and for all. It says that God will make us plenteous in goods. One definition that *Strong's Concordance* gives for the Hebrew phrase "plenteous in goods" is "too much." That sounds like our God to me. One of God's names, El Shaddai, translates into the God of more than enough. God has promised to give us too much when we serve Him.

As if that were not enough, in verse 12, God begins to talk about opening up His good treasure. God's *good treasure* is something that only God can do. The Bible says that only God can send the rain. Rain is the ingredient for a good harvest. No matter how many things that we do right, planting, sowing, weeding, and tilling, it is not enough unless God sends the rain. He let us know that He will. God is promising a miracle that only He can guarantee.

He goes on to tell us that we will do the lending and not the borrowing. This not only relates to lending to individuals but also suggests that God's people would export more than they would import. The blessing was designed to put Israel in the supreme position. That's where God wants to put His children today. He has already seated us in heavenly places with Christ Jesus and placed all things under our feet. We need to live out in the natural, the position that God has already placed us in spiritually.

Verse 13 reinforces power and position. God says that we will be the head and not the tail, above and not beneath. He will give His people power and authority in school, on the job, in learning crafts and hobbies, and in every area of life that He sends them. He will elevate His people to leadership and position them where they can make a difference. He will send promotions to His faithful representatives on the job.

Verse 14 reminds us one last time that these promises are conditional. God will bless us when we are obeying, refusing to deviate even one iota from His commandments. This speaks not only of God's written Word but the words that He speaks to us by that inward voice of the Spirit on the inside. God may tell you to go somewhere or to say something to someone. For these blessings to come to you, you must be obedient to His words. You cannot rebelliously or independently "do your own thing" apart from what God speaks to you.

In Biblical days, people never confused the blessings and the curses. A blessing was a blessing, and a curse was a curse. The people saw someone sick and in poverty and made the statement, "Look, there goes someone who is under the curse of the Law." When the people saw someone prospering and living in divine health, they would make the statement, "Look at that blessed son of Abraham."

It is only in our time that people get so confused in the Church, calling poverty, deformities, and disease "special blessings." Many individuals call prosperity and health "a curse." No, it is clear from Scripture that God says health and prosperity are part of the blessings of Abraham, and sickness and poverty are part of the curse of the law. The curse does not come without a reason.

> As the bird by wandering, as the swallow by flying, so the curse causeless shall not come.
>
> PROVERBS 26:2

The curse is the penalty for breaking God's laws or statutes. The curse is retribution or punishment for sin and disobedience. Christ hath redeemed us from the curse of the Law! The Bible says,

> Christ hath redeemed us from the curse of the law, being made a curse for us: for it is written, Cursed is every one that hangeth on a tree.
>
> GALATIANS 3:13

Our quandary is that we have all transgressed; therefore, we all deserve the curse. However, Jesus came and took the curse for us. He traded our curse for His blessing.

We could never make a better deal! Hallelujah! Now that you know what belongs to you, refuse to live under the curse. Live under the blessings of God as an heir of Abraham, a child of God, and a joint heir of Jesus Christ. Be the blessing on the earth that God designed you to be.

SIX

STIMULATED GIVING

Now about the offering that is [to be made] for the saints (God's people in Jerusalem), it is quite superfluous that I should write you;

For I am well acquainted with your willingness (your readiness and your eagerness to promote it) and I have proudly told about you to the people of Macedonia, saying that Achaia (most of Greece) has been prepared since last year for this contribution; and [consequently] your enthusiasm has stimulated the majority of them.

Still, I am sending the brethren [on to you], lest our pride in you should be made an empty boast in this particular case, and so that you may be all ready, as I told them you would be;

Lest, if [any] Macedonians should come with me and find you unprepared [for this generosity], we, to say nothing of yourselves, be humiliated for our being so confident.

That is why I thought it necessary to urge these brethren to go to you before I do and make arrangements in advance for this bountiful, promised gift of yours, so that it may

> be ready, not as an extortion [wrung out of you] but as a generous and willing gift.
>
> [Remember] this: he who sows sparingly and grudgingly will also reap sparingly and grudgingly, and he who sows generously [that blessings may come to someone] will also reap generously and with blessings.
>
> Let each one [give] as he has made up his own mind and purposed in his heart, not reluctantly or sorrowfully or under compulsion, for God loves (He takes pleasure in, prizes above other things, and is unwilling to abandon or to do without) a cheerful (joyous, "prompt to do it") giver [whose heart is in his giving].
>
> And God is able to make all grace (every favor and earthly blessing) come to you in abundance, so that you may always and under all circumstances and whatever the need be self-sufficient [possessing enough to require no aid or support and furnished in abundance for every good work and charitable donation].
>
> 2 CORINTHIANS 9:1-8 (AMPC)

Paul opened this chapter by noting that it was about an offering. He was one of the first traveling missionaries to teach the Church about giving. He realized that the subject of offerings was every bit as important to the Body of Christ as any other topic. Paul also realized his responsibility in teaching the church of Corinth, bringing them to understand why they were to give, how to be led in giving, how to give, and what to expect after they gave.

Paul did not hang his head or apologize for teaching this to the church, nor did he briefly "touch on" the matter while preaching another sermon. Paul clearly took his time, covering the subject thoroughly. As a matter of fact, chapters 8 and 9 of our text (2 Corinthians) deal exclusively with the theme of giving. I, like Paul, have been given a commission from the Lord to teach on this issue so that the Body of Christ can become the Church she is called to be.

In verse 2, Paul said he realized that the people were eager and willing to give. He went further by saying that the church of Corinth was actually excited to give and that their enthusiasm has stimulated others. Very few churches or individuals ever get to witness that kind of stimulated and fervent giving. That is why we, in the Body of Christ, must once again teach people about godly giving. I believe we are now returning to stimulated giving. In recent years, I have witnessed this empowerment on many occasions.

There are many ways to bring the glory down. It is possible to preach it down. You can also praise and worship it down. You can pray it down. Most people in church know this, but very few realize that you can "give" it down. I have seen a spirit of giving hit a place and witnessed the glory of God rolling into the building. People have been filled with the Spirit, others have run down to the altar to get saved, some have rededicated their lives, and still others have been healed.

One of the most outstanding nights of stimulated, enthusiastic, spontaneous giving that I have ever witnessed took place in September of 1993 in Nome, Alaska. I did not know anyone in that town; I had absolutely no contacts there. In fact, I had not been invited to minister in that church—I went strictly on divine, Holy Ghost direction. My original plan had been to rent a building before the Assembly of God pastor felt led to allow me to preach one night. He then asked me to preach for two more nights. After Friday night's service, he asked me to continue through Sunday. I was scheduled to start another revival elsewhere on Sunday, but the pastor felt it imperative that I stay on, so I arranged for someone else to start my next revival.

On Sunday night, all of Heaven came down and enraptured us. Everyone in the church was out on the floor under the power of God. Every backslider and unsaved person in the house came back to God that night. The Holy Spirit upended both the pastor and the associate pastor. They were basically slam-dunked to the floor, ending up under the front-row pew. The pastor remained there for three and a half hours. During that time, he prophesied about a move of God that he hadn't really even believed in until then. He sang in the Spirit, laughed, cried, spoke in tongues, gave an interpretation of tongues, and was caught up in the rapturous Shekinah glory. Now that was a revival!

Since, technically, I had not even been invited to minister in that church, it was a real miracle that I was there, holding a Holy Ghost revival. I certainly was not going to push the limit by asking to teach on giving. However, I did mention that I usually taught on giving when I held other revivals. At the end of the five days, the pastor asked me to make an opening in my schedule and return as quickly as possible.

When I agreed to return in September, the pastor asked that I include a teaching on giving. He said that he had not really heard the subject taught as God had instructed us but was anxious to. The pastor said that he trusted me and that I had complete liberty.

So when I returned to Nome for those services, I taught on giving each night before we received the offering. I cannot remember if it was the second or third night that the miracle occurred that I am about to relate. However, on one of those nights, I was about five minutes into teaching when a man on the end of the third row jumped to his feet, interrupting me. This was a large man, probably about 6' 4" tall. He was very excited and was jumping up and down, shouting and waving his hands. Quite frankly, he scared me. I thought to myself, 'Oh no, I've really run into a religious devil this time. He's interrupting me, and he's really angry. What do I do at this point?'

I soon realized that I was making a premature judgment. I discovered that the man was not angry at all. He was thrilled and full of joy. This man was beside himself with excitement because of the revelation that had just come to him. He was waving his arms and saying, "I am so sorry to interrupt you, Sister Debbie. I have never interrupted a preacher before, and I know that I should wait until you are through, but I can't stand it any longer. This is the best news I have ever heard. My life would be different if I had been taught this earlier. This is wonderful news. I know that you are in the middle of your teaching, but I have to give now. Please let us give now!"

With that, he proceeded to give a message in tongues along with the interpretation of that tongue. God was admonishing the entire congregation to give with their whole heart. This man led the way in giving. He ran up front and put a one hundred dollar bill in each of my hands. (I have jokingly said many times that I wished I was an octopus that night.) I got to witness one of the most incredible things that I had ever seen. The entire congregation ran to the altar to give their offerings. They were full of joy. They were all stimulated to give. The Holy Spirit fell upon them as they gave, and the entire church was filled with His glory. We experienced another glorious night of revival—one that began with stimulated giving.

The pastor was so excited about the manner in which his congregation gave that he went downstairs to be with the deacons as they counted the offering. He wanted to witness what had actually taken place. The pastor had never before seen his congregation so excited about giving. The night before I left Nome, he came in with a check. "Before I give this to you," he said, "I want to tell you a story. Prior to your arrival, I met with my board and told them that I wanted to believe for five thousand dollars to give you as you left. The news almost sent my board into shock because we had never before given anyone even half that amount. I shared with the board how you go into small villages where you don't even receive the cost of your plane ticket in offerings. We were going to believe to subsidize that village ministry and be a real help in forwarding you on your way. Now, this is a lot for a church of about sixty-five to eighty-five people to believe for, but I thought that we could do it. My surprised board said that they would try not to negate my faith and would believe with me.

"When I saw the spirit of giving break out upon my congregation the other night, I decided to go with the men to count the offering. I could not believe what I was seeing. It was better than I could have believed or even hoped. On the other hand, I know my people. I know where they work and approximately how much they make. I knew that they could not keep up this kind of giving, and if they did, our Sunday morning tithes and offerings would be down.

"As we counted the offerings each night, I was more and more surprised at what God was doing. Not only did the offerings increase, but our own Sunday morning tithes and offerings set a new record high as well. I thought you would enjoy hearing this before I gave you your check."

With that, the pastor handed me a check, not for five thousand, but ten thousand dollars. I was shocked! I had never seen that amount come into my ministry at one time, ever. What a blessing! I never dreamed that a little church like that would be able to give in such a big way. They fulfilled their vision of supplementing the village ministry, and as a result, they became very blessed themselves. The next Sunday, the church received their highest tithes and offerings to date. It set a new record and has continued to stay up every week since.

Then, the pastor called with exciting news of yet another blessing. One day, a lady walked into his office and asked how much they still owed on the church building. When the pastor told her about eight thousand dollars, she proceeded to write out a check and hand it to him. When the pastor looked at it, he thought he read five thousand dollars and was thrilled. He said, "That's great; that is over half of it." She said, "I think that you had better look again." When the pastor looked, he realized that he had missed one of the zeros. The check was made out for fifty thousand dollars. The lady instructed him to pay off the loan on the church building, put twenty thousand into his own account, and the rest into the church account. She told the pastor that he had been a missionary to Alaska for years and that it was time that he was blessed. The pastor called me, thrilled at what God had done.

It was not long before I received another phone call. For quite some time, the blessings continued to rain on the Assembly of God church in Nome. The man who led the way in giving that night also received a great blessing. He was a butcher in Nome's grocery store. Shortly after our visit there, he went into work to find the owner quite depressed. When he asked what was wrong, he was told that they had just received word that a large food chain by the name of Carr's (later sold to Safeway) was coming to Nome. Their grand opening was in just a few months. The grocery store owner did not feel he could compete with a large food chain. He felt that he would be going out of business and that they would all lose their jobs.

The man who had been in our services was now full of Holy Ghost boldness. He boldly proclaimed that because he worked there and because he was in covenant with Jehovah Jireh—the Lord our Provider—God would bless that little store. He told his employer, "This will be the best month we've ever had. In fact, Carr's grand opening day will be this store's best day ever. We will have more people in this store than Carr's has in theirs, even with their cake, ice cream, and balloons. God will bless us; you just wait and see." The owner looked at him as if he were missing a few marbles and said, "Hmmm, we'll see."

Would you be surprised to find out that things happened just as this Holy Ghost-transformed giant of a man predicted? The little store's best month was indeed the same month that the new store opened. Grand opening day was the little grocery store's best day ever, with more people shopping there than at the food chain's store. Now buckle your seat belts; the best is yet to come. That little grocery became so blessed that radical changes were made. Do you remember the man's job as a butcher? There were suddenly so many meat orders that the owner had to hire additional help. That butcher got a promotion and a big raise. Praise God! He had only heard ten days of teaching in the revival, but it was enough to transform him and his family, the pastor and his family, the church, the little community grocery store, and more. Thanks be to God for His Word that changes people, circumstances, and situations. That Word can affect individuals, families, churches, towns, and nations.

And still, the blessings did not end. The pastor called to tell me that someone in the church bought his family plane tickets for an all-expenses-paid Hawaiian vacation. Nothing like this had ever before happened, and they felt extremely blessed.

Still later, someone bought them four plane tickets so the entire family could travel to be with their relatives for Christmas in Anchorage. With all of them together, it was going to be a wonderful holiday time. The pastor, ecstatic that they had been blessed with the trip, did not realize that more was yet to come. Since Nome has only a couple of tourist stores, it was really no place to do Christmas shopping. So they decided to wait and do their Christmas shopping in Anchorage. Upon arriving, they decided to check their bank balance before shopping. When they did, they discovered that someone had anonymously deposited thirty-five thousand dollars into their personal account. What an expected blessing from the Lord!

In one year, the pastor received fifty-five thousand dollars above his salary, the church was paid for, trips were made, the little grocery store was saved, the butcher received a pay raise, and individual people in the church and community were blessed, and more. Among their other blessings, the church was able to give more to missions that year than they usually gave in a whole year. What a big God! Others were blessed as well. After sacrificial giving, a couple in the church was able to sell their home for substantially more than the going rate. They were able to go on to Bible school and have since graduated.

I returned to that church approximately once a year for several years. On one of my visits, they scheduled a missionary to speak the following Sunday. Later, I was told that the missionary thought of canceling when he realized that I would be just leaving. He was afraid that after a week of Holy Ghost revival meetings, the people might be bored with an itinerant missionary. The missionary was in need of funds for the mission field and was certain that after giving for a solid week, the congregation would not have any money left to give to the missionary. The pastor encouraged him to come anyway, stating that they would trust God together. In just one service, the missionary received several thousand dollars, even more than I had been given in a whole week! The missionary was so thrilled that he jokingly told the pastor to tell me he would follow behind me anytime. They both knew that the teachings I had been giving all week helped pave the way for his reaping this tremendous financial blessing.

I do love this part of how we live and what we believe. I can remember days of jealousy and competition in the church when people were afraid that someone else's blessing would result in less for them. That is because that individual's dependency was upon man, not God. When people are taught that God is a God of more than enough, with no limits, they can trust Him to meet not only their own needs but also the needs of others. We are no longer competing with one another but trusting God together. We are members of the same family and have the same Father. We are in the same receiving line along with everyone else. God will be as big to us as He is to others, and vice versa.

If God could do this for a little church situated on the west coast of Alaska alongside the Bering Sea, He can do it for you. If God could take care of this missionary to villages above the Arctic Circle, He can do it for you. He was the same God that year that He had been in previous years.

Why, then, was it this little church's year of blessing? They had discovered a key to blessing. When the congregation began to get a revelation of Jehovah Jireh and their responsibility to trust in Him and to give to Him, their whole attitude about giving changed. The church was now filled with stimulated, enthusiastic givers whose hearts were in their giving. And God began to meet them right there.

I remember another time when people were enthusiastic and stimulated to give. It was in Pastor Rodney Howard-Browne's meeting in Port Elizabeth, South Africa. In recent years, as the value of the rand continued to drop in relation to the American dollar, South Africa had been suffering substantial poverty. Recession hit Port Elizabeth so hard that their poverty made the news. It was reported that there was no gas in the police cars. If a victim of a crime called the police for help, they were advised that in order to help, the police would have to be picked up and driven to the scene. That is how desperate the Port Elizabethan financial situation had become. It was during this recession that Pastor Howard-Browne returned to his South African homeland to hold a revival.

The timing of his arrival placed Pastor Rodney in an interesting dilemma. Either he could let that spirit of poverty intimidate him, causing him to back off from his stewardship teaching, or he could hit it head-on. My pastor knows only one mode, and this is to hit the enemy head-on. He knew the chance he was taking. The people could have reacted with anger, thinking, 'How dare you teach us about giving when we have nothing? Who do you think you are? You started out here but left us and went to America, where you have been blessed. It sure is easy for you to come back now and tell us that we should give, isn't it?'

The people could have become so angry that they wanted to gnash on Pastor Rodney with their teeth, as the people in the Bible did when they persecuted Stephen. Despite all this, Pastor Rodney knew that the only way to break that spirit of poverty was to preach the Word of God under the anointing of the Holy Spirit. Then, the people would have at least been given the choice to act on that Word. Thank God they were given the opportunity! As you will see, it affected the entire local body.

In one particular meeting, Pastor Rodney called an African Anglican lay preacher forward and questioned him about the touch he had received from the Lord during that week. He was very excited because the Lord had totally transformed his life. He said that he had bought several of Pastor Rodney's videos, and he was going to invite the whole small town to view them with him in his double-car garage. Pastor Rodney asked him how much it would cost to build a church building, and he said around R20 000. Pastor Rodney was so moved that he gave the man the first R5 000 and also gave the congregation an opportunity to give an offering to him. The offering ended up being R24 500, which was outstanding for that part of the country!

During another night, the people spontaneously started giving to Pastor Rodney's ministry. They ran to the altar, piling their offerings onto the platform until they stood three and a half feet high. People were so overcome with joy that they laid down their shoes, watches, jewelry, coats, shirts, and other personal items. A professional surfer laid his board on the altar. As he went back to his seat, a person tapped him on the shoulder and told him to come over to the surf shop in the morning to make his choice of any surfboard.

During that week, one of the area's leading newspapers interviewed Pastors Rodney and Adonica and wanted to know all about the meetings.

Some of their reporters had attended the meetings. The next day, the headlines read, *Hundreds Take Off Their Clothes in Port Elizabeth Church*. Needless to say, those headlines drew more people to the revival. Many came to know Christ because they realized that a God who could so move on His people was a God worth serving. For years, they had seen stingy, tightwad people in the church but had never before witnessed people who were stimulated to give.

The amazing thing is how the people gave out of their poverty. The less they had, the more they realized that if they were to survive and prosper, they *must* receive this revelation. Later, reports came back from the surrounding areas relating that those who had received that revelation took it back to their homes and churches, where that same spirit of giving broke out as well.

When this story was shared in our home church, The River at Tampa Bay, that giving spirit broke out again. A little boy brought his brand-new Nike sneakers to the altar. He was weeping, saying that he wanted to give his new shoes to Jesus. Again, people began to "run to give." The worship team was so moved that they laid their instruments on the altar. Of course, Pastor Rodney had to give them back so he could have worship music for the altar call. That is truly stimulated, enthusiastic giving! I believe that we are about to see much more of this all over the world.

We rejoice in our church, The River at Tampa Bay, at offering time. Offering is one of the times of worship that we look forward to most. You will hear people shout and laugh. Sometimes, you can even see them dance. In describing what our giving attitude should be, *The Amplified Bible* even uses the word *hilarious*. Offering time should be a time of great rejoicing; it is a celebration time. When a church has sound teaching along these lines, the people can hardly wait to cheerfully give.

Verse 7 of our text emphasizes that God takes pleasure in this kind of giving and prizes it above other things. Anything that God takes pleasure in and prizes is something in which I want to have a part. The Bible also says that God takes pleasure in the prosperity of His servants. Yet, there are people who are actually afraid to prosper, as if that is not the will of God.

The Bible lets us know that God loves prospering His people, receives pleasure in it, and refuses to do without it.

Verse 8 tells us that God will make all grace and earthly blessings come to us in abundance. The word *abundance* is frequently used in the Bible in connection with God's blessings. God loves adjectives and adverbs. He makes sure that we understand that He has not sent His Son just to give life but to give life more abundantly. God has promised to do exceeding abundantly above all that we ask or think.

The Amplified Bible mentions that these blessings will enable us to be self-sufficient. When the Church gets a hold of this, we will no longer be improperly dependent upon our parents, the government, the welfare system, social institutions, employers, or anyone or anything else for our supply. We will have a total dependency upon Jehovah Jireh, the Lord, our Provider. This teaching will positively influence our entire nation.

More recently, I was privileged to minister in San Diego, California. I was asked to join Pastor Rodney Howard-Browne in his crusade. As we ministered, we could feel that the atmosphere was a little stiff in the area of giving and even in joy. However, Pastor Rodney was not taking the time to teach on giving that he usually does, for in that crusade, he was concentrating on souls. He needed additional time to reach the lost. When it was time for Pastor Rodney to depart, he suggested that an associate evangelist, Richard Moore, and I stay over and hold another meeting on Saturday night. The pastor agreed. That night, once Richard had finished teaching on giving, the offering was received.

Richard did a wonderful job of teaching, and you could tell that the people were beginning to catch what giving was all about. Then, I got up to preach the second message of the evening. All at once, the anointing of God hit me in a fresh way, and I felt led to continue what Richard had been preaching. I told the people that while we were not going to receive another offering, I felt compelled to teach some more on the subject of giving. I was about a half hour into my teaching when the place began to explode in joy and laughter, catching me by surprise. I had been teaching on giving. Yet, the joy broke out. Our ministry team had witnessed this on numerous occasions. When people begin to get set free in one area, they also get free in another.

Even though I had announced that we were not receiving another offering, a little girl came forward weeping. She brought a little purse with some fingernail polish in it that she wanted to give to Jesus. Suddenly, people began running forward to give—I couldn't keep them from it. A person on the praise and worship team came and laid down his keyboard, and so the church continued to give.

In the middle of the giving, a lady ran to the altar and told me that she was not a Christian. She was weeping and said if she had known Christians were like this, she would have become one long ago. The spirit of giving moved her to want to become a Christian. When she asked how she could become a Christian, I led her to the Lord on the spot. I was so surprised! I had not even given the altar call, yet people were being saved. Another lady came up and received her healing right in the middle of this joyous giving.

When the service was over, the pastor asked me to come observe what was taking place in the foyer. I went out there to discover that people were giving to one another. Children were taking the shoes off of their feet and giving them to others who needed shoes. Money was being given to some, clothing to others. It was so precious. That was a night of joyous revival, salvation, healing, and infilling of the Holy Spirit, all a result of stimulated giving. The liberality of some in the congregation had so moved others as they witnessed the church practicing what it preached. Praise God!

In this chapter, I have included several examples of spiritually stimulated giving. I could have given you many more just like them. Over the last eight years, I have rejoiced to see God's people receiving the knowledge of hilarious and stimulated giving. The Church will become the Church that she's called to be. If you are a believer, you, too, are a part of that Church. So, I believe that you, too, are hungry to become all that God has called you to be. I believe that you, too, are becoming a hilarious, from-the-heart, prompt-to-do-it giver!

SEVEN

YOU ARE NOT A BIRD

Let the thief steal no more, but rather let him be industrious, making an honest living with his own hands, so that he may be able to give to those in need.

EPHESIANS 4:28 (AMPC)

Lay not up for yourselves treasures upon earth, where moth and rust doth corrupt, and where thieves break through and steal:
But lay up for yourselves treasures in heaven, where neither moth nor rust doth corrupt, and where thieves do not break through nor steal:
For where your treasure is, there will your heart be also.
The light of the body is the eye: if therefore thine eye be single, thy whole body shall be full of light.
But if thine eye be evil, thy whole body shall be full of darkness. If therefore the light that is in thee be darkness, how great is that darkness!
No man can serve two masters: for either he will hate the one, and love the other; or else he will hold to the one,

and despise the other. Ye cannot serve God and mammon.

Therefore I say unto you, Take no thought for your life, what ye shall eat, or what ye shall drink; nor yet for your body, what ye shall put on. Is not the life more than meat, and the body than raiment?

Behold the fowls of the air: for they sow not, neither do they reap, nor gather into barns; yet your heavenly Father feedeth them. Are ye not much better than they?

Which of you by taking thought can add one cubit unto his stature?

And why take ye thought for raiment? Consider the lilies of the field, how they grow; they toil not, neither do they spin:

And yet I say unto you, That even Solomon in all his glory was not arrayed like one of these.

Wherefore, if God so clothe the grass of the field, which to day is, and to morrow is cast into the oven, shall he not much more clothe you, O ye of little faith?

Therefore take no thought, saying, What shall we eat? or, What shall we drink? or, Wherewithal shall we be clothed?

(For after all these things do the Gentiles seek:) for your heavenly Father knoweth that ye have need of all these things.

But seek ye first the kingdom of God, and his righteousness; and all these things shall be added unto you.

Take therefore no thought for the morrow: for the morrow shall take thought for the things of itself. Sufficient unto the day is the evil thereof.

MATTHEW 6:19-34

Ephesians 4:28 gives us the reason for working. It says we work so that we may be able to give to those in need. For many Christians, this is a brand-new concept. We have been taught that we go to work to pay *our* bills and take care of *our* needs. Every morning, you can see people rushing about their business. Their entire motivation is to make more money for themselves and their families. For them, it becomes all about *my* salary, *my* house, *my* car, *my* vacation, *my* recreation, *my* children's education, *my* retirement, and *my* children's inheritance. Our culture encourages us to be very selfish individuals.

We assume that because we are Christians, we are not worldly. Such is not necessarily the case. To be worldly is to think and behave like the world, to have motivations and heart attitudes like the world, and to treat others as the world would treat them. While the world thinks, ME FIRST, Christians should think, OTHERS FIRST. While the world thinks, I WANT THE FRONT SEAT, we Christians should think, I WILL TAKE THE BACKSEAT. While the world thinks I MUST SAVE MY LIFE, the Christian should think I MUST LOSE MY LIFE.

Most people believe that they go to work to have their needs met, and then, hopefully, they might have a little left over. They may even give a small amount to the Lord after they take care of everything else. They believe that if they do not take care of their own needs, no one else will. Their security is placed in their jobs and in the government. So they go into an occupation that they think will take care of their own needs and the needs of their family. The interesting thing about this is that sometimes, the very job that they believe will meet their needs actually causes them to have more needs.

Take a moment to look at things from a jobless, homeless person's perspective. If you are living in a park without a job, you do not need a car. However, usually, the moment that you get a job, you need a car to take you to work. Now, you need to buy gas to put into the car that takes you to work. You also need insurance and upkeep for that car that you bought to take you to work. Now, because you have employment, you feel it is time to get a house. Now, because you have the house, you must pay the utilities and upkeep of that house.

When you were unemployed, you had very few basic needs. You needed to eat, but not as much as one would think. You needed a few basic clothing articles (depending on the climate where you were living), but you didn't need many changes of clothes to survive. It is when you get a job that you suddenly need decent clothes to wear to that job. So you can see that even in the natural, we do not necessarily have to go to work to take care of our needs. Humans have quite a way of deceiving themselves with "self-seeking attitudes" when they want to. Without God, we are basically very selfish creatures.

If we apply Bible principles to this concept, we find that many of us have been going to work for the wrong reasons. According to the Scripture text, we are to go to work so we will have *more to give*. I assure you that if giving more becomes your motivating heart's cry, you will go to work with far greater joy and anticipation. You will receive fresh vision and determination. Your job will no longer be empty and meaningless —just a way to heap more upon yourself. Your job will become an avenue of blessing for others. You'll be thinking, 'This is so exciting. I'm becoming blessed in my job so that I have more to give. I'm going to become a blessing all over the world.' You'll have new meaning and purpose in your job. You will become very thankful and allow God to use you as never before.

You might find yourself shocked by this line of reasoning. You may be asking the question, "Who, then, is going to take care of my needs? I do still have some, you know." I am so glad you asked that question because the Scriptures have an answer for that as well. The same God who said that we were to go to work so that we may have to give is the same God who tells us who is going to meet our needs. God is!

Matthew 6 tells us all about the supplier of our needs. Jesus is ministering in this passage, telling us to not lay up for ourselves treasures on this earth. Again, "laying up treasure" is a concept of the world that doesn't know any better. It takes many forms.

Some people are saving up for a "rainy day." They need to. The rainy days will surely come, for they are placing their faith there. Others are thinking only of retirement and "laying up" everything they have for that day. They may work their fingers to the bone for the hour when it will be waiting for them.

Still others act as though they can "take it with them." No matter how much they make, it is never enough. They are always thinking of ways to make more and how to prevent someone from taking it away from them. They live in constant fear of losing it all and usually cannot even enjoy what they have accumulated.

Such attitudes are all about "laying it up for themselves." Yet, the Bible reminds us that earthly treasure can disappear so easily through neglect, thievery, or natural earthly occurrences. Many times, people are putting their money away into bags with holes in them.

In the very end, we are going to have to part with all of our possessions. Only those things with eternal value will remain. The rest will be meaningless. That is why the Bible reminds us here that we should be placing the bulk of our deposits into God's Kingdom, where no one can steal them. In His Kingdom, our treasure will be eternal.

Verse 21 is a key verse, not only to this chapter but to our entire Christian life as well. This verse tells us that where our treasure is, our heart is. To be able to see where someone's heart is, all we have to do is look at where his or her treasure is. Here in this country, where we use checkbooks, this is easy to do. Simply pull out our check registers. When we look down the list and see that the majority of our entries are restaurants (Chinese, Mexican, American, fast-food), we know that our heart is in our bellies!

Some of you ladies may view your entries and find that your heart is in your clothing and shoes. Or, you may see that your heart is in your home with expenditures on carpet, draperies, and wall furnishings. (I know some of you men are "amen-ing" right now, but you better not enjoy it too much.) If some of you gentlemen were to look at your check registers right now, you would find that your heart is in your sports activities: golf, football, basketball, and boating. Or, it may be in your big-boy toys like motorcycles, three-wheelers, fast cars, or 4 x 4's.

Some of you may find that your entire heart is in your children and their desires. It makes no difference where you've set your heart's affection; one thing is certain. When the majority of your entries are all about things that have nothing to do with God, your heart is not with Him. It's all right to spend money on any of these things as long as we spend more on giving to God. Most people will find that they need to continue making positive adjustments until the God-focused entries surpass the others.

Verse 24 is another key verse, which states that no one can serve two masters. You cannot serve God and money. God will not share His glory with another. This chapter is not saying that you cannot have money. It is saying that you cannot serve money if you are serving God. Be assured that our God is a jealous God. It is all right to have money but not to serve it. It is also all right to have things as long as things do not have you. Some people do not even know when they stopped having things and when the things began to have them.

I have pointed out many times the example that money is a tool. A tool is not something to be loved or hated. Placed into the wrong hands, a tool can be a murder weapon. In the right hands, a tool can be used to build or improve things. Typically, you do not fear having too many tools. You usually do not have to get rid of them for fear they will cause you to backslide. Neither should all of your time and thoughts be caught up in how wonderful the tools are. They are simply tools. You can have them, and you can enjoy them; just do not let them have you. If you are going to do a lot of building or repairing, you will need lots of tools. Interestingly, the same is true of money.

What if the media reported that a man picked up his hammer and killed his wife with it? Would you suddenly fear having a hammer in the house and feel the need to throw it away? Of course not. The hammer is not evil. It is only a tool. The heart of the man who committed that hideous crime was evil, not the tool. Why should we fear having finances? They are not evil. Money in the wrong hands can create great damage, and money in the hands of a righteous man or woman can accomplish great things. It is all about the heart, not the tool.

We should not fear or fall in love with tools. That would be ludicrous. Can you imagine a man waking up in the morning and saying to his hammer, "Hammer, how I love you. I wouldn't want to live life without you. You are my first thought of the day and my last one at night before going to sleep. You are my everything." No, again, that is unthinkable. However, I was giving that example in a church one time, and the entire congregation started laughing and pointing at an usher in the front row. He got up from his chair, went to the back of the church, put a bag over his head, and came back and sat down. The entire thing was entertaining. It was obvious that the man loved his tools a bit more than most men. Hopefully, he was delivered that night.

Money is very good to have—now, more than ever—because we are living in a day of great harvest, and we need more and better equipment to get the job done. If the enemy can get the church to fear having equipment, he can cripple us and keep us from the great harvest. That is why more teachers and preachers must be raised up to teach what God says about money. We have had plenty of people teaching religious ideas and philosophies that are not based on the Word of God. This is the reason I wrote this book, so the truth can set us free.

Verse 25 begins to get specific about who will take care of our needs and what our expectations should be. It specifically says that we are not to be concerned or worried about what we will eat, drink, or wear. This verse does not say that we are not supposed to eat, drink, or wear anything. That would be absolutely ridiculous. We are supposed to know who our source is and simply not worry about those things.

Many live with the false assumption that if they have hardly anything in terms of material possessions, they will not be overly anxious about money. I know that nothing could be farther from the truth. Some of the poorest people I know worry the most about money. They cannot sleep at night because of worrying about how they are going to put groceries on the table for their children. Their every thought is focused on their lack and how money would make things easier for them. No, being in lack does not cure worry and over-anxiousness. It worsens it. The problem is not whether these people have or do not have money. Anxiety is a heart problem, and it is a trust problem.

Verse 26 reminds us of how God takes care of the birds of the air. It says that the birds do not go to work, they do not sow or plant, and they do not reap or harvest. In order to reap, you must be a sower. The laws of sowing and reaping are God's laws. The birds of the air know nothing about such laws. They do not have spirits. They have no understanding of these things and are incapable of applying such principles to their lives. Birds are busily breathing in and out, flying about, finding food, building nests, caring for their young, flapping their wings, chirping, sleeping, and then beginning the process all over again. Yet, in all their supposed self-focus, God loves and takes care of them. Even though birds seem to live outside the laws of sowing and reaping, God who created them is merciful, loving, and kind. He makes sure that their basic needs of living and eating are met.

In this verse, by way of a question, the Lord Jesus makes something else very clear. He asks, *"How much more will He take care of us?"* People use this very verse to say that we shouldn't expect to have anything decent to wear and should expect very little to eat. They have interpreted this passage to say it is unreasonable to believe for more and that here, God is telling us not to even think of such things. They have misunderstood this entire chapter, preaching and teaching just the opposite of what it truly says. No, no, no, no, no, no, no!

God is saying just the opposite. He is trying to get us to see how wonderfully he has promised to take care of us and meet our needs. God's point is that if He meets the basic needs of birds when they don't plant crops or hold down a job, how much more will He do for us, His own children? The key words here are, "HOW MUCH MORE?" You are not a bird; you do not grovel for worms and seeds, yet even the birds are better cared for than most of God's children believe they can be. You are a child of the King. As a child of the King, how much more will God do for you? Do not let the enemy twist this verse in your head until you think you are not to expect any more than a bird.

Verses 28 and 29 take us to the lilies of the field. We are reminded that lilies are flowers and do not go to work. Even then, Solomon, in all of his glory, was not as beautiful as they were. I was studying about King Solomon a while back and found that he wore shining, white robes sprinkled with actual gold dust. Yet the flowers, which do no labor, are far more beautiful.

Verse 30 tells us that God is the One who so beautifully clothes the lilies of the field. The Lord does not stop there but, once again, brings the comparison back to us, His children. God reminds us that if He can take such splendid and awesome care of His flowers, how much more will He clothe us? Therefore, as God's child, I can expect that I will not lack when it comes to clothing. God will provide me with beautiful clothes, more striking than His lilies in full bloom. I am God's own child, born again, filled with His Spirit, bearing His name and His seal. How much more will He take care of me?

As you can plainly see, this passage of Scripture is talking about godly prosperity and not human poverty. This scripture is not saying, "Do not expect to eat or be clothed." Instead, it's saying, "You can expect to have the best and be well taken care of so that you do not have to be anxious or worried about anything."

The Lord goes on to tell us that those who do not believe He will take care of them in such a manner are people of little faith. If we do not believe God for the things that He promises, we are "shorting ourselves" of a blessing. Worse yet, we are displeasing to Him. God calls such individuals people of unbelief.

Our passage (v. 31) closes by reminding us to not be anxious or worried about what we will eat or drink or wear. This text points out that the Gentiles were worried about all these things. The world is not aware of God's principles and promises. The world does not understand the things of God. They do not sow to the Kingdom. They are full of anxiety and consumed with taking care of themselves. Like the birds, they simply do not know any different. Since they don't, they must be concerned and full of care about providing for their own needs. They are only human and can only do so much.

The Apostle Paul tells us that he had learned that no man or woman could be his source. The job or government could not be his source. Paul shared that whatever the case, regardless of the external circumstance, Jehovah Jireh would still come through for him (Philippians 4:11-13).

Verse 32 settles the questions once and for all. It says that our Heavenly Father already knows that we have need of these things. Aren't you glad that God calls food and clothing a basic need and not a nice little luxury? God does not expect us to walk around naked. When we think of all the different body types running around, I think you will readily agree with me that this is a very good thing. Neither does God expect us to go without food. He is a good Father.

Verse 33 tells us our part in all this. We are to seek God, His Kingdom, and His righteousness first. God always wants the first and best of what we have to give. God wants the first of our worship, thanksgiving, time, talents, wallets … our lives. After we seek God first, he reminds us that *"all these (other) things"* will be added unto us. God does not say, "Seek Me first and then live in poverty." He says that by seeking Him first, our needs will be automatically met. He's even promised to give us the desires of our hearts (Psalm 37:4**)**.

I have found that as I serve God and put Him first, He has always provided for my needs. Remember when I said that as I am traveling "at a run" around the world preaching the gospel, I do not wonder if I will have food to eat or clothes to wear. I have also said that people always comment on my beautiful wardrobe—and I can tell you, I eat too much good food! Not only that, there are so many times God seems to meet my needs in other areas where I haven't even asked.

Just a few months ago, a pastor's wife asked to try my microphone on because she wanted to purchase one like it. I heard the Holy Spirit tell me to give it to her, so I did. At the time, it was a sacrifice to do so. I loved that microphone. It gave me great freedom in preaching. It was a cordless headset model. It saved a lot of strain on my voice because I could turn my head, and the sound would stay with me. But I gave my microphone with joy and enjoyed watching the pastor's wife receive it.

From there, I went to another church in Alaska. When I walked into the church on Sunday morning, I was told they had a surprise for me. They escorted me to a back room, where they pulled a brand-new microphone from a bag. It was like my other one, only better. Instead of having to hook part of the controls onto my waistband, they were included in the headpiece. It was the very kind I was planning to purchase next when I thought that we could afford it. It amazed me that the church felt led to purchase it for me. They were not even aware that I had given my old set away. But God was aware of it. I had been seeking Him and His righteousness and Kingdom first, and He met my needs—beyond clothing and food. What a good God!

I love being a living testimony of the goodness of my Lord and His Word. The important thing for you to remember is that God is no respecter of persons. What He has done for me, God will do for you. He has not shown me favoritism because I am a minister of the gospel but has been true to His Word because I am a giver. My goal is to give more and more. We must be stretching all the time in order to be a blessing.

EIGHT

IF I CAN'T BUILD IT, I WILL PAY FOR IT

And King David said to all the assembly, Solomon my son, whom alone God has chosen, is yet young, tender, and inexperienced; and the work is great, for the palace is not to be for man but for the Lord God.

So I have provided with all my might for the house of my God the gold for things to be of gold, silver for things of silver, bronze for things of bronze, iron for things of iron, and wood for things of wood, as well as onyx or beryl stones, stones to be set, stones of antimony, stones of various colors, and all sorts of precious stones, and marble stones in abundance.

Moreover, because I have set my affection on the house of my God, in addition to all I have prepared for the holy house, I have a private treasure of gold and silver which I give for the house of my God:

It is 3,000 talents of gold, gold of Ophir, 7,000 talents of refined silver for overlaying the walls of the house,

Gold for the uses of gold, silver for the uses of silver, and for every work to be done by craftsmen. Now who will offer willingly to fill his hand [and consecrate it] today to the Lord [like one consecrating himself to the priesthood]?

Then the chiefs of the fathers and princes of the tribes of Israel and the captains of thousands and of hundreds, with the rulers of the king's work, offered willingly

And gave for the service of the house of God—of gold 5,000 talents and 10,000 darics, of silver 10,000 talents, of bronze 18,000 talents, and 100,000 talents of iron.

And whoever had precious stones gave them to the treasury of the house of the Lord in the care of Jehiel the Gershonite.

Then the people rejoiced because these had given willingly, for with a whole and blameless heart they had offered freely to the Lord. King David also rejoiced greatly.

Therefore David blessed the Lord before all the assembly and said, Be praised, adored, and thanked, O Lord, the God of Israel our [forefather], forever and ever.

Yours, O Lord, is the greatness and the power and the glory and the victory and the majesty, for all that is in the heavens and the earth is Yours; Yours is the kingdom, O Lord, and Yours it is to be exalted as Head over all.

Both riches and honor come from You, and You reign over all. In Your hands are power and might; in Your hands it is to make great and to give strength to all.

Now therefore, our God, we thank You and praise Your glorious name and those attributes which that name denotes.

But who am I, and what are my people, that we should retain strength and be able to offer thus so willingly? For all things come from You, and out of Your own [hand] we have given You.

1 CHRONICLES 29:1-14 (AMPC)

In this story, King David desperately wanted to build God's house. David was a worshiper, a man after God's own heart. The king had a godly desire for spiritual things. He was hungry and thirsty for the presence of God. Therefore, it is only natural that he would want to build God's house. However, David had also been a man of war, with much bloodshed in his kingdom. God told King David that He was holy, and such holiness had to be honored. In 1 Chronicles 28:3 , God said, *"Thou shalt not build an house for my name, because thou hast been a man of war, and hast shed blood."*

So God instructed the king that the building of the house of the Lord would be left to his son, Solomon. Upon receiving that news, King David's attitude was to be admired. In essence, his response was this, "God told me that I could not build it, but He did not tell me that I couldn't pay for it."

Many of you are not called to foreign missions. You may never pastor a church. You may never hold revivals or great crusades. Therefore, you may feel that you are excluded from those mighty endeavors. But such is not the case. There is a part in those endeavors for you.

Thank God that David did not take offense at God's decision. He did not walk away in a huff, deciding that if he couldn't do things the way he wanted to, God wasn't getting a penny of his money. He did not threaten to quit tithing because he wasn't permitted to build the house of the Lord. Instead, King David decided that the part he was allowed, he would do with his whole heart. This is a valuable lesson we all can learn. We need more Davids in God's Kingdom. We need people who will say, "I may not be called to go, but I can still help fund the spreading of the gospel all around the world."

In verse 1, David assessed that the work would be great, for it was not to be done for man but for God. There are a number of people who would ask what the magnificence, or lack of it, in a ministry's building, has to do with the cause that it represents. Their logic is that when it comes to ministry, the type or quality of building erected should not matter. Sometimes, I think that people in this New Covenant are of the impression that because God is omnipresent and cannot be housed in a man-made building, only things of the spirit are important. It is clear that such thinking is not pleasing to God. He should *always* be given our best. The efforts that we put into the things that pertain to and belong to God *are* things of the Spirit. We must agree with King David that the work is of great importance because it is not for man but for God.

In verse 2, King David stated that he had prepared for the building of the house of God. This demonstrates forethought and premeditated giving. This was no case of nonchalantly throwing something into the offering plate or just reaching into one's pockets, giving whatever happened to be pulled out. David said that he had provided for the work of his God with all his might. He assessed the size of the project, premeditated what his part could be, and gathered up all his ability and strength to meet that need.

Many verses instruct us that we should think about what we are giving.

> Let each one [give] as he has made up his own mind and purposed in his heart, not reluctantly or sorrowfully or under compulsion, for God loves (He takes pleasure in, prizes above other things, and is unwilling to abandon or to do without) a cheerful (joyous, "prompt to do it") giver [whose heart is in his giving].
>
> 2 CORINTHIANS 9:7 (AMPC)

This means that we need to make up our minds and set our wills and emotions upon our giving. We are to think about it, ask God about it, make our decision based on His instruction, and then do it.

David recounted that he was preparing to give gold, silver, wood, precious stones, and jewels for the temple. Such gifts would involve great preparation. However, for the most part, people have assumed that the actual act of giving is spontaneous and unplanned. It is clear that David's preparations involved time, energy, foresight, organization, attention, strength, and follow-through.

In verse 3, King David said that he had set his affection on the house of his God. What a key verse. If the king had to set his affection there, that means his affection did not naturally go there. *Affection* is a word for desire and love. Our soul has many things for which it longs to be affectionate. However, we must set it, or point it, toward the things of God. This is a key element in how we set our affection on the things of our God instead of the things of this world.

In the last part of verse 3, King David said that he was making sure that he gave to God out of his private treasure or, in today's terms, his personal savings account. It was one thing for him to give from the kingdom. He was already prepared to do that. But he did not want only to give from the corporate treasury. King David knew that for his gift to be acceptable and sacrificial, it had to involve personal sacrifice.

In 1 Chronicles 21:24, we find that when King David was offered free animals for the sacrifice to God, he refused. He told Ornan (the person offering him the animals) that any sacrifice worthy of his God would have to cost something. While it is easy for some people to give from their business or ministry, it is much harder when it comes to personal sacrifice. God requires both.

The Bible continues by telling us how much King David decided to give. I find it very interesting that the Word of God recounts the details. God does not waste His time telling us things that are not important. If the Holy Spirit tells us something, rest assured, there is reason to listen. The Bible could have advised us that the king gave without telling us how much. Notice that the Bible never implied that it was the thought that counted, not the amount. It would never say that, because such sayings are men's religious ideas, not biblical teaching.

No, the inspired Word of God does not leave us in the dark about the details of King David's giving. In verse 4, we read that David gave three thousand talents of gold. Talents do not really mean much to us today because we no longer use that form of currency. However, a few years ago, a man did calculate the amount based on current gold prices. What he discovered was truly amazing. The gift of gold talents alone amounted to three-point eighty-two billion dollars. Yes, I said billions. To bring this into proper perspective, it was as if David sat down and wrote out his first check for three-point eighty-two billion dollars.

Now, if that is not mind-boggling enough, the Bible says that King David then gave seven thousand talents of silver. In other words, he then made out check number two for one hundred eighty-seven million dollars. That was just for the overlaying of the walls of the house of the Lord. When it comes to honoring God with the building of His house of worship, it becomes quite obvious that God does not have difficulty with things reflecting His glory. This verse reveals much to me about how God wants to prosper His people. We've been taught that God's desire is for us to be poor. We've even been taught that Christianity is all being meek and poor. Meek? Yes. Poor? Most emphatically, no! David is both an example and a proof.

You may think you can't relate to this story or that it doesn't apply to you. You might think that as "Joe or Josephine Average," you have nothing in common with David, a king of such wealth. You might even be under the very large misconception that financially, the rest of Israel was barely holding on as perhaps you might be.

Listen, God takes good care of His people! In the 28th chapter of Deuteronomy, God promised Israel that they would be blessed coming in and going out. So naturally, the king would be an example of that prosperity. And he was; David was blessed, blessed, and blessed! He was not ashamed of his prosperity, nor did he make excuses for it. King David used his prosperity to further the Kingdom of his God. He was blessed in order to be a blessing.

After becoming blessed, the king did not forget where his blessings came from or for what they were given. David continued to be a big giver and, in doing so, became more and more blessed. Remember how, during his son, King Solomon's reign, gold became so plentiful that they began to pile up the silver in the streets? They had to take the silver to the silver dump. Can you imagine? Solomon and the kingdom continued to increase in prosperity due in part to King David's wise stewardship.

In verse 5, King David asked who would willingly offer to consecrate his service unto the Lord. You cannot ask something of someone that you are not willing to do yourself. It is not the teachings alone that we are to give people. King David would not even consider merely giving the people a teaching about how they should give. David led by example.

That is what my pastors, Rodney and Adonica Howard-Browne, have done in my life. They have set a clear example that can be followed. I have endeavored to do the same thing. I am not out there just teaching on stewardship. I am, to the best of my ability, being a good steward. I am a giver. I love to give, and I give sacrificially. People in my meetings can see that. Therefore, a special anointing comes when I, or other givers, teach on giving. It is an anointing that people cannot wait to catch.

A person must lead by example and with a servant's heart. The king was not ashamed to ask for an offering. He had no fear that the people might think that he was begging for money or manipulating them to give. King David asked nothing that he was not willing to do himself; he had already proven that.

King David had a heart revelation on the subject of giving. For him, every moment of every day was about giving. It was about worship. It was about intimacy with his God. It was about letting God know how much he loved and appreciated Him. Those qualities make up the very heart and essence of a giver. That is how we are to live and how we are to respond to God. It is no wonder that God could trust David with abundance. I wonder, could God trust you or me with abundance, or would we forget where that abundance came from and what it was given for?

Whenever I am teaching from this text in my revival meetings, I notice interesting responses from the people. As soon as I translate the value of the talents into current dollar amounts, the air gets sucked out of the room. People cannot even comprehend that kind of giving. I long for the day when the air is sucked out of the room because people begin to give with that same kind of intensity. If it could be done back then, it can be done today. After all, the Bible tells us in Hebrews 8:6 that we have an even better covenant established on better promises. In the Old Testament, the children of Israel were God's servants. Today, we are God's very own children. How much more He wants to bless us! As for me, I want to be as trusted with abundance as David was.

The Amplified Bible gives us further insight into verse 5. When King David asked who was willing to consecrate his service to the Lord, the Bible says that it was like one consecrating oneself to the priesthood. God takes our sacrificial giving very seriously. It is costly. Sacrificial giving involves not only finances but the representation of our time and labor, as well. When you work for eight or more hours a day, it is a representation of blood, sweat, and tears. Many things are calling out for those hours and finances. Your home's mortgage, children's education, vacations, and recreational activities are all begging to be made a top priority. When you offer your finances and time to the Lord first, it is like consecrating yourself to the priesthood. That offering involves premeditated commitment, sacrifice, effort, energy, and love.

Some people give, but not sacrificially. They never allow themselves to be stretched, instead giving only what is comfortable. They refuse to walk on the water and trust God. Though they make a hundred thousand dollars per year, they may only put five dollars in the offering: a mere drop in the bucket compared to their income and possessions. Another wealthy person might come in and drop one hundred dollars in the offering plate. They may feel that they've really done something because they gave more than anyone else in the house. The truth is that they could have given tens of thousands of dollars without suffering. The widow woman in the Bible who gave her last two mites is Jesus' example of sacrificial giving. God is not looking so much at what we give but at what we keep. Where is our heart? It is kept where we find our treasure.

Making the decision to be a big giver will call on everything you have and everything you are. Such a decision will require strength and determination. Every devil in Hell will fight you. You will have to decide that there is no going back. You will have to consecrate yourself, and your decision will have far-reaching effects on every relationship you have and every aspect of your life. Consequently, you will reap great rewards. You will begin a depth of relationship with your Lord that you have never experienced before. You will know that He has your all.

Verse 6 tells us that the people willingly offered their gifts. God expects our gifts to be given from a willing heart. God wants our offerings given cheerfully. He requires nothing less (2 Corinthians 9:7).

We have to learn that we should never allow ourselves to be manipulated into giving. *The Amplified Bible* emphasizes that your gifts should be generous and willing, not extorted or wrung out of you. You should never give because of someone's need but always by the leading of the Holy Spirit. Once you understand that your giving is not to be dictated by someone's personal need, you will not be pressed, pushed, or pulled by how well they beg.

Once you truly understand what giving is all about, as a voluntary act of worship, you will give willingly and freely, with generosity and compassion, and never under compulsion.

The people of Israel did not give in a miserly fashion but followed King David's example in great, sacrificial giving. Their giving exceeded their king's giving. Such giving was common in Bible times. When Moses received offerings, the Bible tells us that the people gave too much, and a decree had to be issued ordering them to stop. They had too much stuff (Exodus 36:5-7). I have never been in a church where we had to order the people to stop giving because we had received more than we, ministers or the local banks, could handle. In the New Testament, we also read that the people gave until there was no lack. They had received all the funds necessary to accomplish the work that they had been called to do. This is biblical prosperity. It is defined as having no lack.

Verse 8 related that those who had precious stones gave them into the treasury of the house of the Lord. The people withheld nothing. God never requires what we don't have; He only requires what we do have. It might be precious stones, finances, talents, or special giftings.

Verse 9 is very interesting. Our text says that the people rejoiced over the display of giving that they had been privileged to witness. When they observed the great and sacrificial giving of the others in their midst, they were actually overcome with joy and rejoiced.

If a million or a billion dollars are received in an offering, we should rejoice in the generosity of God's people. If we begrudge a generous offering, then something is wrong. At that point, we are openly displaying jealousy and covetousness. Jealousy and covetousness always come from the iniquity of our own hearts. People who complain in this fashion are, in actuality, saying that even though the people gave willingly, they personally don't like it. They don't like it because they are afraid and really believe that if God gives someone else what they consider to be too large of an offering, there will not be enough left over for their own ministries and programs. What they are really stating is that once God freely abounds toward others, He is no longer capable of doing the same for them. To believe that God can no longer supply for them is not only a display of jealousy but also a lack of faith. This entire thinking process is demeaning to God and comes straight out of the pit of Hell.

Looking back at verse 9, we see that the people of Israel gave with a whole and blameless heart. They did not give out of false motives. They were not trying to impress anyone or gain the favor of the king. Nor were they giving out of guilt, condemnation, reasoning, or remorse. They really loved God and His house as much as their king did. They wanted to let God know how much they loved Him, and they held nothing back. Such is the purity of a giving heart.

Verses 10-22 speak of the national celebration that day. King David was neither offended nor did he feel like he gave under compulsion. The king started by praising and magnifying the greatness of God. In verse 12, he began to speak from personal revelation. David confessed that God gave them riches and acknowledged that he and the people had been blessed by God. King David said that he considered it an honor and privilege to give to the work of the Lord in such a way. King David went on to share that our earthly days are as a shadow, and there is no hope of us living forever or holding onto what we have. Everything they had prepared and given had come from God's hand originally and, so, already belonged to Him. That is the revelation that the Church needs—the only things that remain are eternal. How, then, could anyone begrudge giving something back to God?

I find verse 17 intriguing. David declared that God tries the heart and delights in uprightness. He went on to say that it was in the uprightness of his heart that he freely offered God all these things. All too often, people do not realize that God is still trying the hearts of His people, and offerings are one of His ways of dealing with men. It appears that a lot of individuals, preachers included, are failing the test.

Without a faithful preacher to impart these truths and break the iron bars of fear to release stolen treasuries, how will the Church reclaim her territory and repossess her spoils? If people refuse to let evangelists such as myself teach these truths, how will the church ever loosen itself from the chains and fetters, weights and ties that bind them, and break forth into godly provision for His people, His house, and His work?

In verse 18, King David prayed, asking God to keep forever such purposes and thoughts in the minds of His people and to direct and establish their hearts toward Him. To what purposes and thoughts was he referring? The king did not change subjects between verses, so King David was still talking about freewill offerings set aside to supply the work of God's Kingdom. I pray, with David, that God will bring these purposes and thoughts to his people so that they might learn how to give out of full hearts, blameless and pure.

Verse 21 relates that they gave sacrifices and burnt offerings to the Lord again the next day. In fact, it says that the children of Israel gave them in abundance. You do not see the people complaining that they just gave God billions the day before. Thank God for the example set by hearts like these.

> In the morning sow your seed, and in the evening withhold not your hands, for you know not which shall prosper, whether this or that, or whether both alike will be good.
>
> ECCLESIASTES 11:6 (AMPC)

Throughout the Bible, we see examples of back-to-back offerings given day after day, both morning and night. They continued to be generous offerings as well. These things are issues of the heart. They really have nothing to do with money, but they have everything to do with the hearts of men.

1 Chronicles 29:23 celebrates Solomon's appointment as king and his prosperity. I believe that his success was due in large part to the preparations his father made when he instilled the principles of giving into his son during the transition. Over the last few years, I have found that God's blessings in my life have spoken loudly to those around me. I will never forget the first time that my children saw our brand-new home in Tampa, Florida. They walked throughout the house, tears welling up in their eyes, over the goodness of the Lord unto us.

We had never owned a new home before. When my ministry was first launched in Alaska, we had to live with other people. My sons had sacrificed greatly. We rented many homes that were far less than ideal. My sons knew what it was like not having rooms of their own. We had driven both old and "totaled" cars. I would tell the boys that these sacrifices were temporary and that God would bless us. I reminded them that we would have to hang on to God's promises, continuing to be obedient to give.

There were times when the boys were somewhat skeptical. However, here we all stood, five years later, walking through a brand new home, observing together the goodness of God. After walking through the home, I proceeded to show the boys the new car waiting in the driveway. (Previously, a man in one of my meetings in the state of Washington stood up, declaring that God had instructed him to buy me a new car, which he did!) My oldest son stood with amazement etched across his face. He recollected watching me give sacrificially over the course of the last few years, all the while assuring the boys of the faithfulness of God. He turned toward me and said, "Mom, you were right about God's faithfulness."

The Scriptures report that King David died in a good old age, full of days, riches, and honor. Now, that is the will of God for all of us. David's heart had been tried; he withheld nothing from his God, and his God withheld nothing from him. I want to live my life with my God with nothing withheld, give with all my strength to the great work of His Kingdom, and live to demonstrate that He is faithful to His Word. How about you?

NINE

GODLY CONTENTMENT OR LAZY FAITH?

> I was made very happy in the Lord that now you have revived your interest in my welfare after so long a time; you were indeed thinking of me, but you had no opportunity to show it.
> Not that I am implying that I was in any personal want, for I have learned how to be content (satisfied to the point where I am not disturbed or disquieted) in whatever state I am.
> I know how to be abased and live humbly in straitened circumstances, and I know also how to enjoy plenty and live in abundance. I have learned in any and all circumstances the secret of facing every situation, whether well-fed or going hungry, having a sufficiency and enough to spare or going without and being in want.
> I have strength for all things in Christ Who empowers me [I am ready for anything and equal to anything through Him Who infuses inner strength into me; I am self-sufficient in Christ's sufficiency].
> But it was right and commendable and noble of you to

> contribute for my needs and to share my difficulties with me.
>
> And you Philippians yourselves well know that in the early days of the Gospel ministry, when I left Macedonia, no church (assembly) entered into partnership with me and opened up [a debit and credit] account in giving and receiving except you only.
>
> For even in Thessalonica you sent [me contributions] for my needs, not only once but a second time.
>
> Not that I seek or am eager for [your] gift, but I do seek and am eager for the fruit which increases to your credit [the harvest of blessing that is accumulating to your account].
>
> But I have [your full payment] and more; I have everything I need and am amply supplied, now that I have received from Epaphroditus the gifts you sent me. [They are the] fragrant odor of an offering and sacrifice which God welcomes and in which He delights.
>
> And my God will liberally supply (fill to the full) your every need according to His riches in glory in Christ Jesus.
>
> PHILIPPIANS 4:10-19 (AMPC)

As one of the first traveling missionaries, Paul faced the task of guiding the Church both to understanding and becoming doers of the Word. Recall that in this chapter, Paul was teaching the early Church about giving. The last half of the chapter is wholly devoted to the subject. (The Bible has much to say about giving. The New Testament has more to say about giving than it does about Hell, yet some would think that preachers invented this teaching.) The Apostle Paul, by the Holy Spirit, spent a great deal of time instructing the Church on the subject. He devoted several other chapters to sowing, such as First Corinthians, chapter 9, and Second Corinthians, chapters 8 and 9.

Paul began this passage by telling the Philippian church that he was thankful they were beginning to give again. He said that he knew they were thinking of him but had no opportunity to show him. Many people seem to have the philosophy, out of sight, out of mind.

In verse 11, Paul related that he had learned the secret of godly contentment, regardless of the state in which he found himself. Godly contentment is a very important key, both to prosperity and to keeping our peace. Paul had learned that no man or woman was his source. The job or government was not his source. Only God could be his source. Paul shared that whatever the case, regardless of the external circumstance, Jehovah Jireh would still come through for him. *The Message Bible* puts it this way,

> I've learned by now to be quite content whatever my circumstances. I'm just as happy with little as with much, with much as with little. I've found the recipe for being happy whether full or hungry, hands full or hands empty. Whatever I have, wherever I am, I can make it through anything in the One who makes me who I am. I don't mean that your help didn't mean a lot to me—it did. It was a beautiful thing that you came alongside me in my troubles.

Some people can only be content if outside circumstances are perfect. The only time they seem at peace is when there are no storms. Anybody can be in peace then; you do not need peace in the middle of calm. You only need peace in the middle of a storm. Paul realized that the world had not given him his joy or peace, and the world could not take it away. God gave him the joy and peace that he had, and God would not take it away.

In my years of experience in the church, I have found that many Christians have not gained an understanding of this chapter or the godly contentment of which it speaks. In fact, they use Paul's teaching out of context to propagate a lie. They teach just the opposite of what Paul is saying. They will say things like, "I don't want to hear any of that faith stuff. I don't need any more provisions than I have right now. We have enough for us four and no more. We still have food on our table. Our lights are still on, and we can pay the fuel costs. We have clothes on our backs, and our children are fed.

What more could one want in life? No, I don't need anything else. I'm just like Paul, content where I am in life. I think that to want anything else would be selfish. Don't talk to me about faith, believing God for more, sowing, or expecting a harvest."

What these people fail to realize is that their attitude is as selfish as can be. Their first mistake was that they didn't want to hear about faith and felt they didn't need it. But the Bible says that,

> Now the just shall live by faith.
>
> HEBREWS 10:38

> But without faith it is impossible to please him.
>
> HEBREWS 11:6

We were saved by faith, baptized in the Holy Spirit by faith, and healed by faith. Our entire Christianity is about faith. Faith doesn't just belong to one certain "camp" or denomination. Faith is a big part of all Christianity. Faith will be a large part of our Christian walk from now until we go home to be with Jesus.

Secondly, Paul's comment about contentment did not mean that he did not believe for more. The apostle went on to say that he knew what it meant to be abased as well as to abound. There were times when he went without food and shelter. However, that did not mean Paul was perpetually broke. He had been shipwrecked and knew what it was like to go without food. If you are marooned in the middle of an ocean, there are no McDonald's or Hilton Hotels nearby. He knew what it was to be cold and hungry. Paul was truly abased, but he was not necessarily broke. For periods of time, He was imprisoned and kept in stocks and bonds. That certainly is being abased, but it is not being financially bankrupt.

As a matter of fact, there were times when Paul had great finances flowing through his hands. In Acts 24:26, the Bible tells us that King Felix was waiting for Paul to offer him a bribe. The king knew that there were times when Paul had access to great sums of money. A person does not await a bribe from someone waiting to get out of jail if that person has no money. You can be sure that Felix had Paul thoroughly checked out before beginning that wait for a bribe. Also, Paul was the man who was building churches throughout the Roman Empire. He was taking teams into the world, preaching the gospel. He took Dr. Luke, John, Mark, Silas, Timothy, and others. Back then, it was just as expensive to build churches as it is now. The cost of living is relative to the day.

I think you can see that when Paul said he knew how to be abased, he did not mean that he never had money. Obviously, Paul also did not mean that he only wanted to operate with what he had. In fact, it is clear that Paul constantly believed God for more than he had at the time. If he had not believed for increasing funds, he certainly would not have believed in taking more missionary trips, building more churches, or forming more ministry teams. Paul, a man of faith, was constantly being stretched. If you and I live by faith, we, too, would be stretched.

Paul sets an example of godly contentment. Even while chained in stocks and bonds, he could not have been any happier in Jesus. Can't you hear Paul asking his buddy, Silas, to join him in singing another verse of *"Joy Unspeakable and Full of Glory"*? The Bible says that they sang praises unto God at the midnight hour. Now, these two were not sitting around pouting or being bitter at God. They weren't bemoaning their circumstances, nor were they griping and complaining. They certainly were not saying they couldn't be happy until God blessed them with a nice bed in a nice hotel and made them famous preachers. Paul and Silas could not have been any happier in godly contentment than they were at that moment.

You see, contentment and joy are not produced by outside circumstances; they come from the inside. These attitudes are part of the fruit of the Spirit. They come from a mature relationship with Jesus Christ and are not dependent upon our cash flow or creature comforts. Some people are only happy when all their circumstances are perfect. However, that is not godly contentment; it is merely perfect circumstances. We must learn to give thanksgiving in all circumstances, praising God and worshiping Him, no matter what is going on in this life.

At the same time, we must guard against becoming comfortable or lazy in the middle of positive circumstances. To be a bigger blessing, we have to become more blessed. We must always reach for more, believing we have a big God who continually enables us to become a bigger blessing to others. God did not create us to be stopped up containers of blessing, blocking His blessings from going any farther. We were designed to be open vessels of God, pouring out God's salvation, healing, joy, baptism of the Holy Spirit, peace, and provision wherever we go. We are to be vessels that He can pour Himself through for others.

Paul was every bit as secure and joyous in his relationship with the Lord when things were tough as he was when he was abounding. You could see the love and grace of God at work in him and through him in either set of circumstances. However, Paul always believed for more so that he could become a greater blessing. Now, that is godly contentment.

I feel that I can really relate to Paul in our text. I, too, know what it is like to be abased and to abound. I have traveled through blizzards to Alaskan villages in little two-seater airplanes. Often, we did not even have an airstrip for landing. The pilot would just aim for an ice-covered, gravel road. Sometimes, no one was there to pick me (or my luggage) up. There were times when I stayed in little cabins (and not recreational cabins, as you would think) with no running water or bathroom facilities. My bathroom would consist of an outhouse down the road. It was really difficult to get up in the middle of the night to use them when the temperature was thirty to fifty degrees below zero. Sometimes, I would be left with a stove I had to stoke as my only heat. I didn't start out knowing much about wood-burning stoves, but in order to survive, I learned in a hurry.

I remember one instance in particular. It was in a village called Venetie in the Alaskan Interior. The stove I was using was an aluminum type. As it became hotter and hotter, its color changed from gray to orange. I remember thinking that my first newsletter headline would read, "Debbie Sets Village on Fire!" I didn't know what to do, so I ran outside, got some snow, and stuffed it inside the stove. That put it out, and then I had to start all over again.

My eating habits also underwent drastic changes in those villages. I was not used to some of the native delicacies, but I adjusted. I remember being offered soup in one of the villages. As I began to eat, I couldn't help but notice the distinct taste of charcoal abounding in the soup. I also took note of some charcoal-like flakes floating about the bowl. Then, I made the mistake of asking what kind of soup I was eating. With delight, one of the precious native ladies told me that I was eating moose soup. I said, "Oh, that's wonderful." Now, I love moose. I've had moose steak, moose stroganoff, moose hamburger and loved them all. Just as I was eating another bite, she said the word "head." I realized that she had said that I was eating moose-head soup. I was somewhat surprised because I had never had the pleasure of eating any part of the head before.

Without changing expressions (being the good little missionary that I was), I asked a question that I quickly regretted. "Oh, what part of the head, if I may ask?" Thinking that I was pulling her leg, I whispered to a friend with me, "Probably the nostrils." But I soon found out that I was prophesying. For as quickly as I got out my whisper, the native lady answered, "Oh, it is the nostrils of the moose, the really tender part." At that moment, all I could think was, "I hope that moose didn't have a cold." However, I quickly made an internal adjustment and continued eating my soup. And as the honored guest, I put down two big bowls!

I have eaten muktuk, made out of whale blubber soaked in seal oil. I have also had the native delicacy of "Eskimo Ice Cream," which is basically raw blubber with berries. With its texture, it is similar to eating a bowl of Crisco oil.

I endured walking through the town of Ft. Yukon when the temperature was minus fifty degrees, ministering house to house. At temperatures like that, your breath begins to freeze. I remember walking to services with my friend, Jean Thomas, in a coastal town called Wainwright when the temperature was minus thirty degrees. A gruff man in a pickup truck finally came along and offered us a ride. Thinking he meant for us to get in the rear of the extended cab, we gratefully accepted. However, the man told us he had boxes back there and gestured back behind, to the open bed of the truck. The bed was layered in snow, but we were just grateful to have a ride. So we rode in the snow-filled open bed of that truck, sitting in our dresses in the snow, which swirled around us in the open air as we went.

I will never forget the expression on Jean's face as we moved down the road. I, at least, wore a big parka that someone had loaned me, but Jean's coat was not that heavy. She looked at me as if I had gotten her into yet another one of my big adventures, and she wasn't all too sure about it. Since then, we have had many laughs about that night.

Sometimes, people, caught up in their own time zone, would forget what week we were arriving. We would walk down the usually frozen road, carrying our own luggage until we could find someone to help us. Many times, I would remind the Lord that I was a lady and that I had never been in the Boy Scouts. I would wonder how I had ever received the call of God to such a remote and barren place. One would expect a man to be called to rough it out there. I would laugh and say, "I don't understand it Lord, but I love it."

I can honestly say that those were some of the best days of my life. At times, I would lie on the floor, curled up in an old rug for warmth, tired but ever so grateful and full of joy. I would literally cry and laugh myself to sleep at night in ecstatic joy, *"unspeakable and full of glory."* I would say to the Lord, "Oh, I love what I do. Thank You, Lord, for the call of God upon my life; it's the greatest thing in my life, and I reverence it. Religion would not have given me a second chance, Lord, but You did. I am so grateful that I still get to preach the gospel after an eighteen-year detour. I don't care where You send me, Lord, as long as there are hungry, thirsty people. I don't want to waste Your time, Lord, or mine, so just let them be hungry. I will preach to two people or two million; it makes no difference to me. I just love sharing Your Word. I love seeing people restored and healed. I don't care what color their skin is, what tribe they are from, or if it is hot or cold. Please let me continue to do this all the days of my life until You come."

I could not have been happier at that moment than I would have been if I had been in the largest church in America or in the fanciest hotel. I was experiencing godly contentment that came from the inside, and no one could take it away. The weather, the food, the outhouses, the cold walks—none of those circumstances could take that godly contentment away.

I was content, but I was not lazy and satisfied with where I was spiritually or in any other area of my life. Smith Wigglesworth, the great English revivalist, put it like this: "The only thing I am satisfied with is my dissatisfaction." He meant that he was always aspiring to more in Jesus. That is the way we all should be.

I never slept on the village floor and said, "God, since I am happy in You tonight, I never want any more than I have right now. I am content to save up enough money to be able to come to a village about every six weeks and influence and help a few people. I never want to be able to help many, just a few. It's easier this way because I have gotten used to this and do not have to be stretched in faith."

No, I would not have dared to entertain such laziness and slothfulness. God expects more from us than that. So, while I was content in Him, I was not satisfied. I would lie there laughing with joy, saying, "God, I'm happy in You tonight, but I am believing You for much, much more. I want to build churches and Bible schools. I want to train others to go into the villages. I want to be able to sow thousands into other ministries that are accomplishing more than I am. God, I am believing You for big things. However, I want You to know that when the big things come, I will not be any more content in You than I am right now. It doesn't get any better than this."

My friend, this is godly contentment, not lazy faith. You must not dare become satisfied with where you are right now. God wants to do more through you than you ever imagined. You must become a willing vessel, allowing yourself to be stretched beyond your present level. In the process, you must be grateful for where you are today.

DR. DEBBIE RICH

> For who hath despised the day of small things?
>
> ZECHARIAH 4:10

You must find your identity in Jesus rather than in fame and fortune. Yet, you must believe that God desires to bless you more than you have been blessed thus far so that you can be a greater blessing. Here is the balance: godly contentment versus lazy faith (or the other extreme, greed and lust).

Let me give yet another example to help you more fully grasp this truth. In April of 1993, I held a revival in Nome, Alaska. To date, it has been one of the most glorious of all of our revivals. Nome is a small town with a population of about three thousand people. For the most part, the buildings are simple and old. When compared with our busy metropolises of beautiful cities, some might think that, in some respects, Nome reminds them of a third-world nation. April is still considered the dead of winter in Nome. It was very cold there, and the town was covered in ice and white snow. Everyone there was very hospitable to me and showed me great love; they remain some of my favorite people in the world. However, Alaskan churches are not fancy, and ministers are not necessarily treated in the same manner that they have become accustomed to in some of our more yuppie, metropolitan churches.

After Nome, my next invitation was to a church in "the lower forty-eight," as Alaskans call the other states. I had been invited to minister in Roswell, Georgia, a suburb of Atlanta. When I stepped off the jet that April day in Georgia, I experienced a real shock. From the frozen tundra, I had stepped into a land of green grass, beautiful flowers, and sunny, summer-like eighty-degree weather. I couldn't believe my eyes! I had almost forgotten that beyond Alaska, there was another world out there.

Some dear friends accompanied me on that trip from Alaska. When the pastor told me that we would be staying with some rather well-to-do people, I responded with, "Sure, that would be fine." I had no idea of the beautiful subdivision that awaited my team. As we traveled up the street toward the house, I felt like Granny on *The Beverly Hillbillies*, riding in the back of the truck, heading to her new mansion. We arrived at a beautiful home on a gorgeous wooded property, complete with a private bridge and pond and acres of lush vegetation. Each of us was given our own bedroom-bathroom suite. I had a big queen-size bed of my own and was enjoying being served all of my favorite foods. Then, I was taken to the church.

At that time, the church was not that large. It has grown considerably since then. However, the staff still operated with an attitude of excellence in everything that they did. I was taken to the ready room and told that I was welcome to wait there and pray until I was ready to come into the sanctuary. The room was beautifully decorated, and there was a vase of cut flowers inside. Fresh juices, sandwiches, fruits, and vegetables awaited me. I was asked what kind of juice and hors d'oeuvres I preferred and had my preferences in place each night after that. I was introduced to the head usher and advised that he would escort me to the front row when I was ready. He put out his arm to demonstrate the manner in which he would face. I began to chuckle, asking them if they had confused me with Gloria Copeland, Marilyn Hickey, or Joyce Meyer. I reminded them that I was a simple Alaskan missionary who was used to roughing it. They replied that it was time I was honored, and they were going to give honor where honor was due. I realized that I could as easily adapt to those plush circumstances as I had adapted to village floors.

As I lay upon my spacious, queen-size bed that evening, I found myself praying just as I did in the Alaskan villages. I said to the Lord, "Thank You for my call and Your restoration in my life. I don't ever want to have to do anything except what I'm doing right now, preaching the gospel to hungry people all over the earth. I don't care if I preach to two people or two million people as long as they are hungry people. I don't ever want to waste Your time or mine, Lord. I don't care where You send me, as long as the people are hungry. I am so full of joy tonight. I couldn't be any more content in You than I am right now. I don't have to wait until I am invited to big and famous churches; I am extremely content in You.

"However, I have not yet arrived, and I am believing You for bigger things. I want to be an even greater blessing to the Body of Christ than I am right now. I want to build churches, put people through Bible School, feed the hungry, and sow thousands of dollars into other people's ministries. This is a start, Lord, but I am believing you for more."

As you can see, I was equally content in the barren land of Alaska as I was down south in warm, sunny Georgia. I was as equally content to hold house meetings in villages as I was to preach in metropolitan churches. I could be as equally content sleeping on the floor eating moose-head soup as I would be sleeping in a nice bedroom and eating filet mignon. My contentment comes from the inside, not outside circumstances. Yet, in either set of circumstances, I never became lazy in faith. I always believed God for more with which to bless others. That is the kind of faith and contentment that had become a way of life for the Apostle Paul.

Philippians 4:13 is a very popular verse in the church today. It says, *"I can do all things through Christ which strengtheneth me."*

The Amplified Version adds, *"I am self-sufficient in Christ's sufficiency."*

When the Body of Christ learns how to be content in God and learns the secret of living to give, it will become independent of the world. We will not be dependent upon man but upon God. He is more than enough for every situation. For every situation we find ourselves in, God is the One who will grace us.

In November of 1992, when Pastor Rodney Howard-Browne came to Anchorage, Alaska, he taught me how to be self-sufficient in Christ's sufficiency. He could have chosen to help me out financially, but that would have been only a temporary fix. The next month would have found me in the same taxing circumstances I had been in before he arrived. Instead, Pastor Howard-Browne taught me what God had taught him. Instead of being dependent upon others, I learned the secret of directly facing every situation and becoming self-sufficient through Christ. This was very freeing. In turn, my desire is to pass the same secret on to each of my readers.

In verse 15, Paul began to commend the Philippian church for their giving, saying that no other church had entered into a heavenly debit and credit account. Most Christians don't even realize that they have an account open to Heaven. It's nice to know that even if Citibank in New York fails, Heaven will not go down. No matter what crisis hits us economically, we can make withdrawals from our heavenly bank account. Of course, to be able to make a withdrawal from your heavenly account, you need to have been making heavenly deposits.

Each time that I give, I realize that I am making another deposit into my debit and credit account in Heaven. I never know when an emergency might arise. In such events, I am very thankful that I have been making regular deposits and can make withdrawals as needed. It does not matter if my bank or any other financial institution does not work, my heavenly ATM still will.

Thank God that He is the Rock on whom we can depend. I can stand upon His Word. God's Word will not go under. Therefore, if I am standing upon His Word, I cannot go under. In this world's system, when things are unstable, God is the One to whom we can go. God will never fail us; He is the Friend who sticks closer than a brother. That knowledge gives me unshakeable security in the middle of chaos.

Verse 17 speaks of Paul's eagerness to see the Philippian church abundantly blessed. Paul said that he was not teaching them or accepting their offering so much for his sake as for theirs. When ministers say that today, the church usually looks at them as if to say, "Yeah, I'll bet." Yet, Paul said it first. He taught them by saying that their giving would cause fruit and blessings to abound to their account. Even though Paul was blessed personally, he was more excited about that church's future provision. Paul knew that the Philippian church's sowing to him would bring them great future blessings.

Verse 19 is also a very famous verse in today's charismatic church. It promises that God will meet your every need according to His riches in glory in Christ Jesus. That is a lot of riches!

When people in the Church get into a financial bind of some kind, they tend to quote this popular verse. They will walk the floor, confessing it hundreds of times. The only problem is that most of them are quoting the verse out of context. You can quote this verse out of context until the cows come home and still not have God meet your needs.

So, it is important that we read Bible verses within their proper context. The context of this chapter is vital to the meaning of this verse. Paul told the Philippian church that because they were givers, God would meet their every need according to His riches in glory in Christ Jesus. That word is not an unconditional promise to the Body of Christ. If we want that promise to become a personal word to us, we have to do what the Philippian church did and become givers!

As we become givers, we are assured that God will meet our every need. Paul reminded them at Philippi that they were the only ones to join with him in partnership. When others refused to give, the Philippians picked up the slack. Therefore, they could trust God and be quite confident that as they prayed, their prayers would be answered.

My prayer for you, as you read this book, is that you will learn from the Philippians. The Holy Spirit, the author of the Word of God, includes this chapter for a very specific purpose. He wants us to learn what the Philippians learned, that as we give, regardless of whether anyone else gives or not, we can believe that God will meet our every need.

Meanwhile, though we have not yet arrived at the place we are headed in God, we are learning that we must be content in our current circumstances. We will always continue believing God for more so that we can consistently become a greater blessing. We can learn to be content in our Lord Jesus now while we wait for the greater blessing to come. We know one thing for certain, in whatever circumstances we find ourselves, we must not grow lazy in our faith. I pray that God will continue to stretch us so that we will always be growing in Him.

TEN

GOD'S DESIRE FOR YOU TO PROSPER

The elderly elder [of the church addresses this letter] to the beloved (esteemed) Gaius, whom I truly love.

Beloved, I pray that you may prosper in every way and [that your body] may keep well, even as [I know] your soul keeps well and prospers.

In fact, I greatly rejoiced when [some of] the brethren from time to time arrived and spoke [so highly] of the sincerity and fidelity of your life, as indeed you do live in the Truth [the whole Gospel presents].

I have no greater joy than this, to hear that my [spiritual] children are living their lives in the Truth.

Beloved, it is a fine and faithful work that you are doing when you give any service to the [Christian] brethren, and [especially when they are] strangers.

They have testified before the church of your love and friendship. You will do well to forward them on their journey [and you will please do so] in a way worthy of God's [service].

For these [traveling missionaries] have gone out for the

> Name's sake (for His sake) and are accepting nothing
> from the Gentiles (the heathen, the non-Israelites).
> So we ourselves ought to support such people [to welcome
> and provide for them], in order that we may be fellow
> workers in the Truth (the whole Gospel) and cooperate
> with its teachers.
>
> 3 JOHN 1:1-8 (AMPC)

John, by the Holy Ghost, immediately related that he wished or willed that we prosper. He said that it was God's will for us to be in health. If God did not will these things, he would not have included them in His Word. John said that the prospering of the people's souls should be in equal proportion to their daily prospering and being in health. He was assuming, then, that the souls of Christians were also prospering.

Many people confuse the soul with the spirit of man, but they are not the same. When we ask Jesus into our hearts to live and we are saved, the spirit is the part of man that is born again. Our spirit then becomes alive unto God. Our souls house the will, the intellect, and the emotions. The soul of man has to become renewed to God's Word and to the leading of His Spirit.

> And be not conformed to this world: but be ye transformed
> by the renewing of your mind, that ye may prove what is
> that good, and acceptable, and perfect, will of God.
>
> ROMANS 12:2

Renewing our minds, wills, and emotions to the Word of God and to His Spirit is not accomplished overnight! A myriad of things in life have taken their toll upon the souls of humankind. Man-made religions, traditions, and negativity have all been drilled into the human psyche for years. Certain individuals have been told repeatedly by teachers, friends, and family that they were stupid. They have become convinced that they would never amount to anything, ending up "just like their worthless parents." Others have been abused, rejected, betrayed, and unloved. Still others have become self-conscious and insecure, feeling they had nothing to offer. Cruel words and unkind actions have crippled many people's souls. Only the power of the Holy Ghost and an abundance of God's Word can set these people free. Once you have been abused, in order to gain deliverance from such negative programming, you are going to need to invest time sitting under the preaching of God's Word.

I do have good news. Once we are born again, we become the righteousness of God in Christ Jesus. Then we begin the process of renewing our minds. Again, it takes time, but if we are constantly saturated with the Word of God and allow Him by His Spirit to begin changing us, renewal will take place. That is why it is so important to be consistently present in good Holy Ghost meetings. We need to start seeing ourselves as God does.

When God looks at us, He has a hard time telling the difference between His own Son and us because we have become the righteousness of God in Christ Jesus. We are now joint heirs with Jesus, and the enemy has been placed under our feet. We are victors and saints, the very sons and daughters of the Most High God. We are the King's kids! Thank God, He has a way of looking at us and seeing the finished product.

Usually, there is a huge difference between our God-given position in Christ and the level at which we are living on this earth. We are each in the process of *"working out our own salvation with fear and trembling."* Meanwhile, even though our sins are forgiven, many are still quite broken and bruised, with hurting souls.

Our wounded souls are being healed by the renewing of our minds and by the anointing of the Holy Spirit.

> ...and the yoke shall be destroyed because of the anointing.
>
> ISAIAH 10:27

More can happen under the anointing of the Holy Spirit in one minute than can happen in fifty years of counseling. The Bible says that Jesus came to heal the brokenhearted and set the captive free. I know because I've been there. I was brokenhearted. The joy that came into my life during revival helped heal my broken heart.

I have met women who are hurting. In counseling, many received wrong teaching about inner healing and were made worse off than before. Do I believe in inner healing? Absolutely! If what we are talking about is having our hearts healed on the inside, then I most definitely believe in inner healing. Regretfully, a lot of things have been labeled inner healing that are not healing at all. Some of these things are witchcraft with new Charismatic labels.

One teaching says that in order to receive healing from the rejection you received before you were even born, you must go back into your mother's womb. How ridiculous! You cannot find anything in the Word of God to substantiate such a theory. Another teaching says that you must find out exactly what generational curses are present in your life, how long they have been there, and what your relatives did to bring them on. Then, you must find someone to break those curses off of you. Again, nothing in any New Testament teaching even comes close to that.

When Jesus encountered the Gadarene demoniac, He did not explore what generational curses were present. Neither did He ask the man to go back to his mother's womb and experience anything. Jesus did not call up a spirit guide to walk the demoniac through this experience. When Jesus said, "Free," every demon had to flee. Speaking the Word of God under the anointing of the Holy Ghost and in the name of Jesus will break any bondage, no matter how long it has been around. People need to realign their doctrines with the Word of God.

In some of our meetings, we have had to pick up the emotional pieces of individuals who had been to other gatherings where people taught such idiocy. By the time we encountered these people, some were suicidal. They recounted stories of so-called ministers taking them on these "spiritual journeys." What it amounted to was New Age witchcraft. The people were more bound after the "ministers" were through with them than when they began. These so-called ministers were giving the Devil far too much credit and making him way too big. They had developed the "Honey, I shrunk God and blew up the Devil" syndrome. *We need to remember that it is the anointing and not a trip back into our mother's womb that destroys the yoke of bondage.*

When your soul is hurting, it is quite difficult for your body or your pocketbook to prosper; they follow the condition of the soul. Doctors have related that over 90 percent of all illnesses are caused either directly or indirectly by their emotions. Having these sick emotions is one of the primary reasons that Christians fail to prosper.

Most people are unaware of how much their hurting souls affect the other areas of their lives. Insurance companies label people who have been in several vehicular accidents in quick succession as "high-risk." Even if it has been proven that none of the accidents were their fault, insurance companies are still hesitant to insure them. They feel that there is something about the person that is causing them to attract bad luck and multiple accidents. The carriers are not aware that what they are recognizing is a spiritual problem. Indeed, there are individuals who have unwittingly opened doors to the enemy. Through those open doors, the enemy, in turn, wreaks havoc on their lives. Many times, we see this scenario replayed because people's souls are terribly wounded, and they have not yet allowed God to completely heal them.

There are Christians who cannot figure out why they have such a difficult time getting and keeping jobs. Yet, if you watched their interviews, you could easily understand why they were rarely hired. Their heads hang low; they mumble and do not look the interviewer in the eye. They act apologetic about even taking the interviewer's time, giving the impression that they wouldn't hire themselves either. When asked what they would have to offer the company, they reply with a hung head, "Oh, I don't even know if I could do a very good job, but I will try." Then they slouch out again, expressions grim, expecting not to get the job. Yet, these same people will talk about not understanding why God fails to bless them with a job.

These individuals have depressed, insecure, and rejected souls; it sticks out all over them. Other people can easily pick up on it. Their states of emotion negatively affect everything they are and everything they do. It affects the manner in which they take care or don't take care of their personal hygiene and what types of clothes they buy. It affects their eating and exercise habits. It affects how they study and how much education they pursue. It affects their personal and business relationships, how people react to them, and how others perceive them. It also affects how they treat others and how they react to God. People with hurting souls have a hard time receiving God's love. Deep down inside, they believe that God wants to punish them in just the way they've been punished.

It is only after we are healed on the inside that we can begin to prosper on the outside. I am a good personal example of that. I endured years of abuse while living in poverty. I hated answering the telephone because I was certain a creditor would be on the other end. Even after I was freed from the abuse and started handling my own finances, I could not seem to get ahead. I was no longer negligent about paying bills, but as a single mother and a tither, I still could not figure out how to provide enough for my family. The bills were paid, but there was never any extra. We lived in an old, rented trailer and could not imagine enjoying the life I now live or being a blessing to so many. Then, God sent Pastor Rodney Howard-Browne to Anchorage, Alaska, and everything changed. When I got a hold of giving, God began to bless me in every area, including my finances.

I began to dress differently and carry myself differently. My self-pity began to disappear. Depression was gone. I had new hope and then new faith in God and His Word. I became more outgoing and started operating in a sense of humor that, at one point in time, I had just about lost. I was no longer anyone's doormat. I became confident, expecting God to give me favor with man. I could speak whatever God gave me to speak. I developed the courage to contact pastors and to launch out into villages where I had never traveled before.

I expected to prosper and began doing so right away. In some of the places I have gone, pastors have said that they had never received anything remotely close to the amount of money being received in our offerings. We continue to hear similar stories from areas we have ministered in around the globe. It is no coincidence that the more my soul healed, the more my finances and the finances of my ministry grew. Instead of living with others, now others live with me. I am helping other ministries get started in their own ministries and am financially contributing around the world. Talk about a turnaround! It is important that we get healing for our souls. That's why you will see people who were touched through revival and changed in a powerful way suddenly begin to prosper. There is a definite connection.

The Apostle John continued, saying that he recognized that the people were walking in truth. This gave him great joy. About what truth was he being so specific? John had not changed subjects in mid-sentence; he was still talking about prospering. In verses 5 and 6, he said that it was a good thing to give to traveling missionaries. It helped forward them on their journeys, enabling them to fulfill the call of God upon their lives. That was the truth John was talking about, the truth of giving to the gospel.

Many times, the offerings received from a church enable me to travel to a village or foreign country that I would have otherwise been unable to visit. What a blessing to know that you have enabled someone to take the gospel to a foreign field.

When a person's soul gets healed, that person becomes a giver. They no longer live in bondage and fear. They live in faith, able to trust God. They find it a joy to give. They are now free to give and free to receive. Is it any wonder the enemy can no longer keep a person like that down?

The Apostle John reminded us that those traveling missionaries did not receive anything from the Gentiles. I am going to borrow a few paragraphs from Dr. Rodney Howard-Browne's book *Thoughts on Stewardship, Volume One*. On page 12, he writes:

When we came to America, we were not approached by a large beer company that said, "Brother Rodney, we just love your ministry. We believe in what it stands for people getting drunk on the new wine. We want you to know that we are sponsoring you to the tune of one hundred fifty thousand dollars a year." We were not approached by a large hotel chain that said, "We really believe in your ministry. Wherever you go in the United States, you can stay free of charge." We were not approached by a large restaurant chain where we were sponsored with free food. No, the heathen have done absolutely nothing. We were not approached by Jerry the Rat and Four Fingers Brown. "Hey, Brother Rodney, we believe in this ministry. Me and my cousin Joey were talking about getting behind it." No, the Mafia didn't approach us.

It is clear that the heathen don't support God's work. The support comes from God's people. We do not solicit funds through the mail at all. For us, this makes scriptural sense. God has never failed us. We felt that in ten years' time, we did not want to end up in "Prison Ministries International" for not being good stewards over our finances. So the way we receive our offerings is by giving the Word of God—not by using gimmicks, not under pressure. We receive our provision by just obeying the Holy Spirit and the Word of God.

It is interesting to note that the Mafia has not gotten behind our ministry, either. Joey, the Iceman, has not offered to "ice a guy" because the guy did not give to us or attend our meetings. No cigarette manufacturer or beer companies have offered to financially "bail us out." No hotel chain has contacted us to stay with them "on the house" because we are doing such fantastic work. No airlines have offered free flights because they believe in the fine job we are doing. The Gentiles are not supporting us, nor are any other ministries with any regularity. That is why the Bible teaches us that it is the job of the Church to support ministries so that God's covenant might be established on the earth.

It is a problem, then, that the Church is where the religious people like to hang out. Religious people despise this teaching, so they wouldn't have liked Paul or John either. They think this part of the gospel should be ignored. The moment we mention it, they want to "gnash on us with their teeth." The reason for their reaction is that such a message brings conviction. To avoid being confronted with conviction about giving (or the lack thereof), they insist that we not teach on it. However, I shall continue preaching this truth until the Church breaks free from bondage.

Verse 8 tells us that, in order to be fellow workers in the truth, we need to welcome and provide for these traveling ministries. This is pretty plain. Some are called to go, and others are called to be fellow laborers, sharing in the harvest through our giving. This is one of the ways that we walk in truth, by contributing to those good Holy Ghost, Word of God ministries.

These verses continue on with the subject of prospering and being in health, even as the soul prospers. When a person's body, soul, and spirit, or more accurately, when their spirit, soul, and body receive healing, they become a giver. It is in that giving they become fellow laborers in the truth, walking in prosperity and health.

Every element of the Bible is important, tying into all other precepts and principles of the Word. For example, when God made man a three-part being in the Garden of Eden, man's spirit, soul, and body were all created perfect, designed to enjoy fellowship with God. Then, when man disobeyed God, sin entered into the human race. Eventually, sin tainted every aspect of mankind. Once man was separated from the Light, the death process began. When revival comes, it is also all-encompassing, bringing life to every aspect of a man. Like a chain reaction, what affects the spirit eventually affects the soul and the body. In order to thrive as designed by God, we must be in fellowship with His Light.

As our souls once more become alive unto God, we find that every area of our lives becomes prosperous. Relationships thrive, bodies become healthy, and finances become blessed. It is vital to remember that this blessing came about because of the goodness and the grace of God. It is His anointing, His Word, His name, and His joy that heal us. In this process, we must not forget God and begin to think that it is by our own hand that we have gotten these blessings. Neither must we forget that, in all these areas, we have become blessed in order to be a blessing. We are to become fellow partakers in the gospel, financing the Kingdom.

If your soul is still hurting from abuse, the unkind words of parents or teachers, sick relationships, broken marriages, or any other thing, come to Jesus and let Him heal you completely. Come to Him expecting to be healed, both physically and emotionally. Expect to prosper, but do not forget what you are being prospered for.

ELEVEN

HE'S AN EXCESSIVE, TOO-MUCH GOD

In May of 2002, I attended a portion of a minister's conference in Branson, Missouri. One of the keynote speakers, Rev. Keith Moore, was teaching on the goodness of God and the surplus that God has in store for the believers who will trust Him.

I bought the audio tapes of the services and played those teachings over and over again, meditating on the passages of God's Word that Rev. Moore used for his texts. I was again hit with an urgency to teach those same principles in tandem with others that had become so real to me. God's Word is a public domain. The Word of God used in those messages became Rhema (the Greek word for the spoken Word of God) to me. Rev. Moore's message became my own, burning within me. I knew that I had a new word to deliver to the Body of Christ.

A few weeks later, I attended Pastor Rodney Howard-Browne's campmeeting in Tampa, Florida. Several times at the campmeeting, it was my privilege to be invited to teach on the subject of stewardship. Each time I taught, I mixed faith with the Word of God, believing for my own financial needs to be met and to have an excess to sow into the Kingdom. During several of those sessions, I taught on the subject of an excessive, too-much God.

I was aware that, within two weeks, I was heading to a small church in Tulsa. In the natural, it was not the time to be giving excessively. Remember, though, it is in those times of financial need that God delights in showing us that He is a miracle worker. He is the God of impossible situations. He is a too-much God, and I was determined to prove Him. So, I was sowing excessively at offering time.

Then, I traveled to the July revival in a small church in Tulsa, Oklahoma. I experienced the greatest financial miracle that had ever occurred in my ministry. A couple who were attending the meetings asked to take me to lunch. As we were finishing our meal, they began sharing with me some things they were believing God for in their lives. They said they had a gift for me and handed me a check. When I looked, I was quite surprised, for the gift was ten thousand dollars. I nearly fell off of my chair. The gift was extremely timely, and I cried with joy. The couple asked me if I would wait until Monday to deposit the check, to which I agreed. Upon arriving back at the home where I was staying, I shared the news with my friends who were hosting me, Pastors Todd and Katie Holmes. We rejoiced together, and then I made a statement that even surprised me. (Sometimes, our words come directly out of our spirits before our minds have a chance to catch up with us.) I declared, "This is wonderful, but it is not enough to get us caught up right now. I am believing that this is just a token of what God is about to do. I am very thankful, but I am believing for a lot more. I have been preaching about an excessive, too-much God, and this is still not over-the-top excessive. I believe that someone is about to give me a one hundred thousand dollar check, and I believe that it is going to happen suddenly. It would not surprise me if it came this week before I leave this church." They agreed with me, and my expectations were great. This was Friday afternoon.

The Pastors asked me to extend the revival and go another week. We had one of the best services of the revival Sunday evening. At the end of the worship service, I was overcome with the wonderful presence of God. I began to prophesy, and then everyone present wept because of the strong presence of God. I was totally saturated and *Holy Ghost intoxicated*. Before I could resume preaching, I asked someone to sing while I sat down in the front row, trying to gain my composure. During the singing, the lady who had given me the ten thousand dollar check ran up to the front row where I was sitting. She asked if I had deposited the check yet, to which I replied that I had not. She said, "Good, because we were wondering if we could have it back." Needless to say, my heart sank a bit at the request, but what could I do? I said, "Of course," and retrieved the check. She then said, "Because we were disobedient the first time, and now we want to give you this instead." I looked up to see her drop another check into my lap. When I looked at the amount, it was a check for one hundred thousand dollars! I always wondered how I would react in such a moment. Well, I found out. I kicked off my high-heeled shoes and did a Holy Ghost jig around the auditorium! When I did, a large number of the people in the house followed suit and began to run and dance. They didn't know what had transpired but sensed that something in the spirit realm had occurred. WE SERVE A BIG, BIG, GOD! Some said later that they knew how much it was by the way I danced.

Are you ready to hear about this All-Sufficient, Excessive, Too-Much, Boat-Sinking, Net-Breaking, Twelve-Baskets-Left-Over God? Well, you're in for a treat. God is no respecter of persons. Let this burn in your heart as this teaching has in mine, and watch what God will do. He says in John 10:10, *"The thief cometh not, but for to steal, and to kill, and to destroy: I am come that they might have life, and that they might have it more abundantly."* Why did Jesus come? Was it only to save the lost? No. He tells us one of the reasons in John 10:10. He came to give us more than just life. He came to give us life more abundantly. Eternal life is not eternal existence, consisting of breathing in and out forever on some cloud. It is far better than anything we can imagine. It is a life full of abundance. It is the Zoë life. (Greek, for the God-kind of life.) It is life as God lives it, and God knows how to live. He doesn't just exist or barely get by. He is the ultimate Spirit of joy and laughter, and He wants us to enjoy parties.

In the Old Testament, we see where God commanded the Israelites to party three times a year. They were not even allowed a choice in whether to party or not. God is an extravagant God. He built His streets with gold and built His gates out of pearls. Many people say that God paves His streets with gold, but they are gold all the way through. Our God has never had a bad day, never had to hock some of the pearly gates to make a payment, and never had to give the angels sick pay because they had the Hong Kong flu. The Devil's parties are a joke. He entices people to drink alcohol, take drugs, and have illicit affairs. They spend the night vomiting over a porcelain throne, they wake up with headaches, and often lose their money and families. They call that partying. What a sorry substitute!

Jesus said, *"I am come."* Why did He come? It was not just so that we would miss Hell but that we might have life and life more abundantly. It is important that you not just take my word for this. Let's take a closer look at John 10:10 and see what some scholars have to say about this verse.

Let's examine the commentaries of Drs. Thayer and Strong. Dr. Thayer states that the word *abundance* comes from the word *carizos*. It means exceeding number, measure, rank, and need. It means over and above, more than necessary, superadded. The literal translation means superabundance.

Abundance means "more than enough." So what does superabundance mean? By definition, it means "more than, much more than, more than enough." That translates to good news for you and me. Dr. Strong related that it means, "Superabundant in quantity and superior in quality and by implication means excessive."

According to his definition, John 10:10 says that Jesus said He came that we might have life and that we might have it excessively. Now, I want to ask you a question. Are you living excessively, or are you merely existing? Many of you reading this book did not even know that you had a choice.

Big is a word that you must learn to associate with God. *Big* is a part of His nature. He is excessive and has always been so. He will always be that way. Just take a look at the flowers. Notice their unique designs, sizes, and colors. Why did God make so many flowers? If He was like many Christians today, He would have only made one color of flower—the color gray. He would tell us that it would suffice for our basic needs. He would have made one gray medium-sized tree as well, and it would have been only for protein or medicinal purposes because most Christians think that you can't enjoy something just to be enjoying it. It must serve a function.

Look at all of the animals. I recently had an opportunity to go snorkeling in Barbados. I was amazed at the many shapes and colors of the fish. I saw purple, yellow, and neon blue colored fish. I saw spotted, polka-dotted, and striped fish. Most of them are not good for eating or even on the food chain. They seem to have no purpose except for our entertainment. Why is that? He is simply excessive, and He wants us to be excessively blessed.

It is important to understand that fear always entertains a notion or dread of running out of something. It could be running out of funds, health, relationships, etc. However, faith is always rejoicing in anticipation of running over. The Bible tells us that the just shall live by faith. It says that without faith, it is impossible to please God. It also says that perfect love casts out fear. We are to be people of faith and not fear.

> Thou preparest a table before me in the presence of mine enemies: thou anointest my head with oil; my cup runneth over.
>
> PSALM 23:5

The psalmist is not speaking of a full cup but a running-over cup. Doesn't God know when our cups are full? Of course, He does. He is omniscient and all-knowing. It is simply His nature, and His will for our cups to run over. We could ask, "God, do You not realize that an overflowing cup could cause us problems? It would run onto the carpet and get all over the upholstery of the chairs. It will ruin our tablecloth. Do You not understand?" With that, He would reply, "Yes, of course, I understand what it could do. But it is just part of My nature to fill your cup over the top. I am a cup-running-over kind of God."

> ...open you the windows of heaven, and pour you out a
> blessing, that there shall not be room enough to
> receive it.
>
> MALACHI 3:10

We won't have room for it. That sounds rather excessive, doesn't it? That sounds like a too-much blessing to me. Some of you are already wondering if excess could possibly be the will of God. Yes, in spite of what we have been religiously brainwashed into believing, excess *is* the will of God. We have been taught that getting into excess is equivalent to joining forces with the Devil. While it is important that we not get into error, godly excess is different. I want to be into godly excess all the days of my life because God is into godly excess.

There is a false doctrine that we have been taught throughout our lives. It is the doctrine of "moderation in all things." I am going to prove to you that this is indeed a false doctrine. Some use Scripture wrongly to support their poverty doctrine. There are a couple of places in Scripture that mention moderation, and neither place refers to moderation the way the modern English word implies.

> Be glad then, ye children of Zion, and rejoice in the Lord
> your God: for he hath given you the former rain moder-
> ately, and he will cause to come down for you the rain,
> the former rain, and the latter rain in the first month.
> And the floors shall be full of wheat, and the vats shall over-
> flow with wine and oil.
>
> JOEL 2:23, 24

In these verses, moderately does not mean moderation the way we know it today. What it means is righteousness, fairness, and faithfulness. Even then, the Scriptures tell us that in this day in which we live, He will cause the former and the latter rain to come together.

GIVING

> Rejoice in the Lord always: and again I say, Rejoice.
> Let your moderation be known unto all men. The Lord is at hand.
> Be careful for nothing; but in every thing by prayer and supplication with thanksgiving let your requests be made known unto God.
>
> PHILIPPIANS 4:4-6

The word *moderation* here is sandwiched between verses that speak about rejoicing and not worrying. Paul, by the Holy Spirit, does not change subjects here. Is he saying then that we should not be overly excited but just moderate in our rejoicing? Or do you feel that he is speaking of not only worrying moderately or just a little bit? Absolutely not!

We find the same word that has been translated as *moderation* here in Titus 3:2 and other places. Typically, this word is translated as *gentle*.

> To speak evil of no man, to be no brawlers, but gentle, shewing all meekness unto all men.
>
> TITUS 3:2

So then, this verse in Philippians is actually saying, "Let your gentleness be known to all men."

God is excessive. We're supposed to imitate Him. Therefore, we are to be excessive. God is also self-controlled. It is scriptural to be self-controlled. We are not to be walking in error, not to be living out of control, but we are to be living in excess. There is a difference.

> Now these things were our examples, to the intent we should not lust after evil things, as they also lusted.
>
> I CORINTHIANS 10:6

The things that happened to the Israelites were rehearsed so they could be types and examples for us. We are to learn many valuable things from them. It has been said that the school of experience is good, but the tuition is too high. We can either learn from the Israelites' experiences or be doomed to repeat their same mistakes.

As we look at the life of the Israelites, we see that there are three levels of life they experienced. The first one is a life of slavery and total bondage and captivity. They were in captivity to the Egyptians. They didn't have enough of anything. They didn't have enough food or even enough straw to make bricks. They didn't own anything. They didn't even own their freedom. They were slaves to others. They were bondservants. They didn't own the clothes on their backs, the shacks that they lived in, or even their own bodies. You talk about the epitome of bondage and lack. It was not a pleasant sight, and it certainly was not the will of God. Their level of living was the level of not enough.

Next, we see the second level of life. God is so gracious! Not only did He bring the Israelites forth out of bondage, but He brought them out with silver and gold. And there was not one feeble among their tribes. When they needed food, God rained down manna from Heaven. When they had no water, He miraculously and supernaturally brought water forth out of the rock. What a God! God provided shade in the desert by way of the cloud by day. He provided warmth for them in the night with the pillar of fire by night.

The children of Israel were living in the wilderness. They were there to learn to live by faith and obey God. They were supposed to pass through the wilderness in a few days and then possess the Promised Land. The children of Israel failed the test and wandered around the wilderness for forty years. It would have been far better to be obedient to God and obtain what He had for them. He was leading them, but they refused to follow.

The Israelites did not have a surplus. They only had just enough. It was an exact provision. It was exciting and spectacular, and while it was miraculous, it was not the perfect will of God. It was something they became accustomed to and got comfortable with. They developed a comfort zone of exact provision. They became content with their situation. They told themselves, "This is the will of God for me. I'll just keep walking around in circles for forty years, surviving. God will take care of me." However, they were still in the wilderness, and the wilderness was not the will of God.

Exact provision is not the will of God. Living day-to-day with no extra is not the will of God. I remember, as a child, reading books and hearing testimonies about people who lived in the land of exact provision. Some stories were about families living in poverty with no food to eat or gifts to give at Christmas time. Then, at midnight, someone would bring food to eat and candy canes for the children. Other stories related how someone would start down the road with no gas in their tank. They would be able to drive off the fumes until they arrived at their destination. These were great stories of miraculous and supernatural provision. They were exciting stories of exact provision. I used to think that these types of stories were about God's best provision. But I have learned better now. Revelation is progressive, and we are all still learning.

Barely making it from meeting to meeting, offering to offering, check to check, is never God's best for us. Thank God for His spectacular provision. It is definitely God, and we should rejoice over it. We should be thankful, but make sure that we do not settle for only exact provision all of our lives. This is not the will of God for us. It is still a modern-day wandering in the wilderness. This second level of living is where a lot of the body of Christ is at and think that they have arrived.

The third level of life is God's perfect will for us. Canaan's land is God's best for us; it is His promise to us. What is Canaan's land? It is a land where the grapes are so enormous that it takes two men to carry one bunch; it is the land of too much grapes. That is pretty excessive, don't you think? Canaan's land was a place where the children of Israel owned houses they didn't build and had vineyards they didn't plant. They had wells they didn't dig. God said that He would rain on their land. They didn't even have to irrigate. Canaan was God's promise to His people. It was His perfect will for them. However, their responsibility was to believe what He said and possess the land. We are to learn from them and not repeat their mistakes.

We can see that having "not enough" is not God's will for you and me. Just enough is not God's will, either. Too much is His will for you and me. The land of bondage is not His will. Neither is the wilderness of exact provision. God intends for us to move on into the land flowing with milk and honey, the land of plenty. It is the land of more than enough. It is a land of surplus and excess. We must go in and possess it.

Our enemy hates what I am talking about here. He is the perpetrator of not enough. He loves robbing from us. It makes him happy when you and I don't have enough, especially when it is not enough to effectively reach the world with the gospel. And while he will settle for keeping us in the land of not enough, he positively delights in keeping us in the land of barely enough. The Devil knows that if we break into surplus, we will sow into end-time harvest, and then Jesus will return.

Let us look at some Old Testament examples of a too-much God.

> And Abram was very rich in cattle, in silver, and in gold.
>
> GENESIS 13:2

> And Lot also, which went with Abram, had flocks, and herds, and tents.
> And the land was not able to bear them, that they might dwell together: for their substance was great, so that they could not dwell together.
>
> GENESIS 13:5, 6

God has not changed. Our covenant relationship has changed, but He has not. We have an even better covenant than Israel had. He will never change. If He made Abram and Lot so rich that they could not even stay together for the magnitude of their possessions, He'll do it today.

Do you think that God forgot or does not know how many cows an acre of land can sustain? Does He not realize how many sheep and goats an acreage can handle? Yes, He knows how many sheep and goats an acreage can handle. He has not forgotten His multiplication tables. He just doesn't care. When God starts blessing, He just keeps on, no matter how many ramifications there are. That is the will of God; that we have too many cows, too many goats, and too many sheep.

For those of you who still need convincing, let's look at some more examples. This relates to part of the story of Esau and Jacob.

> And Esau took his wives, and his sons, and his daughters, and all the persons of his house, and his cattle, and all his beasts, and all his substance, which he had got in the land of Canaan; and went into the country from the face of his brother Jacob.
> For their riches were more than that they might dwell together; and the land wherein they were strangers could not bear them because of their cattle.
>
> GENESIS 36:6, 7

God is still in the blessing and multiplying business. After all these generations, God is continuing to bless His people. He didn't pick Abram to bless only. He is still blessing Abram's grandchildren with too many cows, goats, sheep, and substance. He's still a too-much God.

We also see in Scripture that the Philistines came and told Isaac that he needed to move away from his place of residence because he was making the king look bad. He had too much. It's obvious that he, too, served a too-much God.

When we read about Abram earlier, it said in Gen. 13:2 that *"Abram was very rich in cattle, in silver, and in gold."* The word rich terrifies some Christians. They say that we should only say blessed, not rich. Are you afraid to use the word "rich"? Some are afraid to use it in their preaching. Is it a part of our redemption or not? Jesus, by the grace of God, became poor so that we *could* be rich.

> For ye know the grace of our Lord Jesus Christ, that, though he was rich, yet for your sakes he became poor, that ye through his poverty might be rich.
>
> 2 CORINTHIANS 8:9

You cannot hyper-spiritualize this. The entire context of 2 Corinthians 9 is about money and offerings. Some people think that this verse is only referring to becoming rich spiritually, not financially. However, the Bible must be interpreted by the entirety of Scripture and kept within its proper context. The Word of God says that we are made rich. *Rich* is a Bible word that you should not be afraid to use or to believe. Redemption truths should be a reality to us. I don't care what your bank account says. The Word does not say that we are made to just get by.

The majority of the church also believes that *rich* is a very bad word, almost a swear word. But *rich* is not a bad word. *Poor* is a bad word. *Sick* is bad. *Broke* is bad. *Bound* is bad. But *rich* is not. Most people do not even know how to relate to *rich*. When they read the warnings in the Bible that relate to rich people, they misunderstand what it is talking about. The Bible gives a warning to the rich who are proud, who refuse to give or submit to God. The Bible also warns about the love of money. We are to love God but not money. However, having money and loving it are two very different issues. We must always put God first.

According to the Word of God, we are just as rich as we are healed. It is part of our redemption. Faith isn't waiting until you see it hit your account or you see it in your hand. We are rich now, this very minute. It might do you good to say the word *rich* a few times. That way, you can get used to not thinking of it as a bad word. Neither should it be a word to which you cannot relate. Confess what God's Word says about you. Meditate on it. (I'm glad that Rich is my last name. Every time that I tell someone my name, I am prophesying about what God has promised me!)

Sadly, about two-thirds of the Body of Christ identify with lack and not enough. They call themselves faith people because the creditors no longer call, and they have food on the table. They become self-satisfied and lethargic, denouncing any teaching that says they can have more than enough.

> And it shall be to me a name of joy, a praise and an honour before all the nations of the earth, which shall hear all the good that I do unto them: and they shall fear and tremble for all the goodness and for all the prosperity that I procure unto it.
>
> JEREMIAH 33:9

God is a good God who longs to show the world His goodness and His prosperity. Is living a righteous lifestyle a witness to the world? Of course, it is. Is it a witness for our children to be healed? Yes, of course. Well, is it a witness to the world for us to be blessed and have excess? Yes, that, too, is a witness to the world of the goodness of God.

> If ye walk in my statutes, and keep my commandments, and do them;
> Then I will give you rain in due season, and the land shall yield her increase, and the trees of the field shall yield their fruit.
> And your threshing shall reach unto the vintage, and the vintage shall reach unto the sowing time: and ye shall eat your bread to the full, and dwell in your land safely.
>
> LEVITICUS 26:3-5

Christ has redeemed us from the curse of the Law, but we get to keep the blessing. One translation for the word prosperity is *reaching*, which means to succeed. It means it reaches, and it means it lasts.

> For I will have respect unto you, and make you fruitful, and
> multiply you, and establish my covenant with you.
> And ye shall eat old store, and bring forth the old because of
> the new.
>
> LEVITICUS 26:9, 10

The new harvest will come in before you can consume the old. You won't be able to take the old clothes out of the closet fast enough to make room for the new. You can't give away the old shoes fast enough to make room for the new.

This is speaking of excess, of too much. It is speaking of the blessing of Abraham. Old cars must come out of the garage to accommodate the new ones. God's will for us is that we have excess when people come to visit us. We can tell them when they come to our homes to attend meetings, they won't have to rent a car. They can use one of ours. When they visit, they can stay in their own private wing of the house. There will be no sleeper sofa or blown-up mattress on the floor for them because we have an excess of bedrooms. Hallelujah!

If we don't begin to think like this, how will we ever operate in God's excess? He is a big, too-much God who has more than enough for us. When we operate in more than enough, we will have enough to share with those living in the land of not enough and just enough.

A lot of people are never going to believe this, so it falls on us to believe for excess, not only for ourselves, but also for them. We must have a heart for it. God wants this message to become reality to us so that we can accomplish big, excessive things.

Did you know that God has actually planned too much for you? Let's look at several New Testament examples of this, as well as do a quick review of the Old Testament examples we've already looked at.

> And it came to pass, that, as the people pressed upon him to hear the word of God, he stood by the lake of Gennesaret,
> And saw two ships standing by the lake: but the fishermen were gone out of them, and were washing their nets.
> And he entered into one of the ships, which was Simon's, and prayed him that he would thrust out a little from the land. And he sat down, and taught the people out of the ship.
> Now when he had left speaking, he said unto Simon, Launch out into the deep, and let down your nets for a draught.
> And Simon answering said unto him, Master, we have toiled all the night, and have taken nothing: nevertheless at thy word I will let down the net.
> And when they had this done, they inclosed a great multitude of fishes: and their net brake.
>
> LUKE 5:1-6

In this story, Jesus asked Peter to use his boat for the purpose of preaching the gospel. The boat was going to be used for the harvest. What an exciting opportunity for Peter to become part of a worldwide harvest.

Jesus thanked Peter for the use of his boat and then blessed Peter for it. Jesus is no moocher. He owes man nothing. He is a blesser. Peter had been fishing all night to no avail. But when you have Jesus in your boat, everything changes. At the word of the Lord, Peter proceeded to launch out into the deep and once again threw out his nets. This time, he experienced supernatural results. Verse 6 tells us that the net broke. He had to beckon to his partners to come help him. Do you think that God did not know how many fish a net could contain before breaking? Of course, He knew. It's just that, as we saw in our other texts, God is a too-much God, and He just didn't care. When he starts blessing, He just keeps on. He is a net-breaking God.

The Bible tells us that, eventually, the boat began to sink. That is an uncomfortable predicament. At first glance, it seems that God is actually causing them problems. Does He not know how many fish their boat could hold? Again, of course, He does. However, it is not God's fault that their nets were too small and their boat was too little for His blessing. They would learn a lesson here. The next time, they needed to better prepare for the blessings of a too-much God. They needed to carry bigger nets and buy larger boats if they were going to hang out with the Son of the living God. For God is a net-breaking, boat-sinking, too-many-fish God!

Was the story in the Bible of the feeding of the multitudes an isolated incident? In Matthew 14:13-21, we read the account. The Bible says that five thousand men were fed, plus women and children. There could have been at least ten or twelve thousand people in attendance that day. They were all fed with a little boy's lunch of five loaves and two fish. Some people have tried explaining away the miracle by saying the loaves were much larger in that day. Maybe so, but I don't know how they explain away the fish. I guess they think that the boy carried two whales with him for lunch that day.

This was already an incredible, supernatural miracle. God was once again consistent with His excessive, too-much character. He didn't just barely feed the multitude. The Bible tells us that after everyone had eaten, twelve baskets were left over. There are two words for "basket" in the New Testament. One word describes the type of "basket" that was used to let the Apostle Paul down over a wall. Still, the other word describes a very large basket. Did God not know how much food this multitude would eat? Yes, He most certainly did. He is an omniscient God. He knows everything. He did not forget His math that day. He just didn't care. He has no pleasure in just meeting the need. He's not that kind of God, no matter what religion has tried to feed us. He is El Shaddai, the God of more than enough. When He starts blessing, He has no desire to stop until He has gone way over the top. He is a twelve-baskets-left-over kind of God.

God is also pleased with excessive offerings:

GIVING

> Now when Jesus was in Bethany, in the house of Simon the leper,
> There came unto him a woman having an alabaster box of very precious ointment, and poured it on his head, as he sat at meat.
> But when his disciples saw it, they had indignation, saying, To what purpose is this waste?
> For this ointment might have been sold for much, and given to the poor.
> When Jesus understood it, he said unto them, Why trouble ye the woman? for she hath wrought a good work upon me.
> For ye have the poor always with you; but me ye have not always.
> For in that she hath poured this ointment on my body, she did it for my burial.
> Verily I say unto you, Wheresoever this gospel shall be preached in the whole world, there shall also this, that this woman hath done, be told for a memorial of her.
>
> MATTHEW 26:6-13

Other translations say that the gift in Matthew 26:7 was very expensive. John 12:5 in the amplified classic tells us that it was a year's wages. Matt. 26:8 tells us that the disciples responded with indignation. This is why they were not able to stand in the day of temptation. Through disillusionment, deception, offense, judging, and looking after the flesh, they had come to a place where they did not value the things of God as they ought.

All faith giving is based on evaluation. You won't support something that you do not value. In order to give to it, you must value it and believe that it is doing the work of God and is achieving results.

Many only see value in the things of the flesh. They are more interested in their homes, cars, clothes, jewelry, and in building their own businesses.

Jesus said that the things men esteem and hold of high value, the Lord despises, and vice versa.

> And he said unto them, Ye are they which justify yourselves before men; but God knoweth your hearts: for that which is highly esteemed among men is abomination in the sight of God.
>
> LUKE 16:15

Many individuals despise the things that God holds in high regard. This is a case of the spirit versus the flesh. The woman of Matthew 26:6-13 saw value in Jesus. She took the most precious thing she owned and gave it to Him. Her offering was worth a full year's wages. In today's currency, it would probably be at least fifty thousand dollars worth of offering.

Of all the disciples, Judas was the most vocal in calling her offering a waste. He was really saying, "This is too much for a preacher." That same attitude is choking our churches today. What the people must realize is that their prosperity is directly linked to how they honor their pastor and other ministers of the gospel.

> ...for them that honour me I will honour, and they that despise me shall be lightly esteemed.
>
> 1 SAMUEL 2:30

We will not see full prosperity in our churches until people learn these truths. We do the people a great disservice by not teaching them to honor God properly. People who gripe about too much offerings and too many gifts are hypocrites who do not honor God.

In our Matthew 26:6-13 biblical example, it was in the woman's heart to be the biggest blessing that she could possibly be. She loved Jesus and wanted to demonstrate it with a too much offering. Please notice that Jesus did not rebuke her and say, "My Lord, woman! Haven't I taught you better than this? You are supposed to be conservative and moderate in all things." No, He didn't do anything of the kind. What Jesus said was that the woman had done a great thing and wherever the gospel would be preached, this story would be told as a memorial to her. The Apostle Paul never rebuked big givers either. He encouraged people to become partners in the faith and to give as much as they could.

In the Bible, Moses issued a decree ordering the people to stop giving because they had received too much stuff. This is totally amazing. I've yet to be in a church where someone was told to blow the trumpets and proclaim, "Hear ye, hear ye. It is henceforth ordered that no man or woman shall be allowed to give any more offerings or they will be breaking the law. We already have too much money. We don't know what to do with it." God is certainly the God of too much offerings in both Testaments.

Let's go back to one last Old Testament example of too much giving.

> And the children of Joseph spake unto Joshua, saying, Why hast thou given me but one lot and one portion to inherit, seeing I am a great people, forasmuch as the Lord hath blessed me hitherto?
> And Joshua answered them, If thou be a great people, then get thee up to the wood country, and cut down for thyself there in the land of the Perizzites and of the giants, if mount Ephraim be too narrow for thee.
> And the children of Joseph said, The hill is not enough for us: and all the Canaanites that dwell in the land of the valley have chariots of iron, both they who are of Bethshean and her towns, and they who are of the valley of Jezreel.
> And Joshua spake unto the house of Joseph, even to Ephraim and to Manasseh, saying, Thou art a great people, and hast great power: thou shalt not have one lot only.
>
> JOSHUA 17:14-17

It is important to remember that faith never puts pressure on others. If you do this, you're not in faith. You are looking to people rather than God to solve your problems. When people pressure ministers to solve all of their problems, or to get them healed, or to solve their financial difficulties, they are not in faith. The tribe of Joseph was trying to put pressure on Joshua to solve their problems. They were letting him know that he should have given them more land. But Joshua put the responsibility right back on them. He agreed with them that they were, indeed, a great people. He basically told them that there was plenty of land around them. He told them that if they were not yet satisfied, they should go ahead and help themselves. The tribe of Joseph said that they were a great people, but, really, they did not believe it. If they did, they would have already been doing something about the problem.

Many times, we think we know that we are the righteousness of Christ, but we aren't quite sure. We hope that the Greater One lives inside us. We hope that His promises are yes and amen, but we aren't really sure. The reason for that is because these truths are not yet revelation knowledge to our spirits. We're not sure that God wants to give us the things that we need. Meanwhile, we pressure others to provide. We murmur and complain, expecting people to bail us out of our predicaments. But God wants us to learn, once and for all, that He is our source. When people are no longer your source, they cannot disappoint you. God desires for us to press into Him and learn of His great faithfulness.

> And the whole congregation of the children of Israel assembled together at Shiloh, and set up the tabernacle of the congregation there. And the land was subdued before them.
> And there remained among the children of Israel seven tribes, which had not yet received their inheritance.
> And Joshua said unto the children of Israel, How long are ye slack to go to possess the land, which the Lord God of your fathers hath given you?
>
> JOSHUA 18:1-3

In verse 2, we see that seven of the twelve tribes did not yet have their inheritance. God promised the inheritance to all twelve tribes, but many of them were just waiting for the Promised Land to drop into their hands, like ripe cherries off a tree. They were sitting and waiting for their inheritance when God expected them to appropriate the promises of God by faith. I wonder if this is typical of the Body of Christ today.

> Therefore I say unto you, What things soever ye desire, when ye pray, believe that ye receive them, and ye shall have them.
>
> MARK 11:24

The phrase *"believe you receive them"* is a keynote phrase here. The literal translation is *"take them and you shall have them."* Most people are too lazy or ignorant of God's ways to *take them*. If verse 3 were paraphrased, it would read like this, "What are you waiting for? You need to get with the program, stir yourself up, believe for more, and claim bigger things."

Joshua's preaching that day was not in vain. The tribe of Judah was listening. I can just imagine the conversation taking place between the leaders of that tribe. "Hey, did you hear what the man of God was preaching today? He was telling the tribes of Joseph that if they wanted more land, they should go take it." Could you hear them asking each other, "Why don't we do that?"

"Yeah, that's a good idea. Let's assemble our men of war and develop a strategy." Then, they began taking land all around them. By the sweat of their brow, they worked hard, fought hard, and shed blood. When all was said and done, they had plenty of land. But that land didn't fall into their hands. They had to take it. They had that kind of spirit about them. Oh, for more men and women of God who would walk with the same spirit of the Lion of the Tribe of Judah!

> Out of the portion of the children of Judah was the inheritance of the children of Simeon: for the part of the chil-

> dren of Judah was too much for them: therefore the children of Simeon had their inheritance within the inheritance of them.
>
> JOSHUA 19:9

Eventually, Judah had too much land. Judah's portion was too much for them to use, so they allowed the tribe of Simeon to sit on their land. They might have looked up one day and said, "This is too much land. We have more than is needed to do what we've been called to do. Let's bless the tribe of Simeon by sharing our blessing with them. It doesn't matter that we worked hard and were obedient to possess the land. This is what receiving the blessing of God is about. We can enjoy believing for someone else and blessing their socks off."

God is looking today for people with the spirit of the tribe of Judah. The Lion of the Tribe of Judah is Jesus. He is a too-much Jesus. People who are like Him know how to reach out with large faith, large vision, and pray big prayers and claim big things. God wants us to become extremely bold in our claiming. He wants us to believe Him for too many things.

Did you notice that no prophet came to the tribe of Judah saying, "You greedy rascals, you've claimed too much? Moderation in all things, I always say. You should only have enough land to get by. Don't claim any more than you think you can use. There just isn't enough to go around. You've been hanging around those prosperity teachers too long." No, they didn't say that. God loved their faith-filled hearts and tenacity.

Regretfully, so much of the Body of Christ is never going to claim this. They will not operate in the blessings of God. They refuse to sow to the God-kind of life. Therefore, you and I have a responsibility to believe in God for both them and us. We will receive the blessings and the abundance and still have enough left over to share with others. Somebody must be in this position for too-much blessing, or the Body of Christ will never possess the Promised Land that we are meant to possess.

Quite frequently, God's people say things like, "I hope we'll have enough" or "I'm afraid that we won't have enough." If you have been guilty of saying these things, you must quit! If you don't, you will set a cap on your living and blessing levels. You will limit yourself and God. He wants to move so much on your behalf, blessing you until your cup is running over. Are we going to have enough? The answer is most definitely not! Are we going to have too much? Unequivocally, yes! We will have exceedingly, abundantly above what we can ask or think. We shall have too many cows and too many sheep. We will have too much land and too many fish. We will have offerings that are too large and too many people around to help us. We will have food left over and will have to empty our pantries to make room for more. Why will this happen?

Because we serve a **too-many sheep, too-many cows, too-many goats, too-much land, net-breaking, boat-sinking, twelve-baskets-left-over, cup-running-over, too-much God!**

TWELVE

GOD PROVIDES SEED FOR THE SOWER

[Remember] this: he who sows sparingly and grudgingly will also reap sparingly and grudgingly, and he who sows generously [that blessings may come to someone] will also reap generously and with blessings.

Let each one [give] as he has made up his own mind and purposed in his heart, not reluctantly or sorrowfully or under compulsion, for God loves (He takes pleasure in, prizes above other things, and is unwilling to abandon or to do without) a cheerful (joyous, "prompt to do it") giver [whose heart is in his giving].

And God is able to make all grace (every favor and earthly blessing) come to you in abundance, so that you may always and under all circumstances and whatever the need be self-sufficient [possessing enough to require no aid or support and furnished in abundance for every good work and charitable donation].

As it is written, He [the benevolent person] scatters abroad; He gives to the poor; His deeds of justice and goodness and kindness and benevolence will go on and endure forever!

> And [God] Who provides seed for the sower and bread for eating will also provide and multiply your [resources for] sowing and increase the fruits of your righteousness [which manifests itself in active goodness, kindness, and charity].
> Thus you will be enriched in all things and in every way, so that you can be generous, and [your generosity as it is] administered by us will bring forth thanksgiving to God.
> For the service that the ministering of this fund renders does not only fully supply what is lacking to the saints (God's people), but it also overflows in many [cries of] thanksgiving to God.
> Because at [your] standing of the test of this ministry, they will glorify God for your loyalty and obedience to the Gospel of Christ which you confess, as well as for your generous-hearted liberality to them and to all [the other needy ones].
> And they yearn for you while they pray for you, because of the surpassing measure of God's grace (His favor and mercy and spiritual blessing which is shown forth) in you.
> Now thanks be to God for His Gift, [precious] beyond telling [His indescribable, inexpressible, free Gift]!
>
> 2 CORINTHIANS 9:6-15 (AMPC)

As I was growing up, I heard people in the church say things like, "It doesn't matter what you give, as long as you give something. It's the thought that counts." I want you to know that such statements cannot be found in the Bible, only in the book of "I say so."

How do beliefs like, "God helps those who help themselves," or "Money is the root of all evil," and other non-scriptural notions about finances become so rooted in the church? Because the truth of God's Word on giving has not been preached enough. Preachers have been afraid to teach on the subject of giving because they feel people will misunderstand it. They fear that the people will misjudge their motives and decide that they are in it for the money. Because they do not want to become unpopular, they continue to preach only what they feel will be accepted.

> The fear of man bringeth a snare.
>
> PROVERBS 29:25

When we fail to preach the Word of God in a certain area, a vacuum, devoid of truth, is formed. That vacuum sucks in false doctrines, ideas, and perversions of the truth that replace the truth. When those perversions are entertained long enough, a religious tradition sets up in the minds of the people.

Certain church traditions have been adopted from local culture, which in America have been widely influenced and shaped by television. Most of the church now buys into the world's values and viewpoints of how ministers should live and when, why, and how people should give. People in the world and in the church alike have been trained to expect godly persons to live in poverty. And they expect to give offerings only after emotionally charged appeals or effective marketing techniques adequately tug at their heartstrings.

You might be promised ridiculous things for your giving, like oil from the Holy Land or a shower cap of blessing from the Jordan River. Or even worse, you might be offered a word of prophecy or healing in exchange for a specific financial gift.

No one can sell the anointing or a gift of the Spirit. It is unthinkable that anyone would try to manipulate the Holy Spirit and God's people this way. Such practices are an abomination to God's house. They must come to a screeching halt in the Body of Christ. I believe with all of my heart that as God's glory increases, these things will stop. Otherwise, we will be having Ananias and Sapphira services again.

The real harm to the Body of Christ comes when people get accustomed to manipulations and have no objections to them. Then, when instead of manipulating, someone comes in and preaches the Word of God in a certain area, the people are disturbed and suspicious because they have been accustomed to what has become their religious tradition.

In order for the Holy Spirit to lead God's people in the area of giving, we have to change their thinking. When people are trained to give because of what the Word of God says, by the leading of the Holy Spirit, they will give whether there is a current need or not. This will effectively put a stop to talented manipulators who have come in to fleece the sheep. When charlatans are no longer empowered to manipulate the church, we will witness the Holy Spirit once again taking charge of the gift-giving.

Only by the preaching of God's Word on the subject will the Church learn how, when, where, and why to give. I, for one, have been called to teach people God's Word regarding this. Some may not understand, but it is to God that I will be called to give an account, not man. I must do what God has called me to do. I am looking forward to seeing the entire Body of Christ begin to worship God with their giving. The day will come when we are no longer manipulated but are stimulated to give.

The reason I can stand up before people and teach on stewardship is because I know that I am not taking from them; I am giving to them. If listeners will catch what I am teaching, they, their families, and their churches will not just be helped for one night—they will be forever changed. Speaking for ministers, it gives us great confidence and boldness when we know that we are helping people. It also helps us to withstand the great opposition that comes with preaching this message.

Many will accuse us of taking from the poor—most especially from elderly ladies. People with no understanding will ask how we can sleep at night after taking money from the poor.

No wonder Hosea writes:

> My people are destroyed for a lack of knowledge.
>
> HOSEA 4:6

The people making such comments have no perception of God's will or His principles. They have not comprehended that giving is God's specific answer for the poor. The good news is that the poor don't have to be poor anymore!

Rather than feeling guilty, I experience great satisfaction when I teach on giving. I get to witness God's people catching the message. The more poverty-laden the people are, such as in third-world countries, the more excited I get about the opportunity I am laying out before them. It enables me to look those religious and poverty devils in the face and stare them down.

Some still say that we shouldn't teach about the subject of giving. Evidently, then, they would have had a problem with the Apostle Paul. He did not pull any punches, and he made no apology for teaching the church of Corinth about offerings.

In verse 6 of our text, Paul basically tells us that if we give a little, we get a little. He makes it plain that we will reap in direct proportion to our planting. If you plant generously, you will reap generously. If you are a stingy giver, a scarce harvest is exactly what you will reap. Remember that this is what the Bible says and not what some preacher made up.

My pastor says that religious and poverty spirits are Siamese twins joined at the hip. Wherever you find one, you will find the other. I don't ever want religion or stinginess to get a hold of me. I want to be generous, as the Bible commands all of us to be.

Verse 7 tells us that we should make up our own minds about giving. This again means we should not allow anyone to manipulate us. Do not let anyone tell you how much you should give. You must learn to listen to the Holy Ghost and then obey Him and only Him. Consequently, we need to inquire of the Lord regarding our giving.

We never know exactly what will be required to meet the challenges of life or how much will be needed later. So I want to always plant far more than enough. I have been especially glad when emergencies have arisen that I have been generous in my planting. Should even the economic systems of this world go down, I have a heavenly bank account that will not fail.

John Avanzini had many interesting things to say about the laws of harvest in his book *30, 60, Hundredfold*. There, he explained that you have to plant exactly what you expect to reap or harvest. In the natural, for instance, a farmer would not plant soybeans and expect to harvest oranges. Yet, many Christians think that, in the spiritual, they can plant in any manner they desire and still reap a financial harvest.

John Avanzini related that he was teaching along these lines one day when a man interrupted him, insisting that what Brother Avanzini was teaching did not work. When asked why he would say such a thing, the man explained that his mother had been one of the biggest givers around. Yet, now she was living in poverty in a nursing home.

When John Avanzini asked if she had been a tither, he was told, "No." The man stated that both he and his mother believed tithing was Old Testament law, which no longer applies today. He also shared with him that because she did not have much money, his mother hardly gave offerings.

The son said that his mother was a big giver in other ways, though. She would stay up all night, knitting afghans for people. She took pastries to some and cooked soup and stew for others. She prayed for people and often visited people in need, just "loving on them." Oh yes, she was a seed sower in many other areas.

Interested, John Avanzini asked the man another couple of questions. He asked, "Does your mother get visitors in the care facility?"

"Oh, yes," the man answered, "my mother is the most popular lady on the floor. People often come to visit her. In fact, she really has too many visitors, so many that it's hard for her to get her proper rest."

When asked if anyone brought her pastries, he replied, "Oh yes, she gets too many sweets. The nurses have told us to cut back on that." John Avanzini was also told that people brought her soup and other delicious dishes. When asked if she had any afghans, he replied, "You should see all of her afghans. She has them on the floor, on her bed, on the walls, and in the closet. People have brought her more afghans than she can even use."

John Avanzini went on to say that the laws of the harvest certainly do work, and the man just proved it. If you plant pastries, you will get pastries. If you plant afghans, you will get afghans. If you plant soup, soup is what you will reap. If you plant prayers and encouraging words to others, you will reap those. If you plant visits to others, you will never be lonely or devoid of friends. If you plant hugs and kisses, you will reap those. (Some of you had better think twice about going out and planting much of those!)

In keeping with this truth, I do not stop at planting finances. I will always remember "from where I came." I can remember the time when my only dress clothes were from a used clothing store. The store did not necessarily have a huge variety, either. Look where God has brought me. Today, He has given me the best. I continue to sow a lot of my wardrobe every few months. And God quite regularly supplies me with a new one. I buy some of my clothes, but often, people give me beautiful outfits. Sometimes, people take me shopping and let me pick out whatever I want. I have been told that I have some of the most beautiful clothes that people have seen.

I plant in other ways as well. I want to reap a harvest in many different areas. I continue to give God the glory for what He has done for me in a multitude of areas.

Let me say, though, that I do not sow only because I am promised a harvest. This is where a lot of people miss it. God Himself is, first and foremost, a giver. God gave His best for me, His only Son. He did not have three or four more sons. God gave His only One because He loved me. I want to be a giver, just like my Father. He reached out to me before I knew who He was. He loved me unconditionally. God brought me out of a kingdom of darkness and set me into a Kingdom of light. He forgave my sins and remembered them no more. He has redeemed me from the law of sin and death and has given me new life. God baptized me in the Holy Ghost and fire. Now, I have joy unspeakable and full of glory and a peace that passes all understanding. I will spend eternity with God on streets of glory with gates of pearl.

If I never received a harvest, I would be a giver all the days of my life, solely because I am in love with God. To give to God, I would not need one promise in His Word of a return of any kind. I would give to God, and to His people, just because I love Him. That love should always be our heart's motive. Remember, this is not about giving to live—it is about living to give.

Equally true, however, is the fact that I have been promised a harvest in the Word of God. It would be disrespectful to His Word (and pure stupidity) to not believe what the Bible says. Over and over again, the Word reminds us of a harvest.

> Give, and it shall be given unto you; good measure, pressed down, and shaken together, and running over, shall men give into your bosom. For with the same measure that ye mete withal it shall be measured to you again.
>
> LUKE 6:38

The *Spirit-Filled Bible* says this about the above verse:

> God expects you to receive a harvest from your giving. He wants us to expect a miracle return! Jesus opened up a whole new way of giving. He gave Himself totally for the people. We can no longer pay or sacrifice our way into God's mercy. Jesus Christ paid our debt, and His cross is

> a completed work. Therefore, our giving is no longer a debt we owe but a seed that we sow! The life and power source is from Him. Our job is simply to act on the power potential in that seed that He has placed in us by grace.

Notice that when Jesus said, *"Give,"* He also said, *"and it will be given unto you."* Giving and receiving go hand in hand. *Only after we give are we in a position to expect to reach out and receive.* Jesus said the harvest would be *"Good measure, pressed down, shaken together and running over."* Notice that this cannot be talking about a spiritual return only because men (mankind) are the ones who will give back to us. So we give as unto God, and we receive as from God.

Notwithstanding, we should at all times remain sensitive and aware of the different ways in which God may deliver our harvest. A miracle is either coming toward you or going past you at all times. Reach out and take it! Do not let it pass by (Matthew 9:20-22). God's miracle for you may be coming in the form of an idea, an opportunity, an invitation, or a previously unknown or unidentified association. Watch expectantly for the ways in which God may choose to bring about your harvest in His *"due season,"* which, for you, may be today.

Under "Kingdom Dynamics," the *Spirit-Filled Bible* goes on to identify Luke 6:38 as *"The Law of Divine Reciprocity, God's Prosperity."* There is a universal law of divine reciprocity. You give; God gives in return. You plant a seed, and the ground yields a harvest. That is a reciprocal relationship. The ground can only give to you as you give to the ground. You put the money in an interest-bearing account at the bank and the bank returns to you interest. That is reciprocity.

Many people want to get something for nothing in God's Kingdom. Now, they clearly understand that such rationale will never work in the world's system. Yet, they continuously expect God to send them something when they have invested nothing into the Kingdom. If you have not been investing your time, talent, commitment, or money into the Kingdom, why do you expect something back? How can you get something from a harvest when you fail to plant your seed? How can you expect God to honor your desire to receive when you fail to honor His commands to give? Prosperity begins with investment.

> Be not deceived; God is not mocked: for whatsoever a man soweth, that shall he also reap.
>
> GALATIANS 6:7

> Beloved, I wish above all things that thou mayest prosper and be in health, even as thy soul prospereth.
>
> 3 JOHN 1:2

To ignore these Verses is not pleasing to God. We don't receive the harvest to heap upon ourselves. We receive it so that we can be a greater blessing. I want to reap a harvest so that I may have even more to give. It is not selfish to believe that.

If a farmer were out in his field planting seed, he would believe for a harvest. He would not be planting just to plant. If you were to come up to him and ask him what type of harvest he was expecting, he would tell you precisely what he was watching and waiting for. You could not even begin to imagine him saying, "Oh, I'm not believing for anything. I'm just planting for something to do." You would think that he was out of his mind and tempted to ask, "Does your mother know that you're here?"

Anyone who plants can and should expect a harvest. This does not mean that you are selfish. It means that you believe in the principles and laws of sowing and reaping that God established on the earth.

Verse 9 says that the benevolent continue to scatter their seed. They give to the poor and sow into many areas. The positive outflow of such sowing will remain forever, through eternity. When I get to Heaven, I will be able to see how much my seed, along with the seed of others, has accomplished.

Verse 10 tells us that it is God who provides seed for the sower. Therefore, if you have no seed, you should repent before God. When the Bible tells us that God gives seed, we know that He does. If we have none, we must admit that we ate our seed, fed it to someone, made jewelry out of it, or did something with it that we should not have done. The good news is that God is gracious and will give us another opportunity once our hearts are right.

Additionally, God will multiply our seed. This is great news for us. God is not just a God of addition—He is a God of multiplication. Our miracle-working God will exponentially multiply our seed, making a little seed go a long way. We have a perfect example of this when a little boy's lunch was used to feed thousands. It happened again when a widow woman's last bit of cake meal and oil was multiplied to last her throughout the famine.

In order to have more to give in future times, our seed must be multiplied. I want my harvest to continue to grow so that I can give more and more. Many people lose a continuous blessing by totally consuming a one-time harvest. Any farmer worth his salt knows that unless he keeps back some of his seed for sowing again, he will soon be out of business. The same principle is true in the supernatural realm.

It is God who enables us to be generous. It is the gifts of God's grace, His love, His direction, and His miraculous multiplication of the seed which afford us the opportunity to be generous. Verse 11 reminds us that this process will bring forth much thanksgiving to God.

In verse 12, we find that this multiplication process also brings forth the needed funds to the church so that the church may accomplish all that it needs to for Christ. This causes many to praise God and is a faith-builder for all when they see how big God is. The church realizes that they can depend upon God's faithfulness.

Verse 13 says that others will see that we withstood this test. I believe that the world has been "turned off" by watching Christians proclaim one thing and live another. Too many Christians live stingier lives than those in the world. The world wants to see if we are generous, giving people. They are watching to see if we give to those in need and are giving to establish God's covenant throughout the world. We are being watched to see if we are obedient to the gospel. If we truly believe this gospel, in order to get this message out, we will be givers. Our liberality will cause Christians and non-Christians alike to recognize our big God and rejoice.

THIRTEEN

THE RAVENS ARE COMING

Elijah the Tishbite, of the temporary residents of Gilead, said to Ahab, As the Lord, the God of Israel, lives, before Whom I stand, there shall not be dew or rain these years but according to My word.
And the word of the Lord came to him, saying,
Go from here and turn east and hide yourself by the brook Cherith, east of the Jordan.
You shall drink of the brook, and I have commanded the ravens to feed you there.
So he did according to the word of the Lord; he went and dwelt by the brook Cherith, east of the Jordan.
And the ravens brought him bread and flesh in the morning and bread and flesh in the evening, and he drank of the brook.
After a while the brook dried up because there was no rain in the land.
And the word of the Lord came to him:
Arise, go to Zarephath, which belongs to Sidon, and dwell there. Behold, I have commanded a widow there to provide for you.

> So he arose and went to Zarephath. When he came to the gate of the city, behold, a widow was there gathering sticks. He called to her, Bring me a little water in a vessel, that I may drink.
> As she was going to get it, he called to her and said, Bring me a morsel of bread in your hand.
> And she said, As the Lord your God lives, I have not a loaf baked but only a handful of meal in the jar and a little oil in the bottle. See, I am gathering two sticks, that I may go in and bake it for me and my son, that we may eat it—and die.
> Elijah said to her, Fear not; go and do as you have said. But make me a little cake of [it] first and bring it to me, and afterward prepare some for yourself and your son.
> For thus says the Lord, the God of Israel: The jar of meal shall not waste away or the bottle of oil fail until the day that the Lord sends rain on the earth.
> She did as Elijah said. And she and he and her household ate for many days.
> The jar of meal was not spent nor did the bottle of oil fail, according to the word which the Lord spoke through Elijah.
>
> 1 KINGS 17:1-16 (AMPC)

This is an extraordinary narrative of supernatural provision. Everything recounted in the Old Testament was told as an example for us today.

> Now all these things happened unto them for examples: and they are written for our admonition, upon whom the ends of the world are come.
>
> 1 CORINTHIANS 10:11

There is much to be learned from this story. The Holy Ghost described Elijah as "Elijah, the Tishbite." I find that humorous. I wonder if God would describe me today as Debbie, the underbite, or someone else as the overbite.

Elijah was a true prophet of God. What he said came to pass. He spoke the Word of the Lord as the very oracles of God. I have seen videos from the forties and fifties of men of God preaching in the days of "The Voice of Healing Revival." These men operated so precisely in the word of knowledge that they could tell people their doctor's names, the diseases with which they had been diagnosed, the times they arrived at the meetings, and the makes of the cars they arrived in. This supernatural word of knowledge would build such faith in the crowd and create such an air of expectancy. We are going to see that kind of accuracy again in the operation of the gifts of the Spirit. I have experienced that to a degree in several meetings. I want to be able to yield myself in a greater way to the gifts of the spirit.

God instructed Elijah to go to the brook Cherith. An important part of provision is obedience. The place of provision is the exact will and plan of God. You are safer in the middle of a war zone if you are in the will of God than on a peaceful southern farm out of His will. Don't think that you can walk in divine provision without obeying the Lord.

In verse 4, God told Elijah that the ravens would feed him. Do you realize that, typically, ravens are selfish scavengers? It's completely out of their character to deliver food to an individual. It would take God's intervention for them to do something like that. If God can command such creatures to be Elijah's provision, surely He can command anyone or anything to be yours.

Verse 6 related that the ravens brought Elijah bread and flesh in the morning and in the evening. We have no idea where the ravens got those delicacies. Did they sweep through a McDonald's drive-through and pick up a burger? If the details are not given, it is not necessary for us to know where they retrieved the bread and flesh. It *is* necessary to know that the ravens obeyed God, and Elijah benefited.

Verse 7 tells us that eventually, the brook dried up. Elijah couldn't complain about there being no rain in the land. He was the one who prophesied it. But Elijah could have felt that, at this point, God had let him down. He could have believed that God was teasing him with temporary provision, only to later pull the rug out from under him.

God *was not* teasing Elijah. He just didn't want Elijah to become dependent upon the ravens and the brook; they were temporary. Jehovah Jireh (the Lord our Provider) must always be our source. The same God who gave Elijah the brook was about to give him a better supply through something, or in this case, someone else. When one source dries up, prepare to get excited, not downcast. If you lost your job, look to God to give you something better. His plan does not include taking us from glory to defeat, but from glory to glory.

God expects us to look to Him as our source. Our source is not our family, employer, or the United States Government. Faith is not thinking that as long as your job lasts, you'll be okay. Jobs are temporary at best. If every single financial institution went under, our God is still on the throne. The Bible says that He owns the cattle on a thousand hills (Psalm 50:10). The earth is the Lord's and the fullness thereof (Psalm 24:1). God is our eternal source. He will not fail. God can always provide us with what we need, but we must look to Him and not our jobs for provision.

Next, God instructed Elijah to arise and go to Zarephath. In the Hebrew, the word *arise* means more than to stand up. The word *arise* involves preparation. God was saying, "Elijah, get ready for your next step of obedience in regard to your provision. It is going to be good, but you are going to have to get ready."

Your *getting ready* may involve many things. God may tell you to spend extra time in prayer. He may tell you to sow extra time or finances into others. For some, getting ready may mean going to the employment office and applying for a job. It may mean taking specific classes in preparation for the call and assignment that God has for you. God may tell you to go somewhere that makes no sense to you; however, it will be a divine appointment. Abraham left home not knowing where he was going, but

God had divine destiny in mind. Abraham would have missed his blessing if he had not obeyed.

If our temporary source has dried up, the one thing we must refuse to do is stay in bed with the covers pulled up over our heads, feeling sorry for ourselves. The Bible states that Elijah was a man of like passions as we are. This means that he experienced the same emotions we do. Elijah could have chosen the pity party route, but he didn't. Elijah was a man of obedience. No wonder he experienced God's supernatural provision time after time!

God told Elijah that He had commanded a widow woman to take care of him. God loves to take impossible situations and make them possible. He delights in using the most unlikely people in time of need. That way, everyone must recognize that it was God and only God. Consequently, God will receive all of the glory. We can take no credit for the miracle.

This happened to me in the early days of the Alaskan ministry. One day, upon arriving at my office, I was told that we had received five hundred dollars in the mail. Never before had we received such a large amount through the mail. After rejoicing, I inquired about who sent us the money, thinking some wealthy new contributor had hooked up with us.

What I found out next took me by surprise. I was told that one of the men from our prison ministry in Alaska was responsible. I almost went into a state of shock. I had never taught on stewardship or received an offering in that prison ministry. I was aware that those men made a maximum of about 40 dollars a month. So, I couldn't figure out where an inmate would get so much money. To tell you the truth, I was almost afraid to ask. I wondered if the prisoner had become involved in the prison Mafia or something.

It so happened that we were holding a service at that prison the next night. While there, I had the opportunity to ask the man where he had obtained that kind of money. The prisoner shared that he belonged to a native corporation of Alaska. Each person in the corporation had just received five thousand dollars. (Where, but in America, can you find prisoners receiving financial dividends from investments while serving their sentence?) He related that my ministry was the one that had been feeding him spiritually every week for almost three years, so he decided to tithe to us. Praise God! Our need was met through a most unlikely source.

God spoke to me that day and reminded me not to look to churches, offerings, or people for my supply. He instructed me to always keep my eyes upon Him, Jehovah Jireh, my Provider. God reminded me that He was able to bring in provision through the most unlikely sources. It might be a prisoner or a puppy dog bringing a brown paper sack full of money to my door. It did not have to be in the form or source that I was expecting or might even have preferred.

The Bible tells us that Elijah obeyed God and went to Zarapheth. There, he found the widow gathering sticks for her last meal. Things didn't look too promising. Nevertheless, Elijah asked the widow to bring him some water to drink. Most people would not consider that to be too bold. Most of us would probably give a stranger a cold cup of water on a hot day if he or she asked for it. However, remember that this was during a time of drought. He asked her for what was scarce and most precious to her. Elijah took another step in boldness. He asked the woman for something to eat as well. That was getting pretty gutsy, don't you think? After all, the woman didn't know him; she was starving, and he had not been invited to dinner. The widow responded by telling Elijah of her specific situation. She let Elijah know that she had only a little meal and oil left. She said she was gathering sticks to make a last meal for her and her son, and they were going to eat it and die.

What a desperate situation! God loves to take worst-case scenarios and turn them around for His glory. By recording this event in His holy Word, God is letting you know that if He could do this for her, He can do it for you. (It's just about time for you to shout!)

Elijah indicated to the widow that he realized her situation. Even so, he still asked that she give it to him first. What courage! In the natural, Elijah could have been embarrassed to insist that this woman give to him when she was in such dire circumstances. I am sure that Elijah had overwhelming compassion for her. However, there is a difference between compassion, sympathy, and empathy. Having sympathy for someone is simply feeling sorry for them and talking about their situation. Empathy understands how they feel in those circumstances. But sympathy and empathy never intervene. Compassion is a God thing that enables you to do something about the situation. It allows an individual to step into the miraculous, supernatural power of God and to be used by God to change someone else's circumstances.

Elijah could be bold because he knew that he was helping the widow. First-fruit giving is a principle of God's Word that runs from Genesis to Revelation. Her life would never be the same. It has been said that you can either give a man a fish to eat for the day or teach him how to fish for a lifetime. The widow would have had the same problems facing her the next day and the next, for as long as she lived. If, instead, Elijah could pass onto her the secrets of obedience and provision that he had learned, she could receive provision throughout the famine and the remainder of her newly extended life. Of course, the woman could not see the end result. It would be easy for any of us to obey if we knew for sure that everything would turn out all right. Anyone can do things by sight. It was faith that was required for this step of obedience. God requires faith and obedience when a situation looks impossible.

Verse 9 states that God had already spoken to the widow and commanded her to give to Elijah. Then, in verse 13, we find Elijah telling the widow, *"Fear not."* I would think that it would have been necessary to tell her that. Isn't it interesting that even when God has already spoken to us, our flesh still tends to respond in fear to His commandments? It is never an easy thing to step over into the supernatural realm and walk on the water.

Every time we attempt this, our flesh retaliates. Our mind tries to keep us attached to this earthly realm. Then, not only must we remind ourselves, we must surround ourselves with others who will remind us to "Fear not." We must think of God and others first. We gravitate toward wanting to give only after we are satisfied that our needs have been sufficiently met. However, we have been instructed to live after the Spirit and not after the flesh. To accomplish that, we have to tell our heads to shut up, and then we must do what our spirit tells us to do.

After Elijah's brief message of *"Fear not,"* the woman obeyed and gave to the man of God in total abandonment. She made Elijah a tasty dinner while she and her son watched him eat. If Elijah had dropped a crumb on his necktie, I am sure the boy would have reached out and grabbed it and eaten it. He was so very hungry. However, that did not happen.

As Elijah, the widow woman, and the boy were all obedient to God's principles of first-fruit giving, God's powerful hand was at work in the supernatural realm to bring His provision into their realm. The Bible tells us that *they all* had provisions for the remainder of the famine. The widow woman traded one meal for a continuous blessing. Thank God that everyone was obedient! Any one of them could have forfeited the plan of God along the way by simply failing to obey.

Let me share an example of giving in obedience to God's command in the middle of lack. In 1997, I was asked to be the conference speaker for the Assembly of God Women's Conference in Queensland, Australia. I was advised in that conversation that my hotel expenses and airfare would be paid, but I could only teach about and receive one love offering during the conference. Normally, I take care of my own expenses and expect to receive all of the offerings. However, when traveling to another country, I usually attempt to accept their protocol, just as I did in this case.

At the Australia State Conference, we had some of the most dynamic meetings I have ever experienced. We had one thousand women in attendance and received a miraculous offering. I was very pleased with the amount. Later, I was told that this particular offering was much more than the one they had received the previous year for the national conference with four thousand ladies. This was only the state conference.

When we left the United States, I did not tell anyone that our ministry account was drained. But I was quite anxious for the offering to be wired home immediately. When I was asked how I would like the offering to be dispensed, they indicated there would be no problem wiring the offering to my office. I didn't know how much time was required for the bank transfer, but I assumed that the funds would be in our ministry account within a day or two.

Next, I traveled on to another Australian church to hold meetings. I was informed that all of the offerings would come directly to me, and I again requested that the funds be wired directly into our stateside ministry account. On the last night of revival, the pastor was called out of town for an emergency, so his secretary transported us to the airport. She never mentioned the offerings, and I assumed the funds would be wired immediately. I moved on to the next church, thinking that two weeks of offerings were now deposited into our account back home. I thought wrong.

My office called to inform me that we had no more money in our account. When they inquired about the offerings, I told them what we had received. I had no idea why the funds had not yet arrived in our account, but I did not feel free to call and ask. I was in a foreign nation and certainly did not want to alienate anyone. So, I instructed the office to "keep on believing" with me. I went on to another church in Australia. I had a wonderful rapport with the pastors. In fact, we became so close that I felt I could talk with them about anything. I told them of our situation and asked if they could transfer our offerings immediately upon our departure. They said they understood the situation and would be glad to do so.

The night before my secretary and I were to leave, the Lord woke me up from a deep sleep. I heard Him say by way of the Holy Spirit's inward voice, "Give the entire week's offering back to the pastors so that they can go to Dr. Rodney Howard-Browne's campmeeting." I just about went into shock. I reminded the Lord that we were completely depleted of funds and that our other offerings had not yet arrived. I asked Him if He remembered that I was there in a foreign country obeying what He had called me to do?

The Bible tells us to present our case before the Lord.

> Come now, and let us reason together.
>
> ISAIAH 1:18

I did just that. I responded with, "Do You mean I should give back the morning offerings or the night offerings? Surely You can't mean the entire week's offerings, Lord, when we need them so desperately?" The Holy Spirit reminded me that he had never failed me, and He required total obedience. I immediately responded with, "I trust You, Lord. You have never let me down." I had to tell myself, "Fear not," just as Elijah had told the widow woman.

I must admit that I needed another confirmation. I woke up Katie, my assistant, and related to her what The Lord had just spoken to me. I knew that it would affect her paycheck, as well as mine. Part of me was hoping that she would argue with me about why we could not do that. (Yes, even after hearing from The Lord, I sometimes had second thoughts, but I have learned over time not to second-guess). Katie responded with, "That's awesome, Miss Debbie. We need a huge miracle. Let's do it." Katie was born-again and filled with the Holy Spirit under my ministry and never knew religion. She was taught freedom, prosperity, and healing from day one, so she never questioned anything about giving. I was so proud of her, even though the flesh side of me was almost hoping she would argue with me.

The next morning, when the pastor's wife came to take us to the airport, I asked her if her husband had wired the money yet. When she said that he was just getting ready to do so, I inquired whether they had ever had a desire to go to Dr. Howard-Browne's campmeeting. (Yes, I was still testing what I had heard.) She answered that before I came and held revival, they had never considered it. However, I created a hunger in them for more of God, and they decided that they wanted to attend a campmeeting. She further related that they had been sowing heavily into my offerings. They held hands the night before and specifically named their seed. They told the Lord that they wanted to go to the campmeeting. I laughed and told her that God awakened me in the night, instructing me to give back all of the offerings. She wept for joy. It was an awesome moment.

I didn't quite know how I was going to break the news to my office staff. They had always been so good about believing with me for finances and had never questioned my giving. Still, with no money in the account and their paychecks overdue, the offerings would have provided enough to pay them. It is one thing to give away your salary. It's quite another to give your staff's salary, as well. I knew that the staff would be calling soon, and sure enough, they did.

They started the conversation by saying that they had some news. I said that I had some news as well, but I wanted to hear theirs first. I was informed that the funds from the Women's Conference had arrived, as well as the wire from the next three churches in Australia. We had also received money from several other nations that same day. Some of these other offerings were from places I had gone to a year or so before. We don't usually receive additional offerings from places a year later. It was as though we suddenly hit a financial gusher from all around the world.

When I asked when the funds had arrived, I found that it was exactly at the time I had given the week's offering back to the church. I knew it was not a coincidence. There is something about obedience, faith, and trust at the midnight hour that brings about great reward. Your flesh will always try to get into fear if you allow it to. However, the more you need the blessing, the less you can afford to procrastinate in giving.

The next year, I got to see my dear Australian friends at Dr. Rodney Howard-Browne's campmeeting. I was thrilled to see them there. I have learned that giving in a time of lack is both rewarding and fulfilling. Usually, it seems that at the times I am called to give, I need the funds more than the people to whom I am giving. But the truth is, the more I need those funds, the more I need to give them. That is a God principle! God always rewards that type of giving. Every time I give, I move up higher in faith. I wouldn't trade that kind of obedience and giving for anything. I encourage you to discover the excitement of living in this faith realm. You will be blessed as never before.

FOURTEEN

BROKEN ONCE AGAIN

God continually asks me to break open alabaster boxes. The test of my heart that I am about to tell you was one that cost greatly and produced great dividends.

It began in March 2002. I returned to Tampa from the state of Washington, where I had held revival meetings for a month. I was exhausted and had gone without sleep for two days. My plane had been delayed, and I finally arrived on a Sunday morning. Without having time to unpack, I went straight to our Sunday morning service at The River at Tampa Bay. I was determined to not miss church. I love our church and need to be refreshed to have more to give out, and I would only be home this one week. So, I commanded my flesh to stay awake and go.

I was invited to come to the platform and testify about the things God was doing in my meetings. I was so honored but also so exhausted that I asked God for help to deliver something that made sense. He did. He is so very faithful. I thought, "I only have to hang on until church is over, and I can go home and sleep for a few hours." After church, I was also invited for fellowship and dinner with Pastors Rodney and Adonica Howard-Browne. Pastor Rodney then told me about a conference he was invited to preach the following day in Tennessee. He then asked me if I would like to accompany his team to the conference and preach on stewardship for him. Even though it was now 2 a.m. and the trip would require another sleepless night, I replied that I would be honored to attend. I departed for my house and realized that I would have to unpack and subsequently repack in a short amount of time and then meet his team at the airport. I knew that God had something very special for me at this meeting, and I would obey Him at any cost to my flesh.

On the way to the meeting, Pastor Rodney and I were engaged in conversation. We were discussing the great things God had done in all of our lives and ministries over the last year. We talked about where we're headed and the harvest of souls. Before landing, he looked at me and asked me a question. He said, "Debbie, I heard you say once that you have always wanted a Corvette. Why don't you buy one?" I told him I had priced them, and they should have three bedrooms and a living room for that price. I told him I could cut back on some of my giving and buy one, but I was determined to give more every year. Before I could finish my sentence, I heard him begin to pray, "Lord, You know her heart, and You've watched her sowing over the years. She does not heap finances upon her own lusts but gives to your kingdom. I believe You'll allow her to have the one thing she's desired since she was a child. Lord, I ask You to either bless her with a vehicle that she can trade in on a Corvette or the down payment for it." I was startled. I've never heard Pastor Rodney pray quite like that before. He prays for the harvest and the funds to bring it in.

Our jet landed in Tennessee just moments after he prayed that prayer. That evening, as Pastor Rodney was preaching, a man walked over to where I was sitting and sat down beside me. He began to prophesy to me. "Debbie, God told me to tell you that He's seen your giving over the years. If you think you've seen a harvest thus far, you haven't seen anything yet. God is about to open up the windows of Heaven for you and pour out a blessing like nothing you've ever known. As a token of that, the Lord spoke to me to give you my car. It's a Mercedes car that is a few years old and in good condition. I believe that you can get about $10,000 to $12,000 for it." My mouth dropped open. It had only been about an hour since Pastor Rodney prayed the prayer that no one knew about except God and me. I wrote out a $1,000 check for a tithe ahead of time and gave it to Pastor. I was expecting to receive $10,000 or so for the car. Before I left the meeting, another minister called me and said that he was Chris's best friend and wanted to buy his car from me. Instead of him driving it to Tampa from Houston, this other preacher would buy it from him and just send me the check. It would be waiting for me by the time I got home. He only offered me $9,000, but I no longer had the hassle of all the legalities. Also, I would rather tithe too much ahead of time because my God blesses me too much ahead of time.

I began to look on the web for Corvettes, hoping to find a used one with low mileage. I knew that I would save a lot of money going that route. I found several, but they were not the color I had dreamed of since I was five years old. My heart was set on a red convertible with a black interior. The Holy Spirit spoke to me and said, "If I've done all of this for you, do you think that I can't give you the color you want?" I continued to look, and then I saw it. Right before my eyes was a 2001 metallic red convertible with a black leather interior and only 6,000 miles on the odometer. They were asking about $7,000 less for it than a new one, and I bargained with them to drop the price another $5,000. Along with the down payment, I was able to purchase a Chevrolet Corvette for a reasonable, normal car payment.

I sent my secretary to pick up the car for me. I was scheduled to be in a revival for another few weeks and would not be able to see the car right away. I called Pastor Rodney and told him that I had instructed my secretary to take the car to him. I wanted him to be able to drive it before I did. It was part of my first fruits. He did not want to drive it first but finally called me one evening, and I could hear the wind blowing as he told me it was a nice car with a lot of horses under the hood.

I arrived at Tampa International Airport a few weeks later. Upon exiting the terminal building, my eyes beheld a shiny, red Corvette convertible. My secretary had it waiting for me. I began to weep. Please do not misunderstand this. I wasn't weeping over a car, Corvette or not. I hope no Christian would ever be so overcome by something like a car. No, it was what that car represented to me. It was only a symbol to remind me that a big God could take a woman with a totaled car, living with other people, restore her, heal her, send her all over the world, and bless her socks off. I was weeping for joy as I thought of all the things He had brought me through and how He had blessed me. I never chased after a car or any other material thing. I have been chasing after God, obeying Him, and preaching His gospel. I never have even taken the time to exercise faith to ask Him for things. I have been seeking His Kingdom and righteousness, and all of these *blessings* were starting to chase me down.

When I was just a child, I was enamored with red Corvettes. I know that may be somewhat unusual for a little girl. It is the only natural thing that I can ever remember saying that I hoped to have someday. I had almost forgotten about it and would never have asked God for it since I have matured in Him. However, God never forgot.

I am away from home so much in revival that I don't have time to drive any car much. When I did, though, it was my "Calgon, take me away," moment! I put the top down, drove to the beach, smelled the ocean, and thanked God for my wonderful life! My family and friends remember the horrible cars I used to have in pre-revival days. They also remember the vehicles I have given away and bought for others when I could have had a nice car for myself years earlier. They have seen the reward of the Lord, and it has been a witness to them.

I decided that I enjoyed driving my car more than I even enjoyed my home. I told several close friends that if I had to make a decision between my car and my home, I would have to choose my car. It was a dream come true, and I was refreshed every time that I drove it.

In April of 2003, I was once again home in Tampa. On a beautiful Sunday evening, I had my top down on the 'vette and was headed to church at The River. I was busy worshipping God and thanking Him for His presence and the many blessings in my life. I couldn't wait to get into the service and be refreshed after being out on the revival trail.

Pastor Rodney decided to teach on giving for a few minutes before his main message. His text was I Chronicles 29. He talked about King David setting his affection on the house of his God. I was listening intently. I began to say to the Lord, within my heart, "Lord, I've heard him teach this several times before. I've taught it myself hundreds of times. However, I want to receive fresh manna tonight. Speak to my heart. I want to hear what I've never heard before and see what I've never seen before. I must go to another level. There are billions of people to be reached in the harvest. I want to reach them, and I want to be able to fund the end-time harvest. Speak to me through this teaching, Lord." Oh, my friend, *did He ever!*

I heard Pastor Rodney make a statement and then pose a question. He said, "God had access to David's personal treasure. Does He have access to yours?" I replied on the inside, 'Oh yes, Lord. You know You have access to my personal treasure.' What I heard next riveted throughout my heart, soul, and body. "Debbie, would you give Me your dream car?" After only a moment's hesitation, I replied, "Yes, Lord, You can have anything that I have." He said, "All right, I want you to give Me your car." God gave it to me to begin with and if He had use for it, I was going to give it to Him. I began to weep and continued to do so all through the teaching. I was going to put my keys in the offering but then realized that there was some preparatory work to be done first.

I didn't tell anyone what God spoke to me. I decided to take a week to pray and know that my commitment to Him was solid and unshakeable. I wanted to do this with no regrets. I didn't want it to be based on an emotional decision. I decided to purchase the CD by Cee Cee Winans with the song "The Alabaster Box" on it. I played that song repeatedly for days. I wept again and again as I heard her sing, "You weren't there the night He found me. You weren't there when He put His loving arms around me. You don't know the cost of the oil in my alabaster box." Finally, the day arrived when I knew it was time to break open the most precious alabaster box that I have ever broken open over my Lord.

It was a bright and sunny Florida day. I hired someone to come out and detail my car. It was sparkling. The red metallic with gold flecks picked up those sunbeams like no other paint could. The black leather was so shiny that it looked like it was wet. There was no flaw inside or out. I took all of my belongings out of the trunk and removed all of my CDs except for one that I knew would be played one last time for the very special event. When everything was ready, I went into my home and retrieved another smaller alabaster box. My most prized possession in my house was a Thomas Kinkade painting, and I put it in the trunk of the Corvette. I made a phone call next. "Pastor, is it all right if I come out tonight to your home? I have something to show you and Pastor Adonica." Now, there was just one thing left to do. I asked a dear friend to drive out there with me so that I would have transportation to come back home. I had already asked my secretary if she would transport me in her older truck whenever I needed to go somewhere. I had bought three vehicles for other people by this time and knew that I was not in a position to take out another loan for another car. Besides, I'm not home often anyway. I had allowed my youngest son to buy my other car, and I now only had the Corvette, so I knew that I had to be transported by someone else for a while. I didn't care. Tonight, I would break open my treasure for my God.

It was a long drive that night. The evening was perfect. The sun was setting, and the air temperature was about 70 degrees. The wind was blowing through my hair. The car was never running smoother. I was compelled to challenge its speed and power one last time, for just a few seconds, as I passed my friend on the interstate. Then I slowed my pace and put the song on again, "You don't know the cost of the oil in my alabaster box." No one did. The pain of years of abuse, the memories of a broken family because of my ex-husband's sin, living away from my sons, and lonely nights on the road. Oh, but in comparison with what I had been given, it was all dung. I had been called, restored, healed, blessed, and received joy unspeakable and full of glory. I am a revival carrier. The precious anointing of the Holy Ghost, that tangible, transmittable empowerment, has run down my head. I have peace that passes understanding. I commune with my Lord in sweet fellowship and intimacy. I will spend eternity with Him on streets of gold with gates of pearls. I am a nation-shaker and a water-walker. I get to stand in awe of His glory as I watch people come to Christ, get baptized in the Holy Ghost and with fire, see bodies healed and marriages restored. My cost is relatively small in comparison. Besides, my Lord and King paid the supreme cost for me with His very own blood. No, this is not as costly as my flesh would try to make me believe. I would smash open this box and let it run down my Jesus. Then, I will wipe His feet with my hair.

Upon arrival at the Howard-Browne house, I asked them if they would walk outside with me for a moment. I knew that they were wondering what this was all about. The moment had come. First, I asked them to listen to just two lines out of the *Alabaster Box* song. I then took the Kinkade painting out of my trunk and gave it to them. I thanked them for all that they had imparted into my life and for believing in the call of God upon my life. Tears filled their eyes, and now my real breaking began. I told them that the print was the lesser part of the alabaster box and now, I would break the rest. I held out my hand, which was embracing a key. Pastor Rodney looked confused and asked what I was doing. I told him that someone came to Alaska eleven years ago preaching the Word of God. That someone offered me a key to breakthrough. It was a key to unlock the prison I was in. It was a prison of poverty, insecurity, rejection, and pain. Joy and blessings have been a part of my life ever since that day. The key he handed me was one of giving. I've never been the same since. Now, I wanted to break open an alabaster box in gratitude to my Lord. He would have access to my private treasure. I poured that night upon Jesus through the ministry that has sowed into my life so much.

Pastor Rodney and Adonica's eyes swelled with tears. Their gaze was one of humility and thankfulness. My pastor made me a proposition. He said, "I will accept this gift on one condition. Thank you for this Corvette. It is now mine. However, I travel so much myself. I really don't have time to drive it, and I already have the vehicles I need. I will only accept this if you will agree to let a good evangelist friend of mine take care of it for me." I began to wonder who that might be when I heard him say, "She's a wonderful woman of God." At that moment, I had a realization that he was sending the car back home with me. I was disappointed and then crushed. I insisted that it was imperative for me to break my alabaster box. I had prayed about it, thought about it, made the commitment, and then acted upon it. Now, he was rejecting it. I began to cry. Then I heard him say,

"Debbie, you did break it open and pour out. We accept this, and God accepts it. I'm only asking you to take care of it for me. I promise to come and get it from you every once in a while." I finally agreed to the terms. I seemed to have no choice.

I would have gladly sold the car and put the money into the ministry if that had been an option. Unfortunately, it was not. The car was not paid for and wouldn't be for a few years. This was all I could do to break my box and pour.

A few minutes later, I found myself driving down the highway, heading toward my home. I could not believe that I was still behind the wheel of that car. I began to weep and pour my heart out to the Lord. I told Him how much I had wanted to give that car in holy worship that night. I told Him that nothing can compare with Him in my life. I told the Lord that it was imperative for me to go to another level in Him. Deep was calling unto deep, and I loved Him more that night than ever before. I told Him that I had so wanted to pour my love and thanksgiving out upon Him. Then I heard these words in my spirit, "Debbie, you did. I saw it. The angels of Heaven witnessed it. So did the devils in Hell. Yes, Debbie, you broke it, poured and wiped My feet with your hair, and, yes, I am taking you to another level. It doesn't matter that the car will rest in your garage. I saw you give it. You released it. I know that I have access to your private treasure. I know that things do not have you. That's why I can trust you with them from time to time. You have passed another test. Come on up higher. I want to pour My blessings through you. You're asking Me for the nations and the heathen for your inheritance. You want the harvest. That is going to take great finances, and you must be proven faithful before I can allow them to flow through our hands. If you always keep your heart like it is tonight, I will continue to pour through you."

I don't know what your alabaster box is or what God will require of you. God asked Abraham for his only son, Isaac, to be placed on the altar. That symbolic sacrifice would be played out years later as God would be obligated to give His only Son in covenant with us. God doesn't need our sacrifice but wants to give us His best and is prepared to see how far we will go in commitment with Him. It is worth more than anything that He asks of us. I would encourage you to allow Him access to every chamber of your heart, including your private treasure.

This is an interesting postscript to this story. Pastor Rodney had me take the Corvette back home, but he could not stay out of the way of God's blessing. It is no coincidence that he now owns two Corvettes. One is a vintage 1961 red and white Corvette. It has been restored to look brand new. The other is a 2019 Z06. Both were given to him, paid in full. He sent my car back home with me and received two in its place. That is just like our God.

FIFTEEN

THE TWO STREAMS COMING TOGETHER

> And Othniel the son of Kenaz, Caleb's younger brother, took
>   it: and he gave him Achsah his daughter to wife.
> And it came to pass, when she came to him, that she moved
>   him to ask of her father a field: and she lighted from off
>   her ass; and Caleb said unto her, What wilt thou?
> And she said unto him, Give me a blessing: for thou hast
>   given me a south land; give me also springs of water. And
>   Caleb gave her the upper springs and the nether springs.
>
> JUDGES 1:13-15

This is a powerful teaching that Pastor Rodney Howard-Browne did some years ago. He originally got it from Evangelist Reinhard Bonnke. Reinhard Bonnke relayed a story about his life and ministry to Pastor Rodney. The famous German evangelist to Africa's ministry began in Lesotho, South Africa. He had a divine irritation. In the beginning, he had an office that he paid $50.00 a month for rent. He often did not have the money for it in those beginning days. He needed a miracle, and God talked to Him about the two streams.

The Lord spoke to Evangelist Bonnke about both streams. In the natural realm, there are two streams. The upper stream is a visible one that you can see with your eyes. In the natural, that is a running stream that you can see. The Lord was talking to Reinhard about finances. Those, like a stream of water, can be seen with your natural eyes. There is also a lower stream. In the natural, you cannot see underground streams until they come to the surface. Those can be streams of water, minerals, oil, etc. You can't see it with the natural eye. God told the evangelist that spiritually, that represents the anointing. We need both in this hour, the anointing and the finances, to bring the anointing to the people. The two streams need to come together more than ever before in this hour of the end-time church.

Evangelist Bonnke told Pastor Rodney that he had never taught what God spoke to him, and Pastor Rodney said it was so powerful that it needed to be taught, and he would start teaching it. Now, I am passing it on to you.

God told Pastor Rodney, "In the last days, the two streams shall merge to reap the great end-time harvest of souls." Finances are the anointing of the flesh, the empowering, enablement, and ability to complete our assignment. It doesn't take long to see that we can't do anything in ministry without the money. Pastor asked God why the church doesn't have unlimited finances.

The Lord told him that people would go on without God to do stupid things like build water parks, etc. There are leeches that purposely come around ministries. They are parasites and vampires to the body of Christ. They sometimes call themselves the ministry of helps, but they do everything but help. They are disguised as CPAs, Christian sound companies, lawyers, media advertisers, etc. They are anything that supplies services to the church. Today, we have music ministries that won't worship unless they are paid. Some people wouldn't come to church unless they were paid. That makes them spiritual prostitutes!

There was a company in New York City that came around Pastors Rodney and Adonica when they were doing their huge soul-winning crusade in New York City in 1999. The company tried to charge them $750,000.00 to send out a newsletter to help with funding for the crusade. They formulated a letter that said Pastor Rodney was on a forty-day fast. He told them that he was not, and they told him that the people didn't need to know that. They were liars, and Pastor Rodney fired them on the spot. That is why every letter that comes out of Pastor Rodney's ministry or mine is personally written by us. We can't take people's gifts lightly. They are holy. You can't just do what you want to do with it. If you want to lose the anointing, all you have to do is touch the money. You will be dead before you know it. There haven't been unlimited funds because God can't trust hearts. When the just get just, we'll have what we need. Motives must become pure. We must pray, "God, don't give me any slack."

Another problem is that the body of Christ gets motivated to give into trinkets. I was in a nation where they were promising that whoever gave a certain amount would receive a plastic statue that looked like one of the toys from a McDonald's "Happy Meal." It was supposed to be a statue of one of the valiant judges in the Bible, Barak. Another year that I was there, they were offering a reward for people who would buy so many square meters of the church floor. I know of evangelists who are always asking people to give for a certain article that they would be purchasing on the foreign field for a pastor, such as a bus or a motorcycle. I have been amazed to see how quickly people will run to give thousands. Yet, I and many others are purchasing the same things for pastors in the foreign field out of our ministry finances without asking for someone to purchase them directly. We should not be manipulated to give to receive a piece of The Old Rugged Cross, a shower cap of blessing from the Jordon River, or some oil from Israel. We need to teach people to give only as holy worship unto The Lord.

We do need finances to continue the work of The Lord Jesus Christ, and people must understand that. Even in the natural, people such as Bill Gates are equipped to do what others can't. However, you cannot judge success by money. You can be rich and go straight to Hell. One hurricane can blow it all away in a moment. There are certain places money can go, but then it stops.

God's money must have pure hearts to operate in these areas. We, as ministers and Christians, have to be so careful to not let people control or bribe us with finances. Pastor Rodney has told a story about something that happened before he left South Africa to come to the United States. He was in need of finances to make the trip. He thought about how some ministers that he knew had wealthy partners to help fund their ministries. He was talking to The Lord about how it would be so helpful to have a wealthy person contribute or partner with him.

Shortly after that, a wealthy man invited him to a steak dinner at a very nice restaurant. He told him that he believed in his ministry and wanted to help him. He handed him a check for $10,000.00, and that was in the 1980s when it went a lot further. He also told him that he would provide spending money for the trip, a first-class ticket to America, food, etc. Pastor Rodney was thrilled and thought, "This is what I have been believing for." Something happened next that changed everything! The man introduced his son to Pastor Rodney and told him that he was a good preacher. He asked only one thing: that Pastor Rodney would take his son with him and let him preach with him. Pastor thanked him, returned the check, and paid for the dinner himself. He realized that the man would have owned him because he bought him. Pastor Rodney refused to be bribed and do something God did not want. He learned that early on, and it has remained with him.

We know what the Bible says. Your gift will make room for you. We don't need people to open doors. Our God will do it. Remember that with your ministry, you'll get the money, but you can't get a ministry with money. We are a servant to all, but a slave to none. There are many people who think and say that the ministry is easy. Then, they need to go out and have one. They will find out that is not the case. We all need to have people to encourage us, give, pray for us, and come alongside and work with us. When you give someone money, you're anointing and enabling them. In this final hour, the two streams must come together, and people will give with purity, with no strings attached. This will make one powerful, operational church that the gates of Hell shall not prevail against. We will have the anointing and the money to do it.

People in the business world have their own opinions about what the minister should be doing with the money. They don't realize that they have just as much responsibility. It is true that those in ministry will receive a higher condemnation, according to the Word of God in James 3:1. Yet, it does not exempt everyone else. Every single one will have a part to play in the end-time harvest. Just like ministers have to be anointed to bring in the harvest, people in the natural must be anointed to do it. They have to be entrusted. Can God trust you with it? Everyone has to be tested and will be. You will write out exams. Even if God blessed you, you could go back to being selfish. The root problem has to be dealt with. People forget God quickly. Don't forget where He brought you from. Be grateful for everything. The sky is the limit, but you have to make a covenant with God that you will use it for His kingdom. He's going to raise up multi-millionaires out of obscurity to fund the end-time harvest. God will give us creative and witty inventions.

People want to be trusted with the anointing but can't even be trusted with finances.

The only purpose of this spring is for the other spring, the supernatural anointing. Money can't extend your life or keep you out of Hell. We won't think of swapping the pearl of great price, the anointing, for money.

Some took a vow of poverty because of personal conviction that the church was so corrupt. Denominations exist that sell salvation to people. They say they are absolving people for a price. If people have to take a vow of poverty to make sure they make it to Heaven, we shouldn't have a problem with that. However, it doesn't have to be one or the other.

We are not required to make that choice. God's not opposed to you being blessed—but the heart must be pure. The problem we've had with the two streams coming together is that when one comes, people get distracted. Without enough anointing, the best of them have become corrupt. When genuine motive turns to greed, people lose the anointing.

The upper stream is there to help me take the lower (heavenly) stream. There's a responsibility connected with the two streams. Every day, you must check your motive and be careful who you let around you or their motive will get on you. When you want true riches, the other has to follow.

The more money you get, the more you pray. There will be twice as much temptation to pull you away. You think that you are comfortable and safe while driving in a ditch. We need God to continually touch us, purify us, and show us anything that we are not aware of in ourselves.

We need to understand what the lower stream is. You can walk on a field and not know what's in there. There could be oil, gas, copper, gold, diamonds, magnesium, or water. Water can be hidden. Sometimes, there is an oasis in the middle of a desert. This is a generation that will ask for both the upper and lower streams. God can bless us when we have pure motives. It's all about focus because there are many distractions.

Jesus said if you can't be trusted with unrighteous mammon, who will entrust to you the true riches? We must remember that everything we have is God's. You can lose it all overnight. We are just custodians. John chapter 4 and chapter 7 distinguish between springs and a river flowing out of your belly. This river can't be blocked. Underneath streams must be unblocked for the two to come together. The flowing together of the two streams must happen. It is important that we understand the assignment of both the kings and the priests. Neither can do it without the other. The kings are to rule in the administration of things. They have wealth to draw from their kingdom for God's kingdom. The kings are those who are anointed for business to generate funds for God's eternal Kingdom. If it were only for a natural kingdom, it would be so very futile. The church hasn't known how to treat the rich. The priests are anointed to bring in God's harvest and to do the work of the ministry. The priests are those who've been called and anointed to preach the Good News for God's eternal Kingdom. We cannot have one without the other. We need both to get the job done.

Many know of the great revivalist Charles Finney. What few know is that two brothers, called the Tappin Brothers, underwrote his crusades. They paid all of his expenses. That great harvest will be laid up to their account. Those who go and preach, along with those who fund it, will receive of the harvest together. The Bible speaks of women of substance who supported Jesus' ministry.

> And certain women, which had been healed of evil spirits and infirmities, Mary called Magdalene, out of whom went seven devils,
> And Joanna the wife of Chuza Herod's steward, and Susanna, and many others, which ministered unto him of their substance.
>
> LUKE 8:2-3

Evangelist Reinhard Bonnke had partners. One businessman supplied one million dollars for each of the two crusades. What a reward that he will have waiting for him. It is time to see 100 million souls and get into billions of dollars to reach the world for Jesus. There is not enough time to go around with people's $50 donations. They are appreciated, but we don't have enough time or finances to get the job done with those kinds of contributions coming in. The Lord's going to take the church where no offering can go. God has told Pastor Rodney more than once that as long as He can trust him with anything, He'll never lack for anything. God is our source, our provider, our everything. He is going to bring the two streams together in this final hour.

SIXTEEN

PUTTING OUT THE VESSELS

Now the wife of a son of the prophets cried to Elisha, Your servant my husband is dead, and you know that your servant feared the Lord. But the creditor has come to take my two sons to be his slaves.

Elisha said to her, What shall I do for you? Tell me, what have you [of sale value] in the house? She said, Your handmaid has nothing in the house except a jar of oil.

Then he said, Go around and borrow vessels from all your neighbors, empty vessels—and not a few.

And when you come in, shut the door upon you and your sons. Then pour out [the oil you have] into all those vessels, setting aside each one when it is full.

So she went from him and shut the door upon herself and her sons, who brought to her the vessels as she poured the oil.

When the vessels were all full, she said to her son, Bring me another vessel. And he said to her, There is not a one left. Then the oil stopped multiplying.

Then she came and told the man of God. He said, Go, sell

> the oil and pay your debt, and you and your sons live on the rest.
>
> 2 KINGS 4:1-7 (AMPC)

This story is another marvelous example of God providing in the midnight hour. The widow's situation seemed hopeless. Life as she had known it was over. She was about to lose her sons to slavery because of debt. The Holy Spirit made sure that this true-life story was recorded for our example to let us know that He will work a miracle in your life, just as He did for this destitute widow.

In this passage, the first thing I noticed was that this widow cried to the man of God. We often exalt our problems above God's Word and His promises. When you magnify the problem, you diminish God. When we dwell on the problem and talk about the problem, we block God's hand of provision. We make our problem bigger than God's Word. We all may have a moment of crying, but that cry needs to change into a declaration of God's promises and faithfulness.

The widow began by stating the obvious: she was broke, and the creditors were coming to take her children into slavery. Her husband had been a part of the school of the prophets. Elisha was already aware that her husband was dead. She reminded Elisha that she and her husband had loved and served God. They obviously had not expected things to turn out this way. The woman ended with a word that is all too often misapplied. That word is "But." She should have turned her "but" around. Too many people in the body of Christ have never turned their "but" around. When we receive a bad report in any way, whether a medical diagnosis, a financial report of how we are going under, or any other negative report, we need to turn the "but" around and declare what God says. "I know what you are saying, doctor, but my Bible says that with the stripes of Jesus, I was healed. I understand what you are saying, Mr. Banker, but my God says that He will meet my every need according to His riches in glory by Christ Jesus." Too many people do just the opposite. When they are told what The Word of God says about a particular situation, they say, "I know that book says that, but the doctor and the banker say this. My symptoms declare something else. I know that I should believe what God says above everything else, but I believe what man says about my circumstances." It is imperative that you turn your "but" around.

The truth is, the widow was beginning to question and accuse God. She was insinuating that even though she and her husband had done everything correctly in their lives, nothing had worked out. Her husband had died, leaving her a widow who lost her means of support and was about to lose her children. Had she continued in that vein, she would have indeed lost them. However, the woman changed. Someday, you're going to have to shake the dust off your feet and begin to believe in God and cooperate with Him. You must give God an opportunity to work on your behalf. That is what this widow finally did, and that is what revival is all about—change!

Elisha responded by asking the widow what he could do for her. While the question might sound inappropriate, what Elisha was really trying to do was get the woman's attention. He wanted to involve her cooperation, faith, confession, and heart. To the natural mind, God's principles and ways never make sense. God's ways are right side up, and ours are upside down. God says you must give to have, die to live, lose your life to save it, take the backseat to be moved to the front, turn the other cheek when someone hits you, give extra to the one who steals from you, and serve to lead.

It is impossible to walk in the supernatural realm with natural principles. While your flesh will always recoil at obeying God, the rewards reaped are so worth it. Before the widow could say anything, Elisha helped guide her to correct thinking. He asked the widow if she had anything in her house that could be sold.

Verse 2 is a pivotal verse in this story. In that verse, the widow told Elisha that she had nothing at all in the house except a bottle of oil. The key lies in the reality that we are not talking about what could be done in the natural but in the supernatural realm. God needs only a little something to work with. What He desires is our cooperation. In the Old Testament, He promises to bless whatever His people put their hand to.

Then, in the New Testament, Jesus took a little boy's lunch and fed thousands. Again, He seemed to need only a little bit to work with. God is the great Miracle Worker, the Multiplier, and the One who makes a way when there is no way. The interesting thing is that there is also a practical side to this kind of giving. When the amount that you have is not enough to meet the need you have, you might as well sow it. Let God do something with those funds and watch as they are multiplied.

There were many times in this ministry that we only had about five hundred dollars when we needed thousands. I have learned that, in each case, it's almost easier to just give it to God and let Him work a miracle. Five hundred dollars would not even make a dent in paying our bills or making payroll for the many staff members. So, it is very easy for the five hundred dollars to become a good seed for a larger harvest.

Several years ago, I was holding a two-week revival in the state of Washington. At the end of the first week, the pastor came to me with excitement in his voice. He was ecstatic that his people were giving so well. He made an announcement that nine hundred dollars had already come in the offering. I could tell that the amount was more than he usually had come in, or he would not have been that excited. I didn't want to dampen his joy, so I put a smile on my face and said, "Hallelujah." However, I was in a bit of shock. Even then, we were used to receiving at least several thousand dollars a week. Our basic budget required that much. Plane tickets for four people flying in from Alaska were much more than nine hundred dollars, let alone our room and board, office rent, payroll, etc. However, while I knew that we would need much more than that, I did not let the pastor know. It is important that we let our needs be known to God, not man. Put the demand *on the anointing*, not *on the people*. Put your trust in God, not man. More importantly, refuse to become a beggar.

> I have been young, and now am old; yet have I not seen the righteous forsaken, nor his seed begging bread.
>
> PSALM 37:25

That night, while praying about what to preach, the Lord spoke to me. He said, "I want you to give five hundred dollars to that little village ministry in Wiseman, Alaska." I was totally shocked. In the first place, I was not praying about what to give but about what to preach. Secondly, I did not even know the people involved in that ministry. I once received a newsletter that I had glanced at and then thrown into my desk. From that newsletter, I knew that the ministry was located above the Arctic Circle, and the couple that had just gone to head it was of retirement age. As I read about their work, I concluded that they had to have been either directed by the Holy Ghost or insane. Ha! I also noticed that they had experienced a flood and were hand-building new bridges.

Now, it's one thing to fly in and out of the villages doing evangelistic work as I do; it's another to actually live there. My hat was off to them. I remember thinking as I read the newsletter that I would probably sow into them someday. I had no idea, however, that the day I would be called upon to sow, in my own time of need, would be so difficult.

I found myself saying to God, "Lord, the last time I checked, we only had five hundred thirty dollars in the ministry account. If I give five hundred, that will only leave us thirty dollars. You already heard what the pastor told me about the offering; we don't even have enough to cover our plane tickets. Now, You want me to give the little that we have? Also, I don't even really know who these people are. How do I even know they are good ground in which to sow?"

Isn't it amazing how stupid we can get when we are talking to God? He is so patient with us. God simply answered, "I know exactly how much you have in your account. You do not have to inform Me of that. Do you think that I would ask you to give to them if they were not good ground? I only require your obedience."

With repentance, I responded, "Lord, I know that You know my account balance. I didn't mean to imply that You didn't. It's just that Your Word says, 'Come now, and let us reason together.' I was just trying to present my case before You. However, I will not reason any longer. I will simply obey You."

I called my office and instructed them to send the five hundred dollars out to the village ministry immediately. Then I asked how much we had in our account, and sure enough, the confirmed amount was five hundred thirty dollars, leaving us with just thirty dollars. Thank God that He seems to allow us to keep just enough in our bank account to keep it open. That way, we don't have to go through all of the paperwork necessary to open another account time after time.

I started the second week of revival in complete faith. In the natural, I should have been terrified, but I wasn't. I had seen my God be so very faithful time and time again, and I knew that He would never fail me. We had approximately the same number of people in attendance the second week as the first. Usually, when the same people give for two straight weeks, the giving goes down, not up. However, at the end of the second week, I was informed that five thousand dollars had been received in offerings. Hallelujah! Talk about a miracle. I don't believe that it's any coincidence that we gave five hundred dollars and received five thousand. What an awesome and big God we serve. Obedience has great rewards in every realm. Each time that you have an opportunity to act on faith and see its rewards, faith grows.

In verse 3 of this story, Elisha told the widow to go and borrow vessels. He didn't stop there but said, "And not a few." Once again, that sounds just like our God. It is His way of saying that when you expect a miracle, don't expect a "barely-getting-you-by miracle." Expect a big one! God is not the God of barely getting by, but El Shaddai, the God of more than enough, the God of plenty. If you already have to get God involved just to get you by, you might as well really get Him involved. Believe for that great miracle. If you have to pray and ask Him for a way to put groceries on the table, then pray and believe for enough to put groceries on someone else's table as well. Put out a lot of vessels.

God has given me an example to which people can relate, demonstrating a type of putting out vessels. A number of years ago, I was involved in competitive power weightlifting. I competed in three different events: the bench press, the squat, and the deadlift. I was a lot slimmer in those competition days than I am now. At a weight of only 114 pounds, I did a 130-pound bench press, a 175-pound squat, and a 180-pound deadlift. I succeeded in winning over a dozen trophies while competing.

Rhema Bible Training Center in Broken Arrow, Oklahoma, had just completed its new gym. After graduating from that Bible school, I was hired to be their first women's gym instructor. I taught weightlifting as well as high-impact aerobics. I was used to working out with serious competitors who were highly intense. What a shock it was to my system to become a coach to some ladies who were simply unmotivated.

These particular ladies would come to the gym all decked out in the latest sports attire. They completed the look with a sports bandana around their head and a Gatorade or water bottle in their hand. Believe me, they looked the part! Some would bring in magazines and show me how they wanted to look in six months. So, I would show them the machines and weights and demonstrate the workouts. They would smile and say, "What a cute little machine! I'll have to try it sometime." Then, some would have the audacity to flip through their magazines, file their fingernails, and then proceed to the snack bar downstairs for an ice cream cone. I would stand at the weight machines, deserted, with my mouth hanging open. Rather than actually doing anything, these ladies just wanted to look the place over. Others would do about three repetitions, visit with their friends, and then leave. After about two months of that, they would get discouraged and say something like, "You know, this just isn't working for me. I don't look any more like the model in the magazine than I did when I first came in. I don't think I'll work out anymore." Now, you and I can see how absurd that was, but most of them were too blind to see it. (Before I continue, I must tell you that, thank God, not all the ladies were like that.)

The free-weight barbells and dumbbells were my favorite workout tools in the gym. I enjoyed putting the ladies on this type of workout because we would see far greater results than if we used just the machines. For instance, when I put my students under the bench press, at first, they usually could not lift more than the empty bar. (The empty bar weighed 45 pounds by itself.)

Then, after a couple of weeks, I would challenge my students to increase the weight. I would ask them to add a little two-and-a-half pounds weight to each end of the bar, totaling five pounds. Some would readily respond, but not everyone. Some would panic and remind me that they hadn't even been able to complete their sets and repetitions using the empty bar. How could they ever add weight to it and still finish the set?

Some completely refused my direction, even though I urged them to trust me. I assured them that when they ran out of strength, I would be there. I would simply put two fingers under each side of the bar and gently help them push it up. If they could trust me and comply, their strength would increase. If not, however, it would always remain the same.

The ladies who believed me and were *"doers of my word,"* so to speak, saw remarkable results in toning. Within two weeks, their strength would greatly increase. When they went back and lifted the empty bar, it would fly up in the air like a balloon; they would be amazed. The others never saw any results. They stayed weak and flabby and were never toned. They thought they could get those same results just by hanging around the gym, flipping through magazines, wearing trendy sports attire, and eating. It simply doesn't work that way.

Many weight lifters go to great lengths to eat quality products, taking in lots of good protein for muscle mass. They eat massive quantities of steak and raw eggs, take supplements such as amino acids, and drink protein drinks. The combination of good food with good workouts is incredibly rewarding. However, one will not work without the other. Eating lots of protein without diligent workouts will only make one fat, not muscular. And if you eat the best food in the world, you must work hard to increase your size and strength. Your workout must be hard enough to produce a good sweat. In this instance, the old saying, "No pain, no gain," is absolutely true. To achieve the desired results, you must never be satisfied with your present strength level but consistently increase the weights.

We find the same principle in the spiritual realm.

> So then faith cometh by hearing, and hearing by the word of God.
>
> ROMANS 10:17

In other words, the Word of God is our spiritual food, our nutrients. The Bible speaks of *"the meat and the milk of the Word."* The more that you hear sound Word, the more you take in good protein. If you combine that spiritual food with spiritual exercise, your faith muscles will grow. However, if you only take in spiritual food without exercising your faith, you become bloated and fat. There are a lot of Christians sitting around the pews in that very condition. They have not done any spiritual exercises for a very long time. They just sit there half asleep, muttering, "Amen, amen, keep it coming, honey. I like that preaching. I like hearing those testimonies of people breaking through and prospering. Of course, I don't want to do what they did to get that way. I only want to hear about it."

It takes a lot of hard work to exercise physically or spiritually. I have not had the money to do one thing God has ever asked me to do. From the first day of this ministry, God has asked me to lift more weight than I thought I could handle. I have never had the finances ahead of time to pay for one foreign mission trip God has asked me to make. I just said, "Yes," and the finances came later. When God asked me to hire staff and prepare for an increase, I did not have the finances ahead of time. I obeyed, and the finances came later. Typically, when God asks me to give, I don't have it. Much of my giving has been by way of a credit card, and I give believing that I will have it later. I have made commitments to pay people's Bible school tuition when the money was just not there. It seems as though, just when I think that I'm almost able to believe for our present budget, God asks me to give more. It is His way of saying, "Let's put five more pounds on each side of the bar now, Debbie. It's time to press for an increase."

At those times, I've found myself answering like this. "Lord, what if I get this weight only halfway up, and I can't finish it? What will happen then?" I love His answer. It is the same one that He will give you because He is no respecter of persons.

"That is what I am here for, Debbie. I can guarantee that you will not be able to get the load up by yourself. You are not strong enough. My fingers will go directly underneath your load, under each side. Where you lack, I will make up the difference. My fingers are strong, and I will not allow you to drop the weight on yourself. I will finish pushing it up. You can trust Me. If you do what I say to do, you will increase in spiritual strength and be astounded at the results. In a few weeks, the load that you are carrying now will seem like nothing. You will be twice as strong and will be able to do twice as much as you are doing now. You don't want to stay where you are right now, do you? Trust Me and allow Me to add more weight."

Every time God asks me to put someone else through Bible school, to give more, to hire someone else, or to take more mission trips, He is adding more weight to the bar. I must take in quality faith food like Luke 6:38 or Philippians 4:13. Then, it is important to exercise those muscles and begin to do what God has asked me to do. After a few months, I look back on the smaller amount that I had been previously doing, and it seems like nothing compared to what I am doing now.

When I give testimonies of increase, people in the congregation get excited and shout. The Word that I teach brings faith. Then, I give them the opportunity to exercise their faith through giving. Some step forward, and some do not. Some only want to hear the Word. They flip through the pages of the Bible, much like the ladies back in the gym. They want to look like Peter, Paul, or Jesus in a few months but do not want to exercise their faith. After hearing the Word a few times, they give up because they do not look at it the way they thought they would. If only they would exercise. Then, instead of living off of other individual's faith testimonies, they would have their own testimonies to tell.

> And when thou art come in, thou shalt shut the door upon thee and upon thy sons, and shalt pour out into all those vessels, and thou shalt set aside that which is full.

GIVING

> So she went from him, and shut the door upon her and upon her sons, who brought the vessels to her; and she poured out.
>
> 2 KINGS 4:4-5

Elisha told her to shut the door on herself and her sons for a reason. There are too many people who are not in faith who will come along to discourage you. Some have the right motives. They don't want to see you make a mistake. Others are just plain jealous and do not want to see you succeed. Others have no idea what faith is. If you listen to them instead of what The Holy Spirit is telling you to do, you will never step out on the water and see your miracle.

When I was in Alaska and knew that God had called me, people seemed to come out of the woodwork to give me the reasons that I could not do what God told me that I could do. A man of God told me that there were three reasons that I could not preach in Alaska. He said that I was a woman, Alaska was cold and then reminded me that I had no husband. I was aware of all three of those issues. It was not a revelation to me that I was a woman. I should have walked over to a full-length mirror and declared, "Oh, my goodness, I am a woman. I did not realize this until you told me." I also already knew that Alaska was cold. I had been to villages and towns that were sixty-five degrees below zero without the wind chill factor. This man lived somewhere that was warm and only came to Alaska occasionally to minister in warmer seasons for a few days. (Many evangelists come to Alaska in the warm months when they can also go hunting or fishing, and their ministry weekend can pay for their fishing trip.) I did not need this man to tell me that Alaska was cold. I was very aware that I had no husband; I didn't think I had three or four of them running around. Isn't it interesting the things people "feel led" to tell you? This man was a "Word of Faith" minister. I am glad that I did not talk to a "word of doubt and unbelief" person.

Because I had been in that man's service and knew that he was anointed, I was devastated by what he told me. He told me that he had never heard me minister and was not prophesying to me, but he had heard what happened to my family and wanted to give his opinion. I should go back to Nebraska, get my children around grandparents, forget Alaska and what I thought was the call of God, and just go home. I felt like the wind had been knocked out of me. I could not even speak.

Ever since I was a little girl, I looked up to and respected every man and woman of God who spoke from behind a pulpit. I could not differentiate between them speaking "by the Spirit of God" and when they were only giving their opinion. Therefore, I took his opinion very seriously. I have since remembered that and try to be careful when talking to people if I do not have "thus sayeth The Lord." They will take my opinion much more seriously than that of someone who is not a minister.

I went to Noel and Edna DeVrie's home and told them what had taken place. Edna told me to take the phone off the hook (which tells you how long ago it was), get alone with God, hear what He has to say, and write it down. She then told me that the first time I preached in the Alaskan church that I became the pastor of, she and her husband Noel looked at each other and said, "This lady is anointed. She is going all over the world, and we are going to help her do it." She reminded me that even though this man was a man of God, men of God can miss it, and he was only giving his opinion.

I took the phone off the hook, got alone with God, and He spoke to me by that still small voice on the inside. However, it was so strong that it was almost audible. I put a tape in and prophesied to myself. Most of that has already come to pass. God said, "You don't have any money, any reputation, business cards, or contacts. I will raise you up from obscurity so that My glory will be seen. People will know that what I have done for you, I will do for them. I am no respecter of persons, only a respecter of principles. What I do for one, I will do for another if they get hungry, thirsty, and obedient like the first person. Everything that I told you as a little girl, I am about to do. It shall be an international ministry that will expand all over the world. This man was wrong. Man has not called you. I have called, anointed, and appointed you. I will do this thing." I never looked back. I learned that day that I had to shut the door and keep out the Devil.

Several years after that, I was holding a revival in Birmingham, Alabama. The governor at that time was Fob James II. He and his wife were Spirit-filled believers who had been in many of Dr. Rodney Howard-Browne's meetings and were touched in a profound way. Their son, Fob James III, a prominent lawyer, invited me to meetings in his home. Their home was rather large and could hold as many people as some of the churches I was in at the time. I agreed. We had wonderful Holy Ghost meetings. I will never forget one night in particular. Mr. James was flooded with the presence of God. He was what we call "drunk in The Holy Ghost" under the influence of The Holy Spirit. He was under his dining room table, rolling and laughing with joy unspeakable and full of glory. His hair was sticking up, and his tie was backward. The sight of this prominent lawyer (the son of the Governor of Alabama) looking and sounding drunk was quite hilarious. He began to sing a Christian reggae chorus that I had never heard at that time. I only remember this line. "Shut de door, keep out de debil." I was laughing so hard at the sight and sound, as he was pronouncing the as de and devil as debil. Since then, every time that I read about Elisha and this widow woman, I read it through this reggae accent. You must shut de door and keep out de debil. You must also realize that de debil can come in many forms. De debil can be de mudder-in-law, or de preacher, or de best friend. Even Peter was used by the enemy, and Jesus had to say, *"Get behind me, Satan."* So before you listen to what someone says and before you allow it to affect you, you need to hear from Heaven and make sure that they are aligning with Heaven's plan for your life. If it does not line up with what God has told you about your life and assignment, make sure that you "shut de door, keep out de devil."

It is so important that we learn from the widow woman's obedience. She gave the little oil that she had, gathered up many vessels, and then began to pour. As she did, God multiplied the oil and prospered her. We must exercise our faith, giving God something to work with. He will do the rest.

SEVENTEEN

THE MULTIPLICATION OF THE BREAD AND FISH

When Jesus heard of it, he departed thence by ship into a desert place apart: and when the people had heard thereof, they followed him on foot out of the cities.

And Jesus went forth, and saw a great multitude, and was moved with compassion toward them, and he healed their sick.

And when it was evening, his disciples came to him, saying, This is a desert place, and the time is now past; send the multitude away, that they may go into the villages, and buy themselves victuals.

But Jesus said unto them, They need not depart; give ye them to eat.

And they say unto him, We have here but five loaves, and two fishes.

He said, Bring them hither to me.

And he commanded the multitude to sit down on the grass, and took the five loaves, and the two fishes, and looking up to heaven, he blessed, and brake, and gave the loaves to his disciples, and the disciples to the multitude.

> And they did all eat, and were filled: and they took up of the fragments that remained twelve baskets full.
> And they that had eaten were about five thousand men, beside women and children.
>
> MATTHEW 14:13-21

We need to look at what took place just before this story unfolds. John the Baptist has been beheaded. He was Jesus' cousin and close friend. Jesus went to a solitary place to be alone with His thoughts and His grief. However, a minister is never off-duty, and the people followed Him. He could have yelled at them and told them to leave Him alone, but He did not. The Bible says that He was moved with compassion. He is still moved with compassion on your behalf and on my behalf. He healed the sick, and He still heals the sick today. His will has never changed. The people were spiritually hungry and stayed while He ministered and prayed for the sick.

One of the things that I have always found amusing about this story is how ignorant religion can be. I've heard supposed theologians say things like, "Well, you know, the loaves of bread were larger in those days." Are you kidding me? First of all, do they think the fish were whales as well? Secondly, this was one little boy's lunch. He could not have eaten or carried that much food. It takes a lot of teaching in our religious cemeteries (sorry, I meant seminaries) by the blind, leading the blind to get that ignorant.

We don't know what caused the disciples to come to Jesus and talk to him about how the people needed to eat. Perhaps they heard the people complaining that the service was too long or that if they were having such a long service, someone should have brought food or what. Maybe the disciples were getting nervous that if the people got too hungry, there would be some unpleasant episode. They may have thought, "You know how people get when they get hungry." I don't believe they cared that much for the people. The Bible says that Jesus was moved with compassion, not the disciples. Maybe they were hungry themselves and used the people as their excuse. All we know is that they mentioned that the people should be sent away to eat because they were out in the desert with no way to give them food.

People tend to make up their own Bible versions. I've heard people say that Jesus multiplied the bread and fish because they had no money to get food. That is not true.

> He answered and said unto them, Give ye them to eat. And they say unto him, Shall we go and buy two hundred pennyworth of bread, and give them to eat?
>
> MARK 6:37

They were asking if they were supposed to go into town and buy enough food for everyone. They did not say, "We don't have enough money to buy food for all of these people." They were telling Him that it was not logistically feasible to walk into town, buy enough for everyone, and bring it all back to them.

In verse sixteen, Jesus said, *"They need not depart; give ye them to eat."* He basically said to them that they should take care of it. They didn't want to hear that. People don't want to have to face responsibility. They don't want to have to exercise their faith, line up with God's Word, listen, and obey Him. They want to have it easy. Brother Kenneth Hagin said, "They want everything to drop on them like ripe cherries off of a tree." They want someone else to do it all for them, pray for them, exercise faith for them, and intercede for them. Or they want a quick fix by meeting the right person who will make it easy for them. Many times, people think, "If I just knew the right person, someone highly respected, someone in politics or wealthy, etc. I just need someone who would endorse me or introduce me to the right person." They forget that God is their supply. God can open doors that no man can shut, and He knows how to keep the Devil out. It's important that you never start off with an excuse. Always start off in faith. Faith speaks, acts, demonstrates, and never makes excuses, ever. You might feel like making an excuse and want it to come out of your mouth. However, you have to learn to keep your mouth shut.

> And they say unto him, We have here but five loaves, and two fishes.
>
> MATTHEW 14:17

We don't know how the disciples knew about the little boy's lunch. We only know that the Bible tells us in John's Gospel that it was one little boy's lunch.

> One of his disciples, Andrew, Simon Peter's brother, saith unto him,
> There is a lad here, which hath five barley loaves, and two small fishes: but what are they among so many?
>
> JOHN 6:8, 9

They brought up a little boy with five loaves and two fish. The boy had more faith than anyone else. He had more than the twelve apostles. Have you ever wondered how they knew he had five loaves and two fish? Someone among the disciples found out about the little boy.

Pastor Eric Gonan (associate pastor to Pastor Rodney Howard-Browne) believes the little boy said, "Mom, I've heard about Jesus and his miracles, and I want to see it." The mother probably said, "Alright, honey," and packed him a lunch. Why did she pack so much? She probably thought he might have some friends who came to the meeting also, and they might not have enough and she would give him extra so that he could share. He heard the disciples talking to Jesus about how they had a big problem. He may have heard them say. "These people are hungry, and it's not right that You aren't letting them go home yet when it is past dinner time." Maybe the boy said, "Mom packed me a good lunch, and here it is." Maybe they even pushed him away and said, "Get away from me, you stupid boy."

Jesus told them that they needed to feed the people. He put it back on them. We always want to put our problems off on someone else, but Jesus asks, *"What do you have?"* "I don't have anything." They tried to make an excuse to prove they had nothing. "All we have is a little boy's lunch, and it's only two fish and five pieces of bread." They are trying to prove to Jesus how little they have to justify their excuses. They state that it is just a little boy's lunch, and He says, "That's perfect. What you call nothing, I'll feed everyone with." Maybe you don't know how you'll fulfill those dreams, desires, and visions, and you don't have the plan figured completely out yet, but God will help you to do that.

They had something in their hand, five loaves and two fish. That would be a lot to somebody who had less, but they were calling the little they had nothing. It is nothing until you put it in the master's hand. When you put it in the master's hand, it becomes more than you need.

> He said, Bring them hither to me.
>
> MATTHEW 14:18

Do you need a miracle? Jesus said bring it to me. I am sure that the disciples were thinking, "What in the world is He going to try to do?" So they took five loaves and two fish to Him.

> And he commanded the multitude to sit down on the grass, and took the five loaves, and the two fishes, and looking up to heaven, he blessed, and brake, and gave the loaves to his disciples, and the disciples to the multitude.
>
> MATTHEW 14:19

It is so important to be thankful for what you have. They should have said, "Thank you, Lord, that I have five loaves and two fish." What you have is more than a lot of other people have in other nations I travel to. It is hard for Americans to grasp what real poverty is. You cannot imagine what some go through to get their breakthrough. Many get up early in the morning and work until dark just to obtain the basic necessities of life, like food and water. Thank God that we are able to tell them that with God, nothing is impossible.

The person who is not thankful now will not be thankful even when they are more blessed. However, I am not just talking about being thankful for what you have now but also for where you are going. My pastors came from South Africa with only $300.00, three kids, and four suitcases. They have now taken revival all around the world. People think it's a great story, but they don't understand that you have to get the breakthrough for yourself before you can give it to others.

You cannot say, "I don't understand why God gave me this dream, and I have no way to get it done." There is always a way with God. The key is five loaves and two fish. It's what you think is nothing that is the key to your breakthrough.

After thanking God for what you do have, you must break something. Jesus had to break something. You have to break something to get a breakthrough. Everybody wants a breakthrough, but nobody wants to break anything. You have to break your old mindset, poverty mentality, lack mentality, and "I don't have anything" mentality. You have to break all these things to have a breakthrough. When you break it, you enter into His abundance. When you break something, you are initiating a miracle. Five loaves and two fish could not feed everyone. They would have to only take one bite out of it. Jesus took five loaves and two fish and broke them.

The miracle still didn't occur even when Jesus was thankful and broke the bread and gave it to the disciples. Each disciple now only had one-twelfth of the little boy's lunch. The breakthrough didn't happen even when Jesus was thankful and broke it. It never became more until the next step. The physical manifestation of the miracle didn't occur until it went to the guys who said it wasn't enough. They were commanded to now give out what they had. The miracle didn't take place all at once or the way most would expect. The fish didn't suddenly become a whale in each disciple's hands where they could see it before they handed it out.

Every time a disciple put some bread and fish in each person's hand, it looked like it remained the same in his own hand. It stretched and lasted until the end. Most of the time, we want to see how the miracle takes place before we exercise faith. It doesn't work that way. No faith would be required at all if it worked like that. You have to take the step of faith first and give out what doesn't look like enough.

It must have been difficult for the disciple to look at the hungry expression on each person's face as he handed out such a small amount. He may have wondered if a riot was about to be invoked. People can do some pretty strange things if they get hungry enough. Can you imagine the surprise and joy of each disciple as he courageously put another portion in another person's hand and looks at what he has left to see it's exactly the same amount that he started with? He would realize at that moment he was working a miracle with Jesus. That is the same way miracles take place today. We and Jesus work them together. That's why one of the gifts of the Spirit is called the working of miracles. They don't just happen. We work them.

Revival Ministries International sows financial seeds all over the world. It is funded by the seeds they sow. They were able to go to Africa, where they saw multitudes come to Jesus in six weeks. Pastor Rodney set his faith before they went that the trip would be paid for in full ahead of time. It was. Normally, it hasn't worked like that in the past. They almost always believed that they would have a miracle at the end of each crusade. But a new level of breakthrough means that you're going to have the money ahead of time. That's called an acceleration. Pastor Eric used to say, "I can't remember that in any crusade, we had the money to do anything that we've done."

Once Pastor Rodney got a word from God, he set out to do it and floored it. It was peal to the metal time. Pastor waited until he heard from God, and everything came in miraculously by the end of the meeting. It's still like that, except that the next level of acceleration is now where the Pastor prays, "Lord, I'm calling in all the money before it even begins." That's an acceleration and a breakthrough. It is definitely another level. God always funded the Crusades and the finances always came in, but this is at another level. When Pastor Rodney decided to do the remodel of the church auditorium this year, he said, "We're going to open this auditorium for the winter campmeeting. It will be ready, and it will be paid for in full, and it was. To have your dreams and visions fulfilled, you will have to energize your faith. It's time for a lot of acceleration. Jesus is coming soon, and this world is very messed up. You must remember to be thankful, break something, give out what you have, and expect a miracle. Remember that what you call nothing, God calls more than enough. Will you believe Him and break what you have? We serve the supernatural God of the breakthrough.

EIGHTEEN

IT'S ALL ABOUT THE OFFERING

> And thou shalt anoint the altar of the burnt offering, and all his vessels, and sanctify the altar: and it shall be an altar most holy.
>
> EXODUS 40:10

Both the giver and the gift are anointed. We are the altar today. Offerings have everything to do with the holiness of God and the essence of who He is. God is a giver, and His giving is pure with no false motives or strings attached. He wants us to be like Him.

Offerings are holy, and they are attached to the anointing. In the Bible, both the offering and the altar it was received upon were anointed and made holy. Our salvation is all about an offering. God gave us His only Son so that we could have eternal life. He spared nothing. He gave His best, and He gave His only Son. His offering was perfect and satisfied the justice system of Heaven. Without God's offering and Jesus's willingness to be that offering, we would have no hope. It was all about the offering, and it still is. This is not a side subject. Offerings are about the heart. They reveal love, priorities, affection, desires, and honor.

The Devil is the polar opposite of our good God in every way. He understands nothing of giving. He is a selfish manipulator. John 10:10 says that he is a thief who comes to steal, kill, and destroy. He is the author of poverty and hates blessing. He is into curses. He wants to make the lives of people a living Hell on earth.

The Devil hates offerings. He knows what they are attached to. One day, the antichrist will commit the desolation of abomination in Jerusalem. He will stop the daily sacrifice. The enemy of our soul hates worship and offerings unto God. His goal is to cut off all supernatural provision. He is only about himself and is trying to convince the church that we are to be only success-oriented with no thought of God or His people. He wants us to believe that we can bring about success on our own without God's help. Satan is about instant gratification.

My pastor, Dr. Rodney Howard-Browne, has a series about trafficking the anointing. It is powerful and reveals how Lucifer (Satan) has always been involved in trafficking.

> Thou wast perfect in thy ways from the day that thou wast created, till iniquity was found in thee.
> By the multitude of thy merchandise they have filled the midst of thee with violence, and thou hast sinned: therefore I will cast thee as profane out of the mountain of God: and I will destroy thee, O covering cherub, from the midst of the stones of fire.
> Thine heart was lifted up because of thy beauty, thou hast corrupted thy wisdom by reason of thy brightness: I will cast thee to the ground, I will lay thee before kings, that they may behold thee.
> Thou hast defiled thy sanctuaries by the multitude of thine iniquities, by the iniquity of thy traffick; therefore will I bring forth a fire from the midst of thee, it shall devour thee, and I will bring thee to ashes upon the earth in the sight of all them that behold thee.
> All they that know thee among the people shall be aston-

ished at thee: thou shalt be a terror, and never shalt thou be any more.

EZEKIEL 28:15-19

I quote Dr. Rodney: "The Devil was cast out of Heaven because iniquity was found in him. He was a merchandiser and trafficker of the anointing—defiling and contaminating that which is pure and good. Greed, arrogance, and lust are the hallmarks of his nature. He uses the temptation of wealth and power to lure, manipulate, control, and trap those who lust after these things. Those who yield to him, give him authority over their lives and even their eternity. The Devil even tried to trap Jesus by offering Him the wealth and power of the worldly kingdoms. He took Jesus up onto a high mountain and showed Him all the kingdoms of the world in a moment of time and offered them—their authority and glory—to Jesus if He would worship him. Of course, Jesus refused him because the Lord our God is the only one worthy of His, and our, worship and service."

Every one of us must make the decision about whom we will serve. We must submit every aspect of our lives to the Word of God and guard our hearts. We must not give in to our fleshly desires or sell out to the Devil and the world. Many Christians—even many preachers—have already compromised and given place to the Devil even though they claim to be serving God. If the Devil tempted Jesus with this, he will tempt us. We must defeat him the same way that Jesus did, with the Word of God.

The enemy is everything opposite of a giver. He is a thief and manipulator. He knows the power of an offering and will do anything to keep God's people from understanding what an offering is all about.

My pastor has said many times that he can tell how well a revival is going by the offering. That usually causes the air to be sucked out of the room. People with religious spirits become highly offended at the thought of equating offerings with the anointing. However, it is absolutely true. When people get free in the area of giving, they become free in other areas, such as praise and worship and yielding to The Holy Spirit. They are able to receive joy unspeakable and full of glory. The hand that is stretched out in giving is the one that is in a position to receive.

I have seen that the Bible tells us many times that there are two opposite offerings taking place simultaneously. They involve two different kinds of hearts. We will look at several of these examples. Let's start at the beginning in the Garden of Eden with Adam and Eve. One of their first challenges was issued by God. He gave them permission to enjoy everything in that garden except for a tree that he told them not to touch. He said, "Don't touch it." He was saying that it was dedicated unto God. He wanted to remind them that they were only stewards of the garden, not owners. God has shown in His Word that when He declares something to be devoted unto Him, and He declares it to be a *"devoted thing,"* we better be careful not to use it for anything else.

However, it was the first thing they were drawn to. Why is it that man, then and now, is determined to live independent of God? When Frank Sinatra made the song *I Did It My Way* famous, he was speaking for the human race. When Adam and Eve did it their way, the glory of God departed, and they were on their own. Until then, God was the source of their life. Now, they found a new source and decided that instead of having God's absolutes as their anchor, they could now judge what is right and wrong on their own. This should sound very familiar in the hour that we live in. We have a society and even a government that has decided that God Himself will not tell them what to do. They will decide on their own without His help.

After Adam and Eve sinned and were without God's glory and presence, they once again decided that they would take matters into their own hands. We see two different types of appeasement offerings. They came to God wearing fig leaves, which was an attempt to cover up sin. I don't know if they thought that He would not notice or what. However, He definitely noticed and still notices today what people bring Him.

Adam and Eve brought God a man-made offering. They offered what they could do themselves without Him. They thought they were covered, but they were not, and God was not pleased. They did something and thought their something was good enough. They reasoned that at least they tried. It was an offering of sorts, but God was far from pleased. God brought to them animal skins still dripping with blood. He let them know that they could not come without the blood or without repentance. He showed them how fruitless their offering was. They realized that they could not put forth their own man-made best efforts if they wanted to please God. He told them that He required an offering that was given properly. He taught them about the blood and told them that a day would come when His own Son would be the supreme offering. Jesus' blood would run down Calvary's hill for them and everyone who would come after them if they accepted His blood sacrifice. He let them know the difference between bringing their own best effort and what God actually required. This was the beginning of seeing man's offering (fig leaves) and God's offering (the blood) side by side.

It does not take long before we see two more offerings that were given from two different hearts. We have the story of Cain and Abel in Genesis 4:

> And in process of time it came to pass, that Cain brought of the fruit of the ground an offering unto the Lord.
> And Abel, he also brought of the firstlings of his flock and of the fat thereof. And the Lord had respect unto Abel and to his offering:
> But unto Cain and to his offering he had not respect. And Cain was very wroth, and his countenance fell.
> And the Lord said unto Cain, Why art thou wroth? and why is thy countenance fallen?
> If thou doest well, shalt thou not be accepted? and if thou doest not well, sin lieth at the door. And unto thee shall be his desire, and thou shalt rule over him.
> And Cain talked with Abel his brother: and it came to pass, when they were in the field, that Cain rose up against Abel his brother, and slew him.
>
> GENESIS 4:3-8

Cain knew that he was supposed to bring a blood sacrifice. His parents taught him how to please God with the right offering. However, like many today, he thought that he could rebel against God's authority and come the bloodless way. It was not acceptable then and is not acceptable today. To please God, we must do things His way.

The Bible says that Cain brought his offering in the course of time. He was not prompt to be obedient. To him, it did not matter if it was first or last, if he paid his bills first and waited to see if there was anything left, whether it took care of his own wants first, etc. He got around to it eventually and thought that was the only thing that mattered. Abel's offering was the first fruit. He did it right off the top before any bills were paid and before he took care of himself. It takes faith to give God our best and to do it first. Faith is what makes Him happy and moves His hand. Without faith, we cannot please Him. We live by faith. We must believe that God is a rewarder. God demands the first and the best, not the leftovers.

Cain brought what was convenient from his garden instead of what God required. It is not up to us to tell God what we think He should accept. He has already shown us in His Holy Word what He accepts. We must do things God's way if we want God's approval. This passage makes it plain that God looks at offerings and judges them as to whether they are acceptable or not. He was pleased with Abel's offering but was not pleased with Cain's offering.

When we don't do things God's way, we are convicted and have a choice at that point. Thank God for the blood of the Lamb and for His great grace. If we surrender our pride, repent, turn around, and do things God's way, He will accept us, be pleased, and all will be well. However, many run the other way, get bitter and angry, and then blame God and everyone around them. It turns into jealousy toward the person whom God is pleased with and is blessing. Instead, we should look at their life as an example and remember that God is no respecter of persons and will bless us as He blesses them if we do what they do.

Cain became disappointed, depressed, jealous, and then enraged. God urged him to just make a turn, but he would not. He was proud and stubborn about his giving and the fact that he believed God should accept whatever he wanted to do and how he did it.

Cain's rebellion led to the very first murder. It destroyed the first family and sent the parents into grief. It ultimately led to Cain being exiled from the presence of God. That is a terrible price to pay. Was it adultery that caused all of this? No, it was all about an offering. This is a very serious subject.

We find another example with Noah. He was the only righteous man of his generation. A righteous man is also a giver. The people around him were full of sin and iniquity. Their sin had reached such a level that God could no longer strive with mankind and started over again with only Noah and his family. The people on earth at that time were only about gratifying their own flesh. Sin is always selfish. It thinks of only one person—Me! Everything about that generation was the opposite of a giver. They were only giving to their fleshly desires.

Noah was thankful to God for sparing him and his family during the flood. The first thing he did when stepping off the ark was to give an offering. He did not just become that way after the flood. He was already a giver and a worshipper. That is why he was spared. Most people would have celebrated getting off the ark with a party or with a barbeque, or going out and purchasing a home. Some would talk about what a close call they had and how they were going to live each moment to the max. Not Noah. He could only think of giving to his God.

> And Noah built an altar unto the Lord; and took of every clean beast, and of every clean fowl, and offered burnt offerings on the altar.
> And the Lord smelled a sweet savour; and the Lord said in his heart, I will not again curse the ground any more for man's sake; for the imagination of man's heart is evil from his youth; neither will I again smite any more every thing living, as I have done.
> While the earth remaineth, seedtime and harvest, and cold

> and heat, and summer and winter, and day and night shall not cease.
>
> GENESIS 8:20-22

Noah worshipped God with an offering, and The Lord smelled his offering. Again, we see that God loves fragrant offerings, not stinky ones. Those fragrant offerings always get God's attention. They build a memorial that God never forgets. What determines if it smells good to God? The person's heart and the amount of sacrifice and worship that goes into it. The memorial offering that Noah gave caused God to interact with Noah and mankind. The Lord and Noah did eternal business that day. God said that He would never again destroy everything. God established seedtime and harvest. When a person interacts with God, He interacts with that person. It causes great favor to come upon the person's life. In this case, all of mankind has benefitted from one man's giving. The other people of Noah's generation were selfish and perished. Noah was a giver, and we all are blessed as a result. It's all about the offering.

These two types of hearts and offerings continue to be contrasted. In Genesis 22, we read of the story of Abraham being willing to sacrifice his son, Isaac. Abraham called giving his most precious offering, worship. He was prepared to go all the way with his commitment to God. In his case, it was going to cost him more than any parent would ever want to pay. God would not allow him to sacrifice his son. He only wanted to see how far Abraham was willing to go in his commitment and love to God. God is still interested in looking at our hearts to see how far we are prepared to go with our commitment. That is what an offering is all about. It involves love, obedience, sacrifice, honor, and commitment. Because Abraham was willing to sacrifice that which he had waited for so long to have, God said that he knew then that Abraham loved him. Where there is much love, there is much sacrifice.

When Abraham was lifting the knife to slay his son, God called out to him, and Abraham did not have to slay his son. He looked up and saw a lamb caught in a bush. Mt. Moriah (where this was taking place) and Mt.

Calvary were in very close proximity to one another. Years later, the Son of God would be slain on Mt. Calvary for your sin and my sin. I believe that Abraham looked up and saw into the spirit realm many years into the future and witnessed the Son of the Living God hanging between Heaven and earth for our salvation. He called the place Jehovah Jireh, The Lord, My Provider, or The Lord Himself Will Provide. Once again, we see that when man does business with God, God does business with man. Abraham's offering obligated God to offer His Son for all of mankind. I thank God that Abraham was a giver.

When God asked Abraham to leave the country and home that he had known, Abraham took his nephew Lot with him. Lot was blessed because of Abraham. In fact, God blessed both Abraham and Lot for Abraham's sake. They became so rich that they could not dwell together any longer. Lot should have been so thankful to Abraham and honored him whenever he had the opportunity. Thankfulness goes hand in hand with honor and appreciation. Yet when God offered Abraham any land that he wanted, Abraham offered the choice to Lot to choose first. Lot had the perfect opportunity to thank Abraham and give him the better land, but he selfishly chose to take the best land. That did not prevent Abraham from being blessed. Circumstances and selfish people cannot keep a giver down. God's favor rests upon them. Abraham continued to prosper and become richer and richer. Lot lost his wife and encountered an unpleasant turn of events in Sodom. One was a giver, and one was a taker. It's all about the offering.

The contrast between a giver and taker continues with the two sons of Isaac, Jacob and Esau, in Genesis 25. Esau could only think of fulfilling his lust upon himself. He was willing to give up spiritual blessings to have instant gratification with a bowl of soup. He should have considered the blessing of God to be far greater than any natural fulfillment. He lost his birthright and his blessing because he wanted natural fulfillment, and he wanted it now.

We see that Jacob was a giver. When God gave him a revelation of His presence in Genesis 28, the first thing Jacob did was build an altar and pour out to God. He told God that he would give ten percent to him all the days of his life. God was not asking Jacob for anything at that moment. He was only interested in blessing Jacob, but Jacob was interested in blessing God and giving to Him an offering.

Moses was so hungry for God and His glory. He willingly went before Pharoah and risked his life to obey God and deliver God's people. He knew it could cost him everything. He was later willing to climb Mt. Horeb to interact with God. He not only gave sacrifices, but he gave up the royal palace life to be identified with God's people. The pursuit of a holy God was more important to him than creature comforts.

While Moses was in pursuit of God, the entire mountain was on fire. God was presiding over that meeting where the greatest display of heaven until that time was taking place. While Moses was doing business with God, his brother, Aaron, was displaying a different heart. Moses was risking death, he thought, to see God face to face. While he was going after the highest spiritual longing, his brother was causing the Israelites to be naked and commit all kinds of whoredom In God's site. Aaron had the audacity to ask the Israelites for the jewelry that God blessed them with when He delivered them from Egypt. The Egyptians had willingly handed over their gold, silver, and other precious metals to the Israelites because of the fear of The Lord and God's favor upon His own people. It was an offering that sustained them in their years in the wilderness. While Moses was offering God his life and worship on the mountain, Aaron was taking God's holy offering and using it for sin. God's judgment was poured out on those who committed sin, and three thousand people lost their lives. God, in His mercy and grace, still used Aaron, but not to the extent that He used Moses.

In the Biblical scenarios with both Elijah and Elisha and widow women, we can see different hearts presented. The Bible says that Elijah was not sent to any other widows during the famine except this one. They were not taken care of because of their need but their offering.

The Shunammite woman in 2 Kings 4 is another example of how important offerings are.

And it fell on a day, that Elisha passed to Shunem, where was a great woman; and she constrained him to eat bread. And so it was, that as oft as he passed by, he turned in thither to eat bread.

And she said unto her husband, Behold now, I perceive that this is an holy man of God, which passeth by us continually.

Let us make a little chamber, I pray thee, on the wall; and let us set for him there a bed, and a table, and a stool, and a candlestick: and it shall be, when he cometh to us, that he shall turn in thither.

And it fell on a day, that he came thither, and he turned into the chamber, and lay there.

And he said to Gehazi his servant, Call this Shunammite. And when he had called her, she stood before him.

And he said unto him, Say now unto her, Behold, thou hast been careful for us with all this care; what is to be done for thee? Wouldest thou be spoken for to the king, or to the captain of the host? And she answered, I dwell among mine own people.

And he said, What then is to be done for her? And Gehazi answered, Verily she hath no child, and her husband is old.

And he said, Call her. And when he had called her, she stood in the door.

And he said, About this season, according to the time of life, thou shalt embrace a son. And she said, Nay, my lord, thou man of God, do not lie unto thine handmaid.

And the woman conceived, and bare a son at that season that Elisha had said unto her, according to the time of life.

And when the child was grown, it fell on a day, that he went out to his father to the reapers.

And he said unto his father, My head, my head. And he said to a lad, Carry him to his mother.

And when he had taken him, and brought him to his mother, he sat on her knees till noon, and then died.

And she went up, and laid him on the bed of the man of God, and shut the door upon him, and went out.

And she called unto her husband, and said, Send me, I pray thee, one of the young men, and one of the asses, that I may run to the man of God, and come again.

And he said, Wherefore wilt thou go to him to day? It is neither new moon, nor sabbath. And she said, It shall be well.

Then she saddled an ass, and said to her servant, Drive, and go forward; slack not thy riding for me, except I bid thee.

So she went and came unto the man of God to mount Carmel. And it came to pass, when the man of God saw her afar off, that he said to Gehazi his servant, Behold, yonder is that Shunammite:

Run now, I pray thee, to meet her, and say unto her, Is it well with thee? Is it well with thy husband? Is it well with the child? And she answered, It is well:

And when she came to the man of God to the hill, she caught him by the feet: but Gehazi came near to thrust her away. And the man of God said, Let her alone; for her soul is vexed within her: and the Lord hath hid it from me, and hath not told me.

Then she said, Did I desire a son of my lord? Did I not say, Do not deceive me?

Then he said to Gehazi, Gird up thy loins, and take my staff in thine hand, and go thy way: if thou meet any man, salute him not; and if any salute thee, answer him not again: and lay my staff upon the face of the child.

And the mother of the child said, As the Lord liveth, and as thy soul liveth, I will not leave thee. And he arose, and followed her.

And Gehazi passed on before them, and laid the staff upon the face of the child; but there was neither voice, nor

> hearing. Wherefore he went again to meet him, and told him, saying, The child is not awaked.
>
> And when Elisha was come into the house, behold, the child was dead, and laid upon his bed.
>
> He went in therefore, and shut the door upon them twain, and prayed unto the Lord.
>
> And he went up, and lay upon the child, and put his mouth upon his mouth, and his eyes upon his eyes, and his hands upon his hands: and stretched himself upon the child; and the flesh of the child waxed warm.
>
> Then he returned, and walked in the house to and fro; and went up, and stretched himself upon him: and the child sneezed seven times, and the child opened his eyes.
>
> And he called Gehazi, and said, Call this Shunammite. So he called her. And when she was come in unto him, he said, Take up thy son.
>
> Then she went in, and fell at his feet, and bowed herself to the ground, and took up her son, and went out.
>
> 2 KINGS 4: 8-37

The first thing that we notice is that the woman perceived that this man was a holy man sent by God. She perceived the anointing. She recognized that he was from God and had been sent to help them. She did not despise the anointing. Many have no breakthrough because they despise the anointing and do not have enough spiritual perception to recognize that people are sent to help them.

She convinced her husband that they needed to give a substantial offering to the man of God. They put an addition onto their home for him to come and stay in comfort. They wanted the anointed man of God to be in their home as often as possible. They built him a bedroom and bought furniture for the room; a bed, table, stand, and candlestick. It takes money to build a bedroom onto your home. It takes money to furnish it with nice furniture that would allow the man of God to be comfortable. I'm sure they supplied him with the best mattress available. Today, someone would furnish the man or woman of God with not only furniture but an iPad, laptop, chargers, and, for me, a Coca-Cola. They also cooked for him every time that he came. He came often, so she must have been a good cook. The Shunammite woman had a gift of hospitality. That gift, combined with the offering of finances, brought the anointing to her very door and home. It brought her even more than that. She had no idea of what was in store for her beyond her wildest dream.

The prophet of God was so moved by her giving and hospitality that God impressed upon his heart to inquire of whatever she had need of. Elisha's servant, Gehazi, sent for her. She stood before the man of God, and he asked what she wanted. She let him know that she did not give to him and God to get anything. She was content. She said that she didn't need to be spoken of before the king or anything else. Yet, God knew that she had a secret desire, and God was about to meet that desire. The servant told Elisha that she was married to an old man and could not have a child. Elisha told her that she would deliver a son at the same time next year. She did. You can know that God does not lie. He always comes through with what He promises.

However, the enemy of our souls does not give up that easily. No one gets a free run up the side. We have to learn to stand our ground to obtain the promises and to keep them. Her son had a heat stroke in the field with his father one day. The woman did not despair and get bitter toward God. She knew that God gave him to her, and God would bring him back. She also knew that what it takes to get, it takes to keep. She found the man of God. He came and laid upon her son, and he came back to life. That was still not the end of the story. We see later in 2 Kings 8 that she received direction on what to do and where to go during the famine that was coming upon the land, and when she returned, she was spoken of to the king and received all of her lands back.

> Then spake Elisha unto the woman, whose son he had restored to life, saying, Arise, and go thou and thine household, and sojourn wheresoever thou canst sojourn:

> for the Lord hath called for a famine; and it shall also come upon the land seven years.
>
> And the woman arose, and did after the saying of the man of God: and she went with her household, and sojourned in the land of the Philistines seven years.
>
> And it came to pass at the seven years' end, that the woman returned out of the land of the Philistines: and she went forth to cry unto the king for her house and for her land.
>
> And the king talked with Gehazi the servant of the man of God, saying, Tell me, I pray thee, all the great things that Elisha hath done.
>
> And it came to pass, as he was telling the king how he had restored a dead body to life, that, behold, the woman, whose son he had restored to life, cried to the king for her house and for her land. And Gehazi said, My lord, O king, this is the woman, and this is her son, whom Elisha restored to life.
>
> And when the king asked the woman, she told him. So the king appointed unto her a certain officer, saying, Restore all that was hers, and all the fruits of the field since the day that she left the land, even until now.
>
> 2 KINGS 8:1-6

It looks to me like it's all about the offering.

Earlier in this book, when I was teaching on the tithe, we looked at Malachi 3. The chapter starts out with Israel asking God how they can return to Him. They found themselves in a backslidden condition, and God let them know that it was all about the tithe. Which came first, forsaking the tithe or backsliding? They both happened simultaneously. The reason is because the heart that quits giving has already quit putting God first.

We read in Malachi 3 about being blessed or cursed. The person who tithes is guaranteed a tremendous blessing where there is no room to even contain it. The blessing has power behind it. The person who does not tithe is guaranteed a curse.

> Ye are cursed with a curse: for ye have robbed me, even this whole nation.
>
> MALACHI 3:9

It is very simple. It comes down to love and obedience. The person who loves much wants to please and obey. The giver knows that God will always take care of him. The person who does not tithe is a person taken by fear. That one is afraid to prove God. We cannot please God unless we are in faith. The person who does not tithe is in fear and disobedience and will reap a curse. The person who is a tither is in faith and obedience and will reap the blessings of God. It's all about the offering.

The offerings were so important in the Old Testament. There were many specific rules and instructions about it. Some of these are as follows: The animals used in the sacrifices could have no blemish or defect, they had to be the first and the best, and they had to be clean. The person who presented the offering had to be clean. It was important that the offering was a first fruit and not a leftover. The animal had to be male, the first of the year, and had to cost something. There couldn't be any leaven in the Passover bread.

The most intriguing offering was the burnt offering, the first of the Levitical offerings. In this offering, the worshipper voluntarily devoted his whole offering to God through the fire. The Burnt Offering is for the sanctification of the whole man in surrender to the Lord, even unto death. It brought a sweet savor to the Lord.

> And thou shalt burn the whole ram upon the altar: it is a burnt offering unto the Lord: it is a sweet savour, an offering made by fire unto the Lord.
>
> EXODUS 29:18

The whole offering "went up in smoke." The animal being sacrificed had to burn overnight in its entirety without its skin. With nothing returned to the worshipper, this made the Burnt Offering distinct from other offerings. Parts of the other sacrifices were also burned on the Altar, but the Burnt Offering was totally consumed by the fire. Everything was totally burned to ashes, with nothing left. We can see this pattern continue into the New Testament.

> And Jesus sat over against the treasury, and beheld how the people cast money into the treasury: and many that were rich cast in much.
> And there came a certain poor widow, and she threw in two mites, which make a farthing.
> And he called unto him his disciples, and saith unto them, Verily I say unto you, That this poor widow hath cast more in, than all they which have cast into the treasury:
> For all they did cast in of their abundance; but she of her want did cast in all that she had, even all her living.
>
> MARK 12:41-44

Earlier in this chapter, Jesus talked about the scribes and chief priests being hypocrites. They exploited widows, loved pretension, and showed off with long religious prayers. Next, Jesus went into this story. He purposely sat where He could watch how people gave in the offering. (I believe He still looks at what people give and the attitude of their heart, yet today.) He contrasts the hearts again. He said the widow who gave two mites gave more than them all because she gave one hundred percent. God doesn't look so much at how much we give but rather at how much we keep in proportion to how much we give. He does not only comment on her giving, but He also commented on the religious, pretentious giving of the rest. He said that they only gave from their abundance. It cost them nothing. There was no sacrifice, worship, or love involved. It was just extra creme off the top. Many do that today while patting themselves on the back because they gave at all.

I shared earlier in this book about the breaking of an alabaster box. Everyone is either more like Judas or Mary. What the woman called worship, the thief, betrayer, and embezzler (Judas) called waste. In John 12, Mary poured out everything that she had on the Master, whom she loved and honored. Judas decided to collect an offering for himself instead of joining in and acting upon what this woman did. He refused to give an offering and was selling Jesus while Mary was worshipping Him with a year's wages. Judas sold Jesus for $21.70 while Mary poured a year's worth of wages on him and dried his feet with her hair.

In Luke 7:36-47, we read about the sinner woman who broke open an alabaster box. Her heart and her offering are contrasted against the backdrop of a pharisee named Simon. The woman gave a costly offering, wiped Jesus' feet with her hair, and kissed his feet. She was thankful and humble. When Simon complained about the entire offering, Jesus rebuked him. He didn't just commend the woman. He made an object lesson for both the woman and Simon the Pharisee. Jesus told everyone who was present at the dinner that Simon never even gave him water for his feet (the custom of the day), never greeted Jesus with a kiss, or anointed him for burial. Jesus reminded everyone present that the person who has been forgiven much is so thankful and shows it with worship and offerings. The religious people only complain and criticize. They do not give.

The greatest contrast of all is when we talk about the breaking of the alabaster box. We see Mary and Judas being contrasted, but we also see Jesus and Judas being contrasted. While Jesus was in the Garden of Gethsemane, His will surrendered to The Father or you and I, Judas was plotting the betrayal of Jesus. We have already talked about when Judas first allowed offense to poison him. It was all over an offering. He wanted the perfume to be sold so that he would have more to steal from the offering bag. Jesus was only thinking of pouring out His entire life's blood on Calvary's tree. Judas was filled with covetousness and greed, and Jesus only wanted to bless all of mankind. Jesus was God's offering to us, and Judas was only thinking of stealing an offering. The greatest betrayal since Lucifer's was Judas's betrayal, and it occurred over an offering. The offering seems to be either the rock of offense or the ultimate consecration.

We see yet another example with the Philippian church and other churches that didn't do their part.

> Now ye Philippians know also, that in the beginning of the gospel, when I departed from Macedonia, no church communicated with me as concerning giving and receiving, but ye only.
> For even in Thessalonica ye sent once and again unto my necessity.
>
> PHILIPPIANS 4:15, 16

The Apostle Paul said that none of the other churches contributed with offerings except the Philippians. He not only commends the Philippian church but also states that the other churches did not have the same heart. Because of the giving of Philippi, Paul said:

> But my God shall supply all your need according to his riches in glory by Christ Jesus.
>
> PHILIPPIANS 4:19

This verse does not apply to those who did not do what the Philippian church did when they gave offerings, not only once but a second time.

We see in another passage where Paul rebuked other churches for not doing their part.

> Have I committed an offence in abasing myself that ye might be exalted, because I have preached to you the gospel of God freely?
> I robbed other churches, taking wages of them, to do you service.
>
> 2 CORINTHIANS 11:7, 8

DR. DEBBIE RICH

The Apostle Paul reminds the Corinthian church with a rebuke that they should have been givers, but others had to make up for their lack. The church at Corinth was known for being an immature, carnal church, while the church at Phillipi made Paul proud. I wonder if the difference between giving hearts and selfish hearts had anything to do with it.

> And Jesus entered and passed through Jericho.
> And, behold, there was a man named Zacchaeus, which was the chief among the publicans, and he was rich.
> And he sought to see Jesus who he was; and could not for the press, because he was little of stature.
> And he ran before, and climbed up into a sycomore tree to see him: for he was to pass that way.
> And when Jesus came to the place, he looked up, and saw him, and said unto him, Zacchaeus, make haste, and come down; for to day I must abide at thy house.
> And he made haste, and came down, and received him joyfully.
> And when they saw it, they all murmured, saying, That he was gone to be guest with a man that is a sinner.
> And Zacchaeus stood, and said unto the Lord: Behold, Lord, the half of my goods I give to the poor; and if I have taken any thing from any man by false accusation, I restore him fourfold.
> And Jesus said unto him, This day is salvation come to this house, forsomuch as he also is a son of Abraham.
> For the Son of man is come to seek and to save that which was lost.
>
> LUKE 19:1-10

Zacchaeus was a man who was rich, but he had another problem. He was short. When Jesus came through town, Zacchaeus wanted to see Him but could not see over the crowd. He did not let that deter him. He decided to climb a tree to view Jesus. He was not content to just hear the crowd saying, "There He is." He wanted his own appointment. That is always a key to any kind of breakthrough: hunger and desperation. Some of you need to get in a tree-climbing mood to have an appointment with Jesus.

Zacchaeus was a renowned sinner. The Jews despised the tax collectors who usually were stealing from them. Zacchaeus was able to get wealthy off the backs of the people he cheated. He doesn't sound like a likely candidate for Jesus to visit his home. However, Jesus came to save sinners. Zacchaeus realized that he was a sinner in need of a savior. He received Jesus with joy. He did not run from Him. Jesus did not even ask Zacchaeus to give back the money. When Zacchaeus received Jesus with joy, he had an experience with Him and, subsequently, had a new heart toward everyone. The first thing he wanted to do was to give an offering. He didn't get angry about giving finances. It was the first thing on his heart once he was converted. That makes me wonder how converted people are if giving is the last thing they want to do.

I believe that giving singles a person out and pulls him out from the crowd. Giving gets Jesus' attention. It caused several people to be listed in the Bible for us to read about later. It puts a microphone in your hand, so to speak. God is not interested in the story of people who say they went to the meeting and didn't get touched. He's not interested in recording the story of people who refused to give or participate. He knows they will have no breakthrough to record. The Holy Spirit made sure that the offerings of many people would be recorded in His holy Bible. These are just some of those people. We can see how important offerings are to God.

In Mark 10:17-22, we have the story of the rich young ruler.

> And when he was gone forth into the way, there came one running, and kneeled to him, and asked him, Good Master, what shall I do that I may inherit eternal life?
> And Jesus said unto him, Why callest thou me good? There is none good but one, that is, God.
> Thou knowest the commandments, Do not commit adultery,

> Do not kill, Do not steal, Do not bear false witness, Defraud not, Honour thy father and mother.
> And he answered and said unto him, Master, all these have I observed from my youth.
> Then Jesus beholding him loved him, and said unto him, One thing thou lackest: go thy way, sell whatsoever thou hast, and give to the poor, and thou shalt have treasure in heaven: and come, take up the cross, and follow me.
> And he was sad at that saying, and went away grieved: for he had great possessions.
>
> MARK 10:17-22

In this story, we have a man who seems to be spiritually hungry. People can appear one way, but Jesus looks at the heart and knows the truth. No one can fool Him. The man came to Jesus inquiring about eternal life. This would be most evangelists' dream in a crusade. Jesus loved him and wanted to help him. He was not trying to be hard on him. He was not after his money but his heart. He knew that he could not serve Him without a fully committed heart. His love of money was his blockage to receiving eternal life. Jesus went straight to his heart and asked him to give everything.

I can only imagine what would happen today if a preacher told someone at the altar that they could not be saved unless they gave everything. It would be blown up on all media outlets that a preacher dared to refuse salvation to someone unless they gave everything. Yet, that is what Jesus did. It had nothing to do with his money and Jesus wanting it. It had everything to do with Jesus wanting the man to consecrate his heart and life to God. That is still the case today. Many times, it is the minister who is accused of loving money and wanting to get it from the people. Most of the time, it is the individual who loves money, not the person who is trying to get them set free from the love of money. A genuine minister of The Gospel wants to help people have a breakthrough, not take from them. However, the Devil knows that and plants the lie in people's minds that preachers are only in it for the money. The Devil is a liar.

The Bible says that the man walked away sad because he had great possessions. I have noticed that people who are not givers are sad, depressed, and bitter. Cain had the same disposition. You cannot be a radical giver, in love with Jesus Christ, and remain sad. Givers are joyful people. Nothing is extracted from them. You cannot keep them from giving.

This story is right across the page from the story of Zacchaeus in my Bible. Both men were rich. Both get the attention of Jesus. Both had the same opportunity for eternal life, but one was a giver and received eternal life, and the other refused to give and lost eternal life and will spend eternity in Hell. Offerings are not a side issue. It's all about the offering.

> And Jesus looked round about, and saith unto his disciples, How hardly shall they that have riches enter into the kingdom of God!
> And the disciples were astonished at his words. But Jesus answereth again, and saith unto them, Children, how hard is it for them that trust in riches to enter into the kingdom of God!
> It is easier for a camel to go through the eye of a needle, than for a rich man to enter into the kingdom of God.
> And they were astonished out of measure, saying among themselves, Who then can be saved?
> And Jesus looking upon them saith, With men it is impossible, but not with God: for with God all things are possible.
>
> MARK 10:23-27

After the meeting with the rich young ruler, the disciples and Jesus had a discussion. Jesus told them how difficult it is for people with great riches to enter the kingdom of God. The disciples were suddenly concerned about who could receive eternal life. If the disciples were poor, they would have felt comforted and said, "We don't have to worry about it since we don't have anything." However, that is not what they said. They asked, *"Who then can be saved?"* The implication is that they might have too much to be saved.

> Then Peter began to say unto him, Lo, we have left all, and have followed thee.
> And Jesus answered and said, Verily I say unto you, There is no man that hath left house, or brethren, or sisters, or father, or mother, or wife, or children, or lands, for my sake, and the gospel's,
> But he shall receive an hundredfold now in this time, houses, and brethren, and sisters, and mothers, and children, and lands, with persecutions; and in the world to come eternal life.
> But many that are first shall be last; and the last first.
>
> MARK 10:28-31

Jesus let them know that they would not only be blessed in Heaven but that they would receive a hundredfold now. He even got specific and mentioned houses and lands. This is what they could believe for while they were still on earth. He let them know that what they gave to follow him, their jobs and income with them, their homes, and any other kind of offering would be rewarded now, on this earth. He let them know that they not only had eternal life but rewards on earth and in Heaven for their giving, unlike the rich young ruler. Offerings and sacrifice are all about the heart.

Offerings are very sacred. There have been serious consequences, as there were for Ananias and Sapphira.

> But a certain man named Ananias, with Sapphira his wife, sold a possession,
> And kept back part of the price, his wife also being privy to

it, and brought a certain part, and laid it at the apostles' feet.

But Peter said, Ananias, why hath Satan filled thine heart to lie to the Holy Ghost, and to keep back part of the price of the land?

Whiles it remained, was it not thine own? And after it was sold, was it not in thine own power? Why hast thou conceived this thing in thine heart? Thou hast not lied unto men, but unto God.

And Ananias hearing these words fell down, and gave up the ghost: and great fear came on all them that heard these things.

And the young men arose, wound him up, and carried him out, and buried him.

And it was about the space of three hours after, when his wife, not knowing what was done, came in.

And Peter answered unto her, Tell me whether ye sold the land for so much? And she said, Yea, for so much.

Then Peter said unto her, How is it that ye have agreed together to tempt the Spirit of the Lord? Behold, the feet of them which have buried thy husband are at the door, and shall carry thee out.

Then fell she down straightway at his feet, and yielded up the ghost: and the young men came in, and found her dead, and, carrying her forth, buried her by her husband.

And great fear came upon all the church, and upon as many as heard these things.

ACTS 5: 1-11

This occurred in the early church. I must remind you that this was in this present-day age of grace. Both husband and wife found out that it's all about the offering. They should have realized that earlier. The hearts of people in the book of Acts were pure, and people were great givers, according to Acts 4. There was great power and grace in the church.

However, two hearts are contrasted in the middle of that, and they belong to Ananias and Sapphira. They held back part of the price of the sale of their land and lied about It. Stinginess tends to lead to other sins. This incident ended up costing them their lives. The Holy Spirit made sure that this was included in the Bible for us to learn what to do and what not to do. Evidently, The Holy Spirit did not take these things lightly. Neither should we. Jesus talked about finances in nearly two-thirds of His teachings for a reason.

We go back to the Old Testament for another example of how sacred offerings are to God, where we read about a man named Achan who touched *"a devoted thing"* unto The Lord.

> But the children of Israel committed a trespass in the accursed thing: for Achan, the son of Carmi, the son of Zabdi, the son of Zerah, of the tribe of Judah, took of the accursed thing: and the anger of the Lord was kindled against the children of Israel.
>
> JOSHUA 7:1

> Israel hath sinned, and they have also transgressed my covenant which I commanded them: for they have even taken of the accursed thing, and have also stolen, and dissembled also, and they have put it even among their own stuff.
> Therefore the children of Israel could not stand before their enemies, but turned their backs before their enemies, because they were accursed: neither will I be with you any more, except ye destroy the accursed from among you.
> Up, sanctify the people, and say, Sanctify yourselves against to morrow: for thus saith the Lord God of Israel, There is an accursed thing in the midst of thee, O Israel: thou

canst not stand before thine enemies, until ye take away the accursed thing from among you.

In the morning therefore ye shall be brought according to your tribes: and it shall be, that the tribe which the Lord taketh shall come according to the families thereof; and the family which the Lord shall take shall come by households; and the household which the Lord shall take shall come man by man.

And it shall be, that he that is taken with the accursed thing shall be burnt with fire, he and all that he hath: because he hath transgressed the covenant of the Lord, and because he hath wrought folly in Israel.

So Joshua rose up early in the morning, and brought Israel by their tribes; and the tribe of Judah was taken:

And he brought the family of Judah; and he took the family of the Zarhites: and he brought the family of the Zarhites man by man; and Zabdi was taken:

And he brought his household man by man; and Achan, the son of Carmi, the son of Zabdi, the son of Zerah, of the tribe of Judah, was taken.

And Joshua said unto Achan, My son, give, I pray thee, glory to the Lord God of Israel, and make confession unto him; and tell me now what thou hast done; hide it not from me.

And Achan answered Joshua, and said, Indeed I have sinned against the Lord God of Israel, and thus and thus have I done:

When I saw among the spoils a goodly Babylonish garment, and two hundred shekels of silver, and a wedge of gold of fifty shekels weight, then I coveted them, and took them; and, behold, they are hid in the earth in the midst of my tent, and the silver under it.

So Joshua sent messengers, and they ran unto the tent; and, behold, it was hid in his tent, and the silver under it.

And they took them out of the midst of the tent, and brought

> them unto Joshua, and unto all the children of Israel, and laid them out before the Lord.
>
> And Joshua, and all Israel with him, took Achan the son of Zerah, and the silver, and the garment, and the wedge of gold, and his sons, and his daughters, and his oxen, and his asses, and his sheep, and his tent, and all that he had: and they brought them unto the valley of Achor.
>
> And Joshua said, Why hast thou troubled us? The Lord shall trouble thee this day. And all Israel stoned him with stones, and burned them with fire, after they had stoned them with stones.
>
> And they raised over him a great heap of stones unto this day. So the Lord turned from the fierceness of his anger. Wherefore the name of that place was called, The valley of Achor, unto this day.
>
> JOSHUA 7:11-26

God commanded Israel to not keep any spoils from the battle in Jericho. That first city was devoted to The Lord. God would not let them partake of the spoils of the next Babylonian clothing, silver, and gold, and hide them in his tent. I have wondered what he thought he could do with them. He couldn't put the enemy's clothing on and not have anyone in Israel notice. He couldn't say he ran down to Walmart to buy them. He would have been found out anyway. However, he forgot that God is always watching. Not only his life and his family's lives were lost, but Israel lost men in battle that day because someone did not understand how sacred offerings are to God.

Offerings are all about consecration, dedication, priorities, or the heart of a person. It's the willing and obedient that shall eat of the good of the land. We are a consecrated and divine meeting place for God. We are more than just the altar. God has called us His temple. You are a far more consecrated altar than the altar of Bethel. The church of The Lord Jesus Christ is a place where His glory is manifested and where He dwells. The church is far more holy than the holy of holies in the Tabernacle. It is separated and consecrated.

That should cause us to see something far more glorious than any earthly interests. We need to recognize that we have not moved into everything God has for us. We must get rid of every excuse and say we can be who we are called to be. We can have no mixture of motives. We can no longer mix what God said to do with what I would like to do. There can be no mixture of faith and unbelief. We must get desperate for God to use us and be willing to do things His way.

God is calling us to move up higher. Living in the realm of the Spirit is not relegated to only a few. Part of living in this realm is the revelation of offerings and realizing that our entire lives are an offering to be spent for our Savior. I am hungering and thirsting for that realm. When He calls you up into the realms of His glory, you have to say, "Lord, I want these things." You must begin to get hungry and desperate for the things of God. You must be willing to risk everything to lay hold of the promise. That disposition becomes a consecrated place.

Just as fire was involved in the Old Testament offerings, fire is involved with our hearts and offerings today. We must have clean, pure hearts. There can be no manipulation or false motives involved. God loves to interact with givers.

> Who shall ascend into the hill of the Lord? Or who shall
>   stand in his holy place?
> He that hath clean hands, and a pure heart; who hath not
>   lifted up his soul unto vanity, nor sworn deccitfully.
>
> PSALM 24:3, 4

God will only use people with pure hearts who have been poured out and hold nothing back from their Lord. We must give ourselves over to His divine will and purpose. We must say, "Not my will, but thine be done." I want The Holy Spirit to take over and only Jesus to be seen.

I had the privilege of taking the Gospel to seven nations in Europe at one time. When I returned home, a friend of mine (who is also an evangelist) told me that she watched some of the services online. She said that she was profoundly moved by the purity in my stewardship messages. That touched me deeply. I told her that I witnessed something in one of the nations that grieved my heart. I sensed the opposite of purity. I knew that the message had been perverted, and I could not be a part of that. When I arrived home and was sitting at The River at Tampa Bay Church (Pastors Rodney and Adonica Howard-Browne's church), I was weeping while listening to Pastor Rodney deliver a stewardship message. It was as pure as it was the first time I heard it, over thirty years ago. It has never changed. This was the message that set me free from poverty so that I could be blessed to be a blessing all over the earth. There is nothing tainted about this message, and I shall continue to guard my heart so that it never becomes tainted. It's all about the offering.

God has given us a certain amount of finances to see how we would manage them. He wants us to manage them under His wisdom and His judgment. We must not manage anything based on our own desires and wishes. We must refuse to walk in our own way. When we do things God's way, He'll cause us to ride upon the high places.

We have seen over and over again that all offerings must have a sweet savor unto God. We've seen that all offerings have a smell. We're living in the new covenant, and there is more than just enough to do all that God wants us to do. Throughout this book, you see two offerings: the one done God's way and the one done man's way, which is really the Devil's way. The Devil hates worship to God, which is what the offering is all about. Giving is an expression of obedience, gratitude, trust, and increasing joy. God seeks out and recognizes those who worship him. He wants the worship.

NINETEEN

RECENT FINANCIAL MIRACLES

Pastor Rodney Howard-Browne did a short series on New Year's weekend, 2022. The subject was making vows and consecration. He declared that this was the year of El-Shaddai, the God of More than Enough, The All-Sufficient One. It was the most powerful preaching that I have ever heard. I was more affected than at any other time in my life. I have prayed prayers of consecration many times in my life, but never with the brokenness and consecration that came from my heart that weekend. I realized like never before that everything that I have or will ever have is by God's grace and power. I also saw with a new reality how big our God is and how much He wants to bless me when He knows that He can trust me. A gift of faith fell on me and enveloped me. I felt that I could believe God for anything. I knew this would be a year of great increase for the ministry and also a year of personal dreams becoming reality.

I distinctly heard The Lord (on the inside of me) say that it was time for the restoration in my life of everything the enemy stole from me years ago. The only part of that restoration that had not come back was the Corvette that you read about earlier. After Pastor Rodney sent it back home with me, I made a terrible decision and trusted someone that I should not have. It cost me greatly, including financially. I sold my dream car to pay off someone else's debt in 2006. I learned many lessons and have received God's grace and restoration. However, I felt the guilt and condemnation from making a stupid decision, and that prevented me from even dreaming of having a car like that again. Besides, I have reached an age where I feel a sports car is not feasible and would look ridiculous. I have also raised the level of my giving and felt that would be detrimental to my giving. I didn't think I even cared about a nice car anymore. I cared about building the kingdom of Heaven. I could have paid cash for three corvettes after I sold my home in Washington State following the death of my husband in 2020. Instead, I gave over half of the money. I moved from Washington State to the Tampa area to be a part of the River at Tampa Bay Church with Pastors Rodney and Adonica Howard-Browne. I put a down payment on my home in Riverview (a suburb of Tampa, FL) and bought furniture for the home. That depleted the rest of the money from the sale of my home in Washington. If I bought a new car, it would not be possible to pay cash for it. I had just enough for a down payment.

However, after the New Year's messages, I knew that it was time to expect God to bless me with a vehicle like the one I gave to Pastors Rodney and Adonica many years prior. The condemnation was gone, and I knew that God wanted to bless me. I thought that I was believing for some wealthy person to give me one or buy one for me. These are the kinds of testimonies we hear every week at The River. People are often given cars. Since I had sown five vehicles to others, I felt that it was time for me to be given one, or at least given the down payment for one, like I was given the first time. We seem to think that when God moves, He will do it the same way every time. However, He doesn't want us to get too comfortable but to stay totally dependent on Him. He has many ways that He can give us a miracle.

Sometime in February, I heard Pastor Rodney say, "Some of you just need to go out and buy your car." That hit me like a sledgehammer. I knew this was for me. I told my assistant, Heather, "I'm going to buy a Vette today. Do you want to come?" She was totally shocked. She never heard me speaking of wanting one. However, I knew that it was time for me to buy it myself. When I arrived at the dealership, a salesman told me that a man had brought to the dealership a 2022 Z51 performance package Corvette convertible with only 350 miles on it. It was red with a black and red interior. It also had a black racing stripe on the red hood. It was a beautiful car that surpassed what I was looking for. I knew that it was the one God was directing me to.

I had enough money left from the sale of my Washington home to put a down payment of twenty thousand dollars on the car. I financed the rest with a seven-year loan. The payments were higher than any car payments that I had ever made, but I knew that God was gracing me to make those payments. This was on February 22, 2023. I did not realize the significance of the date until the next day. I had closed on my new home on February 2, 2022. Exactly one year later, God enabled me to purchase my dream car. I felt that The Lord was showing me that in one year, He replaced everything that the enemy ever stole from me or that I gave up willingly. What a gracious and big God! My pastor told me that he believed God that I would be able to pay it off within the year. I told him that I would agree in faith for that miracle.

A series of financial miracles took place over the next four months. Many times, when I have taught on the subject of stewardship, people have been blessed financially. Sometimes, congregations began to give to individuals spontaneously. However, it had never happened to me until July of 2023. My church, The River at Tampa Bay, and my pastors, Rodney and Adonica Howard-Browne, host two campmeetings and two ministers' conferences a year. July is the summer "Fire Conference." I had the privilege of teaching in several of the services. In one of the evening services, Pastor Rodney spoke my name and asked me to step onto the altar area, and he prophesied to me about going to Alaska again for ministry. He said that God was going to honor all of my years of pioneering in that cold state, and the ministry would be blessed, and planes would be given. I fell out under the power of God, and people immediately began to pile an offering on me. Several thousand dollars were given to me personally. The next day, I received a notice from my bank that several thousand dollars had been deposited into my account from the government. I had no idea why and knew that I better check into it. It turned out to be something that had to do with my late husband, who was a war veteran retired from the United States Navy. I never opened that case or even inquired about it. I knew that God was bringing funds in supernaturally. Every time that I saved extra finances or was blessed with a gift, I applied it to the loan. The loan was supernaturally paid off in seven months instead of seven years.

The Corvette has been a soul-winning tool. Everywhere I go, someone asks about it, and many want to take a picture standing beside it. I tell them my testimony of being a single mother, living with other people, driving a totaled car in Alaska, and how God has blessed me. I have found no one who is unsaved having a problem with God blessing me with that car. In fact, a homeless man walked up to me, congratulated me on the car, and mentioned that he could see how God had blessed me. However, it should surprise no one that religious people are the ones who have a problem. One woman posted a picture of a corvette that is similar, with a price tag. She had plenty to say about how shameful it was of me to buy such a car. The interesting thing is the fact that my car was nicer, and I paid less for it. I told her that she verified that I got a very good deal on the car. I also told her that I did not use offerings or ministry funds to pay for it. It came out of my salary. (Not that it is anyone's business.) No one has a problem with anyone from any other profession buying a nice car. Religious people seem to think that Christians, especially ministers, should live in poverty and drive junk cars.

I flew to Alaska earlier in July to visit family. While there, I had the opportunity to minister in two churches. I discovered that a pastor friend, previously from Pt. Barrow, Alaska, had moved to the same area that my sons live in. He attended the meetings and asked to take me to dinner with himself and his wife. During the dinner conversation, Pastor McKenzie mentioned that he had recently been given an Alaskan bush plane. He is getting older and wants to make sure that when he goes to Heaven, the plane will be used for Godly purposes. He mentioned possibly giving the plane to Pastor Rodney, and I told him that God spoke to me about ministering in Alaska again. He and Pastor Rodney agreed that the plane should come to me. It is a Cessna year 1970, single-engine plane that seats six people. This is the first plane that has been given to me. I have flown in many two-seater planes through snowstorms and heavy turbulence. I felt like this was God rewarding me. Pastor Rodney prophesied a few weeks later that this would be the first of many planes and that hangars and pilots would be coming with them. I believe it.

I was ministering in a small church in northwest Arkansas recently and was told by the pastors that a man brought in a heavy box for our ministry. When I opened it, I found it to be a box full of silver coins. It amounted to several thousand dollars for the ministry. God has a way of bringing the funds in from different sources in unique ways.

I am willing to preach to thirty like I do to three thousand or thirty thousand. I go to churches of many sizes in many different locations. It is always a step of faith to go to a small church when you have employees and commitments all over the world. However, God has always been faithful, and many of our largest offerings have come from the smallest of churches. It always amazes me. It has been that way from the beginning but even more apparent lately. As God has blessed this ministry, some think that I can no longer afford to go to the smaller churches because the budget has increased. I am so thankful that we still can. Many of those churches are churches that feel that they do not dare ask proven ministers, who carry the anointing of The Holy Spirit, to come to their church. I still enjoy being able to go to those churches and making a difference in people's lives. Recently, a church of about thirty people gave thirty-five thousand dollars in one week. God is so faithful!

As I write this chapter, I am in the middle of two large transactions that are taking place as a result of growth. I hired an assistant this year, as well as a media person. I already have a secretary who is in Washington State at this time. I felt to give one of my assistants, Heather Mosely, my second car, which is a Chevrolet Impala with very low mileage and has the highest trim level. I have loved that car. It was the last thing my husband purchased for me when he saw how much I liked it. So, it also has sentimental value. A week before Heather started to work for me, she was hit by a driver with no insurance. She only had liability insurance on her vehicle, and it was totaled. She came to me with no vehicle, and I invited her to live in my home and use my car. The Lord spoke to my heart a few weeks ago to give her the Impala, even though I knew that I was getting ready to purchase a vehicle for the ministry that could hold our luggage and book table. The Impala would have made a nice trade-in, but I wanted to bless her and felt led to give it to her. The ministry just purchased a new mini-van that will hold our luggage and drive us to nearby states instead of always having to fly and deal with TSA. It is a beautiful vehicle, and God has blessed us again.

I also invited Emma (the media person) to live in my home but have come to realize that we all need more space. I probably should have bought a larger home when I moved back to the Tampa area but felt it was more than adequate for a lady living alone. However, I should have thought about how many guests I host at the campmeetings and ministers' conference time. I also should have realized that I now need a filming studio in my home, a room for working out, and space for when my children visit. So, I am leasing another home in the same neighborhood for my studio and my employees to live in. I signed on both the vehicle and the home today, just weeks before Christmas. It is time to kick it up another level again, and that always involves expense. It would be easier at my age to begin to coast, but I continue to push myself in every way. It is not time to retire. It is time to re-fire. These shall be the best days of Debbie Rich Ministries yet. We will continue to plunder Hell and populate Heaven. I will continue to walk on the water and shake nations. I want to encourage you to do the same. The body of Christ cannot afford to pull back now. We are the restraining force against the spirit of anti-Christ in the world today. It is time to take territory. To do so, we must continue to exercise our faith.

TWENTY

FOLLOWING IN THE STEPS OF MY PASTORS

When I first met Drs. Rodney and Adonica Howard-Browne, they were in Broken Arrow, Oklahoma (a suburb of Tulsa) at Rhema Bible Training Center. Dr. Rodney was preaching on The Coming Revival. I was a student. The message created a powerful spiritual hunger in me. I never dreamed that I would ever see the Howard-Brownes again. After I graduated from Rhema Bible Training Center, I worked for Kenneth Hagin Ministries for over a year and then traveled to Alaska as a missionary in October of 1990. In November of 1992, I received a telephone call that changed my life, the life of my family, and now, countless other lives. A good friend invited me to attend meetings in Anchorage, where a great revival was taking place. I found out that Drs. Rodney and Adonica Howard-Browne were the evangelists conducting the revival. I was so surprised that they were ministering in that cold state. They are originally from South Africa. They were a long way from home. It was the middle of the Alaskan winter, and as few evangelists came to Alaska in the winter, I knew they were true evangelists who wanted to minister to the people. They did not just want to go fishing and hunting and book a weekend of ministry to pay for their trip.

DR. DEBBIE RICH

At the beginning of this book, I shared that Pastor Rodney's stewardship teaching changed my life. God delivered me from poverty and has blessed me to make me a blessing. It was not only my pastors' teaching but their example of faith and their giving hearts that gave me the breakthrough. I know that what it takes to get, it takes to keep. I continue to follow them as they follow Christ. I have watched God continually stretch them in their vision and in their giving. Everything about their ministry, Revival Ministries International, is increasing exponentially. Every time that I come home from ministering somewhere, I see an increase at the church. The blessings of God are surely chasing after them and running them down, as Deuteronomy 28:2 says. *"And all these blessings shall come on thee, and overtake thee, if thou shalt hearken unto the voice of the Lord thy God."*

Pastors Rodney and Adonica paid off the note that held the church mortgage a few years ago. It was approximately twelve million dollars. It took about twenty years to pay it off. Next, they decided to buy an outside pavilion with a canvas roof during COVID. It is huge. It will house 747 jets. They did that to make a stand against tyranny and wicked people trying to shut the church down. It has been going now for over three years, and he said that they will have church every night in it as long as there are people anywhere in the world who are free to worship. The pavilion, equipment, astroturf, and everything else associated with the pavilion came at great expense. After the pavilion was purchased, they felt that it was time to remodel the church auditorium and build balconies to accommodate a growing congregation. The remodel cost was very close to the same amount as the initial mortgage. Yet, they paid cash for the remodel and balconies in only four and one-half months. What took twenty years to pay was almost the same amount that was paid in only four and one-half months. Talk about things being expedited! They introduced a video of the third phase of the building a few months ago. It will sit between the pavilion and the main auditorium and will house youth, children's church, offices, Bible school rooms, restaurants, businesses, kingdom business fellowship, etc. It will cost more than the other two phases. While taking on such a large project, The Lord directed them to go to ten cities in Africa, where they not only held crusades but also met with kings, presidents, and businessmen. He took 500 tons of food into Kenya to help thirty-six thousand families. In Eswatini (Swaziland), he gave three hundred blankets for the winter, supplied widows with blankets, took fertilizer into another country, and paid for the crusades. Pastors Rodney and Adonica gave the offerings back to the nations they ministered in. Pastor Rodney was led to give an African minister, who was sitting in one of the meetings, ten thousand dollars. This is all while he was paying cash for the building project. God told him that he could believe to do both at the same time.

During the ministers' and leaders' conference in October of 2023, I witnessed my pastor give thousands to visiting ministers, some to build people's churches, and more. It looked impossible for him to do that at this time, but he obeyed God. I was astounded at how many hundreds of thousands he gave while believing God for his own financial miracle. Every day, he pointed at someone and said, "I want to give you ten thousand," to another one, he said, "I am giving you one hundred thousand for your ministry." He needs millions of dollars in the days ahead for the third phase of our building project and for all of the crusades coming up, both here in America and overseas. Pastors Rodney and Adonica Howard-Browne have never let up in their giving. They realize that what God showed them in the beginning is still the case. What it takes to get, it takes to keep. If giving was the key to a breakthrough when they had nothing, it is still the key to a breakthrough into a greater blessing.

When Pastors Rodney and Adonica went on a ten-city tour to Africa in September of 2022, he chartered an Airbus to take a team of nineteen people. No preacher has ever done that before. It so impressed the kings and governmental leaders of those nations that it opened doors for Pastor Rodney to speak to the governmental leaders about current international problems and the way to solve those problems. The blessing of The Lord has opened many doors. The Bible says in Ecclesiastes 9:16 b, *"The poor man's wisdom is despised, and his words are not heard."* Poverty had no influence on Pastors Rodney and Adonica when they were starting out. The blessing of God has brought them to a place of great influence. It has also brought them into a place of being able to be a blessing to countless people all over the earth. Likewise, no one listened to me when I had nothing and was dependent upon others for basic survival. The blessing of The Lord has allowed me to bless others and speak into their lives. When people tell me that this doesn't work, I have to say, "you've come too late to tell me this doesn't work. I've been there and I've been here, and here is better."

When Pastor Rodney and Adonica's daughter Kelly went home to be with Jesus on Christmas Day, 2002, Pastor Rodney made a vow to The Lord. He told the Devil that he could not steal her. He would lay her down as an offering to God, the best offering that he could ever give. He told The Lord that he vowed one hundred million souls into the kingdom and one hundred billion dollars for God's work to accomplish his assignment. They are well on their way to accomplishing both. They have come at a great price, including Pastor Rodney's arrest in March of 2020 for not shutting the church down because of the COVID restrictions. They will not compromise and continue to believe God for big things, and they are accomplishing big things for the kingdom of God.

I will continue to follow my pastors who have set the example in laying down their lives, giving everything they have, and staying true to God, His Word, and His Spirit without compromise. I will follow them as they follow Christ. Every time I see them being stretched, I stretch. When I see them go to another level, I know that I am going to another level. The blessings of God and the revelation of His Word flow from the top down. I am so thankful for the message they first brought to me all of those years ago in Alaska, and I am privileged to continue to sit under them today. It is as pure as it was the day I first heard it. It is all part and parcel of revival. I am so honored to be associated with these five-star generals in the faith.

TWENTY-ONE

WATCHING OVER YOUR SEED

I am a bit saddened that this book is drawing to a close. Giving is a subject especially dear to my heart and is found throughout the Bible, from Genesis to Revelation. There is no way that I could exhaust the subject in this one book. I've already thought of so many more texts from which I would like to have taught. However, it would add countless chapters, and you wouldn't have the time and energy to read it. Yet, there is much to be explored in this area. As far as most of the church is concerned, we are in uncharted waters. I hope that many others will *get in the boat*, teaching in tandem with me.

Teaching alone will not guarantee that people will live to give. Revival must be caught, not taught. Those who have been called and appointed by The Lord to preach and teach the Gospel have a responsibility to teach this. However, each one must first catch the spirit of giving themselves.

I thank God that when Pastor Rodney came to Alaska with this teaching from the Word of God, I was in a state of desperation. If I had been like most of the people in that audience, I would have remained just as I was. Most of them had not plunged to my level of poverty. They were not single mothers who had a call of God upon their lives but no natural way to fulfill it. They had jobs and careers, and most lived in double-income earning households. Most ministers in the audience had churches from which they received comfortable salaries.

Interestingly enough, those people have not progressed. They have remained in the same financial situations. I, however, was at the bottom of the barrel. Actually, let me rephrase that. I was sitting underneath the barrel. I had to believe God's Word, or it was going to be all over for me. I have continued to increase because God's Word became real to me.

Some people think that in order to prosper, all you have to do is give. That's only one part of it. I have known too many people who were *big givers*, yet continued to *live in poverty*. Some of the reasons were quite obvious. Some still had a poverty mentality, refusing to see that God wanted and willed to bless them. Other people were good givers but lousy receivers. They enjoy giving but would not humble themselves to receive. Still others were so abused and beat up by life that their souls were not prospering. Others know nothing of mixing faith with their giving. Many times, the pitfall is pride and wrong teaching.

God cannot bless someone who will not receive. I've had a difficult time getting certain people to receive from me. I have a relative who gets angry every time I pay for dinners or purchase anything. Even though I was in a better position to pay than he was, he would still not receive. Yet, I've heard him say on many occasions, "Nobody ever gave me anything in my life, and nobody ever will. I believe in carrying my own weight. I'll never ask anyone for anything."

Remarkably, that same person becomes bitter when others succeed. I've also heard him say repeatedly that only the lazy make money. He has said that hard-working people will never have anything. Obviously, he cannot prosper when he practices embracing such lies, nurturing such attitudes, and verbalizing so much negativity.

> Death and life are in the power of the tongue.
>
> PROVERBS 18:21

> . . .
>
> But the word is very nigh unto thee, in thy mouth, and in thy heart, that thou mayest do it.
>
> DEUTERONOMY 30:14

Our tongues are powerful weapons. We repeatedly cancel our blessings by the words of our mouths. Just as it is possible to cancel or incur penalties by withdrawing a certificate of deposit (CD) before it reaches maturity, it is also possible in the spiritual realm to cancel your harvest by speaking words of doubt and unbelief.

Maybe the circumstances of life have tainted how you have received God's Word. Bitterness will block your faith and block God from working on your behalf. I know a very good man who worked hard all his life and didn't have a tightwad bone in his body. He was a tither and a giver. This man had an accident that resulted in physical injury but was unable to receive any reimbursement for the incident. Then, he was turned down the first time he applied for Social Security.

He watched people around him taking advantage of our government. He drank coffee with men who were receiving disability and Social Security for so-called "bad backs." These same men could be seen out playing sports every day. They were having a good ol' time at the taxpayers' expense. Yet, here sat this seriously hurt, honest tither and giver unable to get the help he needed.

To the observer, it just didn't make sense. But you know, this dear man could be heard saying that it was always those kinds of people who got ahead in life. He would rehearse and repeat the phrase that "the working guy never had a chance."

It was my impression that he thought that because there was a devil out there who hated Christians, life would always have to be hard. (At least he was clear that poverty and sickness come from Satan. He just didn't comprehend that we don't have to stand for it.) That precious man fought what he calls "the prosperity message" and has never prospered. I know that he wanted to give more to the Kingdom, but he had nothing left to give. It's sad that he never laid hold of this message.

It takes more than being a giver to receive.

In order to receive the promised results, God has principles by which we must abide. In addition to keeping your mouth lined up with the Word of God, you must water your field with the Word. Pluck out those weeds of doubt and unbelief. Fertilize your crop with the Holy Spirit. Work your fields and don't give up, for, in due time, you will reap your harvest.

I remember holding a revival in the Seattle area. It was a good-sized meeting with crowds of five to six hundred attending every night. We saw many salvations, healings, and people being blessed and filled with the Holy Spirit. At the end of the week, I received twelve thousand dollars, which, at that time, was an enormous offering for our ministry. When I asked when I could return, we scheduled a time in December.

Meanwhile, I received an invitation to bring revival to the country of Nepal shortly after the New Year. However, I was asked not to receive any offerings there. I agreed because I felt that God was opening a door of ministry into that region. I determined that the fact that I would not be receiving offerings would not prevent me from teaching on stewardship. I knew that, especially in these poverty-stricken nations, the teaching must begin somewhere.

When we returned to Seattle during the first two weeks of December, we once again experienced an awesome revival. The crowds were even bigger than before. God was moving in a very demonstrable way.

Aware of the return to Seattle in December, I thought about how God arranged to give me an invitation to a large church shortly before I was to depart for Nepal. God knew that a large offering could carry us through several weeks on the foreign field where no offerings would be received. (These are things that people who are not in the ministry often do not understand or comprehend.) When they hear that someone received a large offering somewhere, they do not realize that often, the offering must carry their ministry through lean times in the foreign field. Or maybe it must carry them through periods of time when they continue to labor in small churches here in the United States.

I realized that if God had given me twelve thousand dollars in one week in Seattle, I could believe Him for twenty thousand for two weeks. Larger crowds were in attendance, so this shouldn't be a problem. I was preaching two services a day and praying for hundreds of people each night into the wee hours of the morning. I did not ask the pastor how much we received in the offerings. On Thursday night of the second week, the church secretary delivered some disappointing news. She asked, "Has anyone told you about the offerings yet?"

I replied, "No, they haven't."

She said, "Well, we thought you should know that, for some reason, the offerings are really down. We didn't want you to be shocked tomorrow when you received the check. We don't know what's wrong. It could be that it's getting close to Christmas, but only six thousand dollars has come in." Believe me, I was shocked. This made no sense whatsoever. Here I was, ministering to larger crowds for twice as long as before with only half the amount. I decided that I needed to go talk to God.

I went out to the trailer where I was staying and began to pray. I reminded God that He was a good God and His Word was true. I reminded Him that I was a giver and had been sowing even more than usual. I reminded Him how this offering was going to be used. I was not going to consume it on my own lusts. The offering would be used to preach the gospel to multitudes on the foreign field.

I took a few minutes to quote God's Word back to Him and to fortify my own spirit. I was pulling out weeds of doubt and unbelief that were mixed in with my harvest. I was fertilizing and irrigating my crops with the Word of God. I came out of that trailer knowing that I would have my miracle. I did not speak words of doubt and unbelief. I did not murmur, complain, or accuse God; I kept my mouth aligned with His Word.

The next day was Friday, the last day of our revival. I taught just as I always do in the morning service. I did not mention that our offerings were down and that we needed a miracle. Nor did I indicate that we needed to raise a certain amount of money. After the morning service, the same secretary came running up to me. She asked if anyone had told me what had happened with the offering that morning. I let her know that they had not. She told me that she had no idea what I had taught, but something must have really moved the people. They gave much more than in any other service. I began to shout, but she said, "Oh, there's more. That's not the really, really good news. Someone gave one thousand dollars all by themselves." I really got happy, and she stopped me again, saying, "No, you don't understand. That's not the really, really, really good news. Someone else gave five thousand dollars all by themselves."

In one morning meeting of only forty or fifty people (the larger crowds of about six hundred people attended at night), over six thousand dollars came in. We received more in that small morning service than had been received in two weeks of day and night meetings. Hallelujah! God did even more than that. That night, another seven thousand dollars came in. In one day, about fourteen thousand dollars was given, bringing the total received up to over twenty thousand dollars. It was just the amount that I needed for my miracle.

Everyone loves to hear incredible, miraculous stories like this. The problem is that few want to operate in this realm of faith. Even fewer want to tend to their fields. These people do not prosper because they are just plain lazy. They want everything to come easily. They think that everything with God should be automatic. However, this is not so.

I've heard my pastor tell how he and his wife, Adonica, started out in ministry right after they were married. Someone from their native South Africa asked them to come and hold a revival. When they got to the man's church, he had taken off to America to raise funds. Now, others might sit down and have a pity party or get bitter and quit, but not the Howard-Brownes. They rented a building and then went door-to-door, passing out fliers and inviting people to come to their meetings. Only twelve people attended the first service. Pastor Rodney led the worship with his guitar. He prayed for people and then caught them when they "went out." He did whatever he had to do to get the job done.

I've done the same thing. At the beginning of my ministry, I worked at a used clothing store, saving up money to go into the villages of Alaska. At the same time, I ran a prison ministry. In case you didn't know it, prison ministry does not make you rich or famous. In the three years I ministered there, I never received an offering. However, God was watching it all. Faithfulness does pay off.

I went into villages where the churches would not allow me to preach. I met with people in their homes and held my own worship, walking door to door in sub-zero climates. I flew in little two-seater airplanes through blizzards. I went to "sing-spirations" in villages that lasted until 4:00 a.m. Many times, I couldn't minister. The people didn't trust me yet. I would go, listen to them sing, and then go to their potlatches (native version of our potlucks). I would spend hundreds of dollars to sit down beside them and eat Muktuk, an Eskimo dish made of whale blubber and seal oil. These actions enabled me to return and minister to the people. I was faithfully tending my fields.

Remember, God has no favorites and is not a respecter of persons. He is only a respecter of principles. You must be a doer of His Word in all areas, not just in your favorite ones. Thank God, there are those of us who have not despised the days of small beginnings when we labored with little or no pay. We were willing to pay the price, no matter what it was, to win the lost.

There's been a lot of arguing back and forth about "the hundred-fold return." The Bible speaks of it, so I will continue to teach it. Remember that in the time of famine, Isaac sowed into a parched desert land and reaped a hundred-fold return (Genesis 26:1,12). You don't have to calculate that. It is so!

Nevertheless, I've never told anyone in my meetings that it was the hundred-fold night and that if they gave, they would receive a hundred-fold. No. I don't believe in that. There are too *many factors in individual lives that determine their harvest.* However, in my giving, I will continue to believe that a hundred-fold return is possible. Why? Because I've witnessed it take place.

I saw the hundred-fold return come to a young woman in Ukraine who had just been saved in our meetings. In sharing her testimony, she related giving the last of what she had (which amounted to five cents in their currency) in the offering. She realized that she had no money or food whatsoever for the next day but decided to trust God and give. (I love the faith of new believers. There was no time for anyone to get to her and discourage her faith.) The next morning, the young woman heard a knock on her door. When she answered, a lady asked the young woman if she could sew some clothing for her. When she replied that she would, the lady said that she felt impressed to pay her ahead of time—just because she liked her. The lady paid the young woman a more than generous amount. Just moments later, the new convert heard another knock at her door. Someone who had owed her money for more than four years came by to repay it. In just one day, she received a 5,000 percent return on what she had sown. Hallelujah!

It's important to give even when it's not convenient. I held a revival in Long Beach, Mississippi, in January of 1997. It was a blowout that lasted for six weeks. Fourteen states and sixteen denominations were represented, with many saved and great miraculous demonstrations.

I had to cancel several previously planned meetings in other states to continue in Mississippi. One of the places that was canceled was a little village church in Alaska called Hoonah. I promised the pastor that I would come the following January and that I would bring the Mississippi pastor and his wife with me. The pastor and his wife had always wanted to minister in an Alaskan village, so I told them I would buy their plane tickets.

January was a slower season financially. Evangelists usually don't have meetings in the month of December because of the Christmas season in churches. (It's difficult to have revival when churches are busy celebrating Jesus!)

I had no income for several weeks. My youngest son was traveling with me at the time, as well as my secretary. Since I was also taking the Mississippi pastors with me, I had five plane tickets to purchase to go to this village church of about forty people. I not only had to buy five plane tickets to get to Juneau, Alaska, but I also had to purchase an additional five plane tickets to take us from Juneau to Hoonah in a small plane.

I did not have the finances for it but kept my word to bless the pastors. I put the tickets on my credit card. After purchasing the tickets, I attended Dr. Rodney Howard-Browne's Winter Campmeeting in January before making the Alaskan trip. I gave sacrificially in the offerings and believed God for a miracle. People told me that I could no longer afford to go to such small villages now that my ministry was much larger. A large ministry makes for a larger budget. However, I felt in my heart that if I can no longer afford to go to the bush of Alaska where no one else is going and where this ministry was birthed, something is very wrong. Church offerings are not my source. God is, and I will trust in Him.

We had an awesome revival in that village. By the end of the week, the church was packed, and the mayor of the city was there. We saw many salvations and healings. At the end of the night, the pastor's wife approached me with a question. She asked, "May I ask what your budget is?"

I was shocked that she would ask me such a question. I thought to myself that if I told her what it was, she would go into cardiac arrest. At the very least, she would feel terrible to realize that their little church could not begin to meet the needs of my ministry budget. I told her that I wasn't exactly sure what it was. It differs from week to week, depending on how many tickets we buy, where we stay, and other factors. She said that she appreciated that but would like for me to give an approximation. I replied that I was uncomfortable with that and reminded her that they were not my source and God would take care of me some other way. He could make it up to me in the next church with an offering through the mail or through a variety of ways. Once again, she said she understood that but would just like me to tell her the amount of my budget. I finally said, "If you don't mind, I would like to just keep that between God and me."

She replied with, "Okay. We were just wondering if this would help much toward your budget." With that, she handed me a check. I opened it up and saw an amount that staggered me. It was a check for fifteen thousand dollars. That was the largest amount we had ever received in the history of our ministry at that time, and it was in a little village church!

I looked at her with total astonishment on my face and asked her a question. "How did you do this? Did someone sell their home or something?"

She answered, "If you don't mind, we'll just keep that between us and God." The Lord spoke to my heart that He had watched me continue to be faithful in my giving in difficult circumstances, and He brought in an awesome harvest.

There are many reasons that could cause a person not to prosper. However, the one who abides in the secret place of the Most High, stays under the anointing, and constantly yields his or her heart to God can do nothing but prosper. Do I now become comfortable since God has blessed both my ministry and me personally? Do I settle back and quit pressing in? God forbid! I have a greater responsibility to accomplish much more. I desire to be a blessing around the world.

At the present time of writing of this book, I have ministered across this nation and in over fifty nations. I have a heart to build churches and Bible schools. It's my heart to have many more crusades and to help with other ministries' crusades. I am seeing multitudes come to Jesus. This is not the time to relax.

For every story that I have told you, there are about ten more that come to mind: of things my pastors and I have experienced. I know that I cannot tell them all. There will be many more that I have not yet lived out. This will be another year of giving and watching God do some of the greatest things that I've yet to witness. He truly is a God who has, and who will continue to do exceedingly, abundantly above all I ask or think (Ephesians

3:20). What a Holy Ghost adventure I am living in this life of giving! I'm certainly never bored. Wouldn't you like to join me on this adventure and have your own stories to tell and write?

I believe that as you have been reading these pages, your giving has changed dramatically. You have come to realize that you do not give habitually or out of compulsion or manipulation. Your giving is a holy worship unto a holy God. You gladly give 10 percent right off the top of your earnings and offerings above that, as led by the Holy Ghost. You ask Him how much to give, mix faith with it, and give joyfully. You give expecting that He will bless you so that you can have more to give.

You continue to care for your fields and keep your mouth lined up with the Word of God at all times. You learn to weed out doubt and unbelief. You water your crops with the Word of God and do not cancel out your harvest with negativity.

You have become one who lives to give and searches daily for ways to bless others. You are the one who rushes from the table to pay for the meal ticket. In fact, sometimes you do it for strangers anonymously. You begin to buy people clothes. You are the one who can easily take off your favorite tie or give away your favorite piece of jewelry at just the slightest prompting of the Holy Spirit. You could give your car or house away if God asked you to. You are in a contest to out-give God, even though you know that He will always win and you will always lose. You keep your heart right and constantly allow Him to examine your heart, changing you from glory to glory.

My pastor told God a long time ago that if He would bless him, he would make duplicates of the keys to that blessing and pass them out wherever he went. I was given those keys in Anchorage, Alaska, in November of 1992. Now, I am making duplicates and giving them to you. I trust that you will make duplicates and continue to give them to others. We all have a responsibility to give what we have received.

I caught revival over thirty ago, and with it, I caught a spirit of giving. I have tried to teach and transfer this spirit of giving to you, but the rest is up to you. Many hearing me have caught it. Many have not. Which will you be?

I hope to read your book someday or attend your service. You might be one who says, "I was set free from poverty when I listened to Debbie Rich," or "I was set free when I read her book." That is exactly what I say about Pastor Rodney Howard-Browne. And someone else can catch this from you. But you have to be red hot to light someone else on fire. No wet piece of wood ever lit another. This is a contagious anointing that flows like electricity. Such as I have, I have given you. Now, what will you do?

At the time of writing this book, I sat down with Pastor Rodney and reviewed some of his testimonies with him. As we finished, I looked up into my pastor's face and heard him say these words, "Debbie, I cannot wait any longer for the church to get the message of giving and funding the end-time harvest. The harvest is ready now. We must have the funds now. I must do it myself." I agreed with him and told him that I would believe to do it as well.

Pastor Rodney has formed a new corporation solely for the purpose of funding the end-time harvest. God has given him a plan and the wisdom with which to achieve it.

On December 25, Christmas morning, of 2002, Pastors Rodney and Adonica Howard-Browne gave their largest offering. They held their eighteen-year-old daughter, Kelly Mae, in their arms, as she was dying, Pastor Rodney said, "I'm not going to let the Devil steal her. I'm going to offer her up to Jesus as seed. This is going to cost the Devil. I'm going to believe God for one hundred million souls and over one billion dollars for the gospel." He laid his daughter into the arms of Jesus that Christmas morning. He gave his best gift. He said he could never outdo that gift.

Pastor Rodney has always lived his life with one foot in eternity, but that is more pronounced now than ever before. His daughter, who was born with cystic fibrosis, is already waiting for him in Heaven. There is only one reason he is still living. That reason is to see as many souls as possible brought into the kingdom of Heaven.

God has given Pastor Rodney favor, and several businessmen have sought him out and are being set in position around him to help fund this end-time harvest. As several corporate businessmen and a governor met, one of them asked the others if they knew why they were all there. They replied that all they knew was that God was putting them all together. The gentleman replied, "Yes, He is, but it goes farther than that. We are here because a man with a heart for the lost gave his best gift on Christmas morning and vowed that he would have a hundred million souls and a billion dollars for the harvest. We're here to help him accomplish that."

He will do it! I am confident of this one thing. The church is being given an opportunity to catch this message and be a part of funding the end-time harvest. However, if the majority of the church fails to catch it, there will be a remnant who will get the job done. Dr. Rodney Howard-Browne will be one of those, and I will be right behind him. The question remains, will you be a part of it as well? Will you have anything to lay at the feet of Jesus on that day?

TWENTY-TWO

ADDITIONAL SCRIPTURE RESOURCES
WHAT GOD SAYS ABOUT YOU PROSPERING

These are just a few of the verses in God's Word that let you know that He desires to prosper you and me. There are many more, but this is enough to settle the matter once and for all! Let faith come as you read these, and let God speak to you by the Holy Spirit until you know that you know that it's His divine will for you to prosper.

> And I will bless them that bless thee, and curse him that curseth thee: and in thee shall all families of the earth be blessed.
>
> GENESIS 12:3

> That in blessing I will bless thee, and in multiplying I will multiply thy seed as the stars of the heaven, and as the sand which is upon the sea shore; and thy seed shall possess the gate of his enemies.
>
> GENESIS 22:17

And his master saw that the LORD was with him, and that the LORD made all that he did to prosper in his hand.

GENESIS 39:3

The keeper of the prison looked not to any thing that was under his hand; because the LORD was with him, and that which he did, the LORD made it to prosper.

GENESIS 39:23

And he will love thee, and bless thee, and multiply thee: he will also bless the fruit of thy womb, and the fruit of thy land, thy corn, and thy wine, and thine oil, the increase of thy kine, and the flocks of thy sheep, in the land which he sware unto thy fathers to give thee.

DEUTERONOMY 7:13

Blessed shall be thy basket and thy store.
Blessed shalt thou be when thou comest in, and blessed shalt thou be when thou goest out.

DEUTERONOMY 28:5-6

The LORD shall command the blessing upon thee in thy storehouses, and in all that thou settest thine hand unto; and he shall bless thee in the land which the LORD thy God giveth thee.

DEUTERONOMY 28:8

The LORD shall open unto thee his good treasure, the heaven to give the rain unto thy land in his season, and to bless all the work of thine hand: and thou shalt lend unto many nations, and thou shalt not borrow.

DEUTERONOMY 28:12

Keep therefore the words of this covenant, and do them, that ye may prosper in all that ye do.

DEUTERONOMY 29:9

Only be thou strong and very courageous, that thou mayest observe to do according to all the law, which Moses my servant commanded thee: turn not from it to the right hand or to the left, that thou mayest prosper withersoever thou goest.

JOSHUA 1:7

And they rose early in the morning, and went forth into the wilderness of Tekoa: and as they went forth, Jehoshaphat stood and said, Hear me, O Judah, and ye inhabitants of Jerusalem; Believe in the LORD your God, so shall ye be established; believe his prophets, so shall ye prosper.

2 CHRONICLES 20:20

And he sought God in the days of Zechariah, who had understanding in the visions of God: and as long as he sought the LORD, God made him to prosper.

2 CHRONICLES 26:5

And he shall be like a tree planted by the rivers of water, that bringeth forth his fruit in his season; his leaf also shall not wither; and whatsoever he doeth shall prosper.

PSALM 1:3

Delight thyself also in the LORD: and he shall give thee the desires of thine heart.

PSALM 37:4

Blessed be the Lord, who daily loadeth us with benefits, even the God of our salvation. Selah.

PSALM 68:19

Pray for the peace of Jerusalem: they shall prosper that love thee.

PSALM 122:6

Give, and it shall be given unto you; good measure, pressed down, and shaken together, and running over, shall men give into your bosom. For with the same measure that ye mete withal it shall be measured to you again.

LUKE 6:38

The thief cometh not, but for to steal, and to kill, and to destroy: I am come that they might have life, and that they might have it more abundantly.

JOHN 10:10

Even so hath the Lord ordained that they which preach the gospel should live of the gospel.

> 1 CORINTHIANS 9:14

For ye know the grace of our Lord Jesus Christ, that, though he was rich, yet for your sakes he became poor, that ye through his poverty might be rich.

> 2 CORINTHIANS 8:9

But this I say, He which soweth sparingly shall reap also sparingly; and he which soweth bountifully shall reap also bountifully.
Every man according as he purposeth in his heart, so let him give; not grudgingly, or of necessity: for God loveth a cheerful giver.
And God is able to make all grace abound toward you; that ye, always having all sufficiency in all things, may abound to every good work:

> 2 CORINTHIANS 9:6-8

Be not deceived; God is not mocked: for whatsoever a man soweth, that shall he also reap.

> GALATIANS 6:7

Now unto him that is able to do exceeding abundantly above all that we ask or think, according to the power that worketh in us.

> EPHESIANS 3:20

> But my God shall supply all your need according to his riches in glory by Christ Jesus.
>
> PHILIPPIANS 4:19

> Beloved, I wish above all things that thou mayest prosper and be in health, even as thy soul prospereth.
>
> 3 JOHN 1:2

END

RESURRECTED

OVERCOMING DEATH, DESTRUCTION, AND DEFEAT

Have you ever had a defining, soul-shattering moment when you knew that life would never be the same? Perhaps you received a fearful diagnosis from a doctor, or your spouse just walked out the door, leaving you devastated, torn, and alone. Maybe the career that you chose is no longer possible. Possibly, your life savings were lost, either through someone's treachery or your own misguided decisions. Was the love of your life snatched from this earth far too early, leaving you to grieve and cope alone? Have you lost a child you nursed, loved more than life, and never expected to bury? Has your body betrayed you and refused to function or allow you to do the everyday things you used to enjoy? Perhaps the company that you believed you would retire from abruptly shut the door on your future. Maybe a friend or loved one has betrayed you and shattered your trust and confidence. Have you found out that one of your children is in trouble, and there is nothing you can do to rescue him? Have your life-long dreams been shattered, never to be realized?

If you ask the question, "Why do bad things happen to good people," you are reading the right book. Perhaps you have found yourself looking at endless mounds of self-help books to realize that there is nothing anyone can tell you to ease the pain or bring hope. So, you walk away slowly, feeling dead inside. Everyone you observe seems to have it together, laughing, talking, sharing, and oblivious to your pain. It seems you are in a terrible movie, watching everything take place in slow motion, unable to change the outcome. You ask yourself about a hundred times a day, "Will I ever really live again?" If you still have breath and can read this, I tell you, most certainly, that you can and will live again. What my God has done for me, He will do for you. He is no respecter of persons.

Everyone goes through times of trial, pain, and suffering in their life. Yes, even Christians. We live on a planet that is dying. God meant for man to live in a paradise, subdue the earth, be fruitful, enjoy His presence, and live forever. However, man decided to do it his way. Adam's way has cost every one of us dearly. Ever since Eve was deceived and she and Adam sinned, humanity has had problems. When we don't do things God's way, we cannot expect His results.

The book is an account of my journey. As such, it will cover in detail some of my life's most challenging and painful episodes and the highest of highs. I will be honest with you about my mistakes—episodes on which I look back now and think, "How could you be so stupid?" But it will also convey the mighty ways in which God rescued, forgave, restored, and used me to fulfill my calling to preach the Gospel.

I hope that someone reading this book, who may be going through similarly difficult circumstances, will read things on these pages with which they can relate. And, more importantly, I hope they will learn that they, too, should never give up and that we serve a God of second chances, a God who can undo any scheme or trap the Devil has used to derail our lives. You walk away knowing that we serve a big God, a God who gives up on no one, a God who is working endlessly to bring every last human on earth into restoration with His plan for his or her life.

Who is Debbie Rich? I am a nobody with a big God. I believe God gave me the assignment to write this book to give you hope and inspiration. It is time to get on with the plan and purpose of God in your life. For others, it is time to quit feeling sorry for yourself, give up your hospital bed to someone else who needs it, and let God powerfully use you.

Let's make history. Let it be said that we never gave up. Will you be quick to repent and forgive? Will you refuse to give up in the hard places? Will you refuse to take no for an answer and never give in to the enemy? Let God forgive you, heal you, restore you, and use you beyond your wildest imagination. I and many others are waiting to read your book.

Available in Paperback and eBook from Your Favorite Bookstore or Online Retailer

ABOUT DEBBIE RICH

Known as a fiery preacher who flows in the Holy Spirit while ministering the Word of God, Dr. Debbie Rich is an international teacher, evangelist, and revivalist who has carried the fire of revival to over fifty nations.

Dr. Debbie received her Ph.D. in Theology from Life Christian University following her graduation from Rhema Bible Training Center in Broken Arrow, Oklahoma. She also attended Open Bible College in Des Moines, Iowa.

As a pioneer missionary in the remote "Alaskan Bush," she traveled where few dared to go. Ministering in prisons, she saw inmates filled with the Holy Spirit after receiving Jesus as their Lord and Savior. Her ministry ignited a fire of revival across the state of Alaska as she boldly ventured into remote villages, towns, and cities where she felt called to go but had not been invited. While some local pastors initially opposed her efforts, many have since become long-time friends.

Dr. Debbie pioneered Faith Life Church and Word & Spirit Institute Northwest in the state of Washington. She teaches in Bible schools around the world.

Currently, she ministers out of Revival Ministries International in Tampa, Florida, with Pastors Rodney and Adonica Howard-Browne.

For Ministry Information Contact:

Dr. Debbie Rich Ministries
13194 US HWY 301 S,
Suite 107, Riverview, FL. 33578
Web Info: debbierichministries.org
E-mail: office@debbierichministries.org

facebook.com/debbierichministries
instagram.com/debbierichministries
youtube.com/debbierichministries

www.ingramcontent.com/pod-product-compliance
Lightning Source LLC
Chambersburg PA
CBHW042248240426
43672CB00020BA/2988